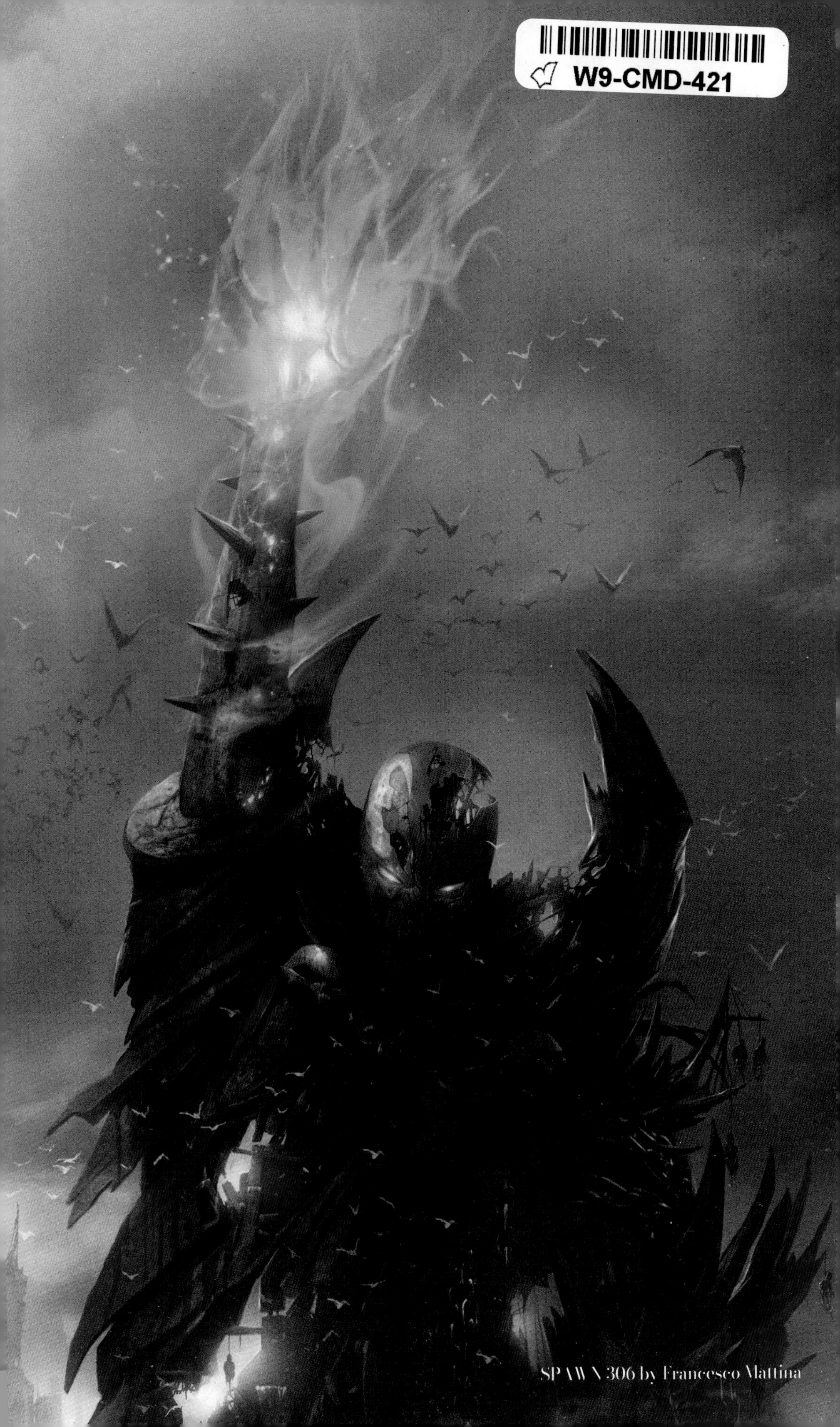

SPAWN 306 by Francesco Mattina

SPAWN®

AFTERMATH

WRITER
TODD McFARLANE

ARTISTS
JASON SHAWN ALEXANDER
PHILIP TAN

COVERS BY
TODD McFARLANE
FRANCESCO MATTINA
GREG CAPULLO
JASON SHAWN ALEXANDER
PHILIP TAN

Creative Director
TODD McFARLANE

Senior Production Artist
KRISTEN DENTON

President of Comic Operations
SHANNON BAILEY

Editor-In-Chief
THOMAS HEALY

Associate Editor
YVETTE ARTEAGA

Publisher for Image Comics
ERIC STEPHENSON

SPAWN CREATED BY
TODD McFARLANE

Spawn: Aftermath. June 2022. FIRST PRINTING. Published by IMAGE COMICS, 2701 NW Vaughn St, Suite 780 Portland, OR 97210 USA. Originally published in single issue format as Spawn issues #302-307.

image
TODD McFARLAN
PRODUCTION
McFARLANE.CO

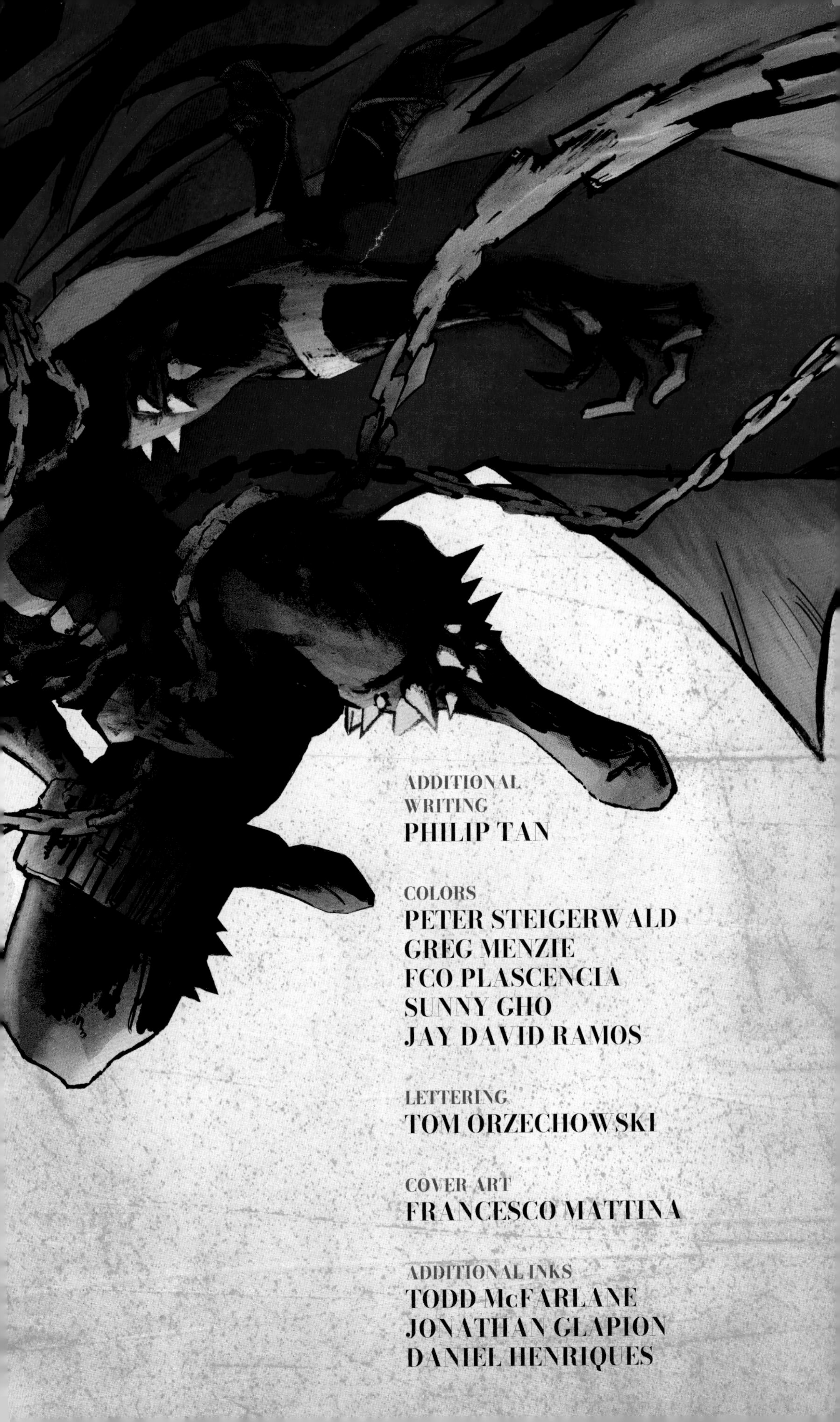

ADDITIONAL WRITING
PHILIP TAN

COLORS
PETER STEIGERWALD
GREG MENZIE
FCO PLASCENCIA
SUNNY GHO
JAY DAVID RAMOS

LETTERING
TOM ORZECHOWSKI

COVER ART
FRANCESCO MATTINA

ADDITIONAL INKS
TODD McFARLANE
JONATHAN GLAPION
DANIEL HENRIQUES

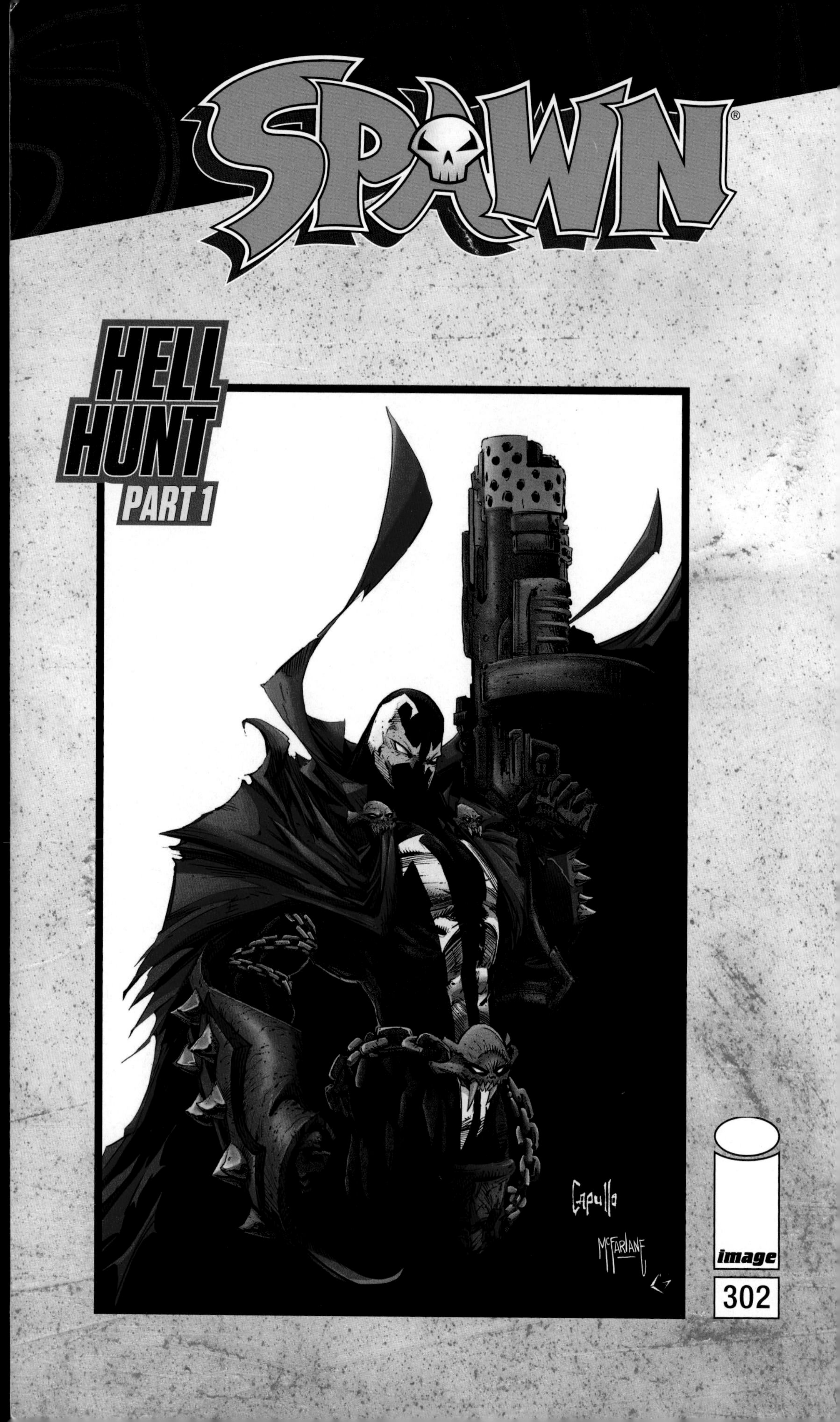
SPAWN®
HELL HUNT
PART 1
Capullo
McFarlane
image
302

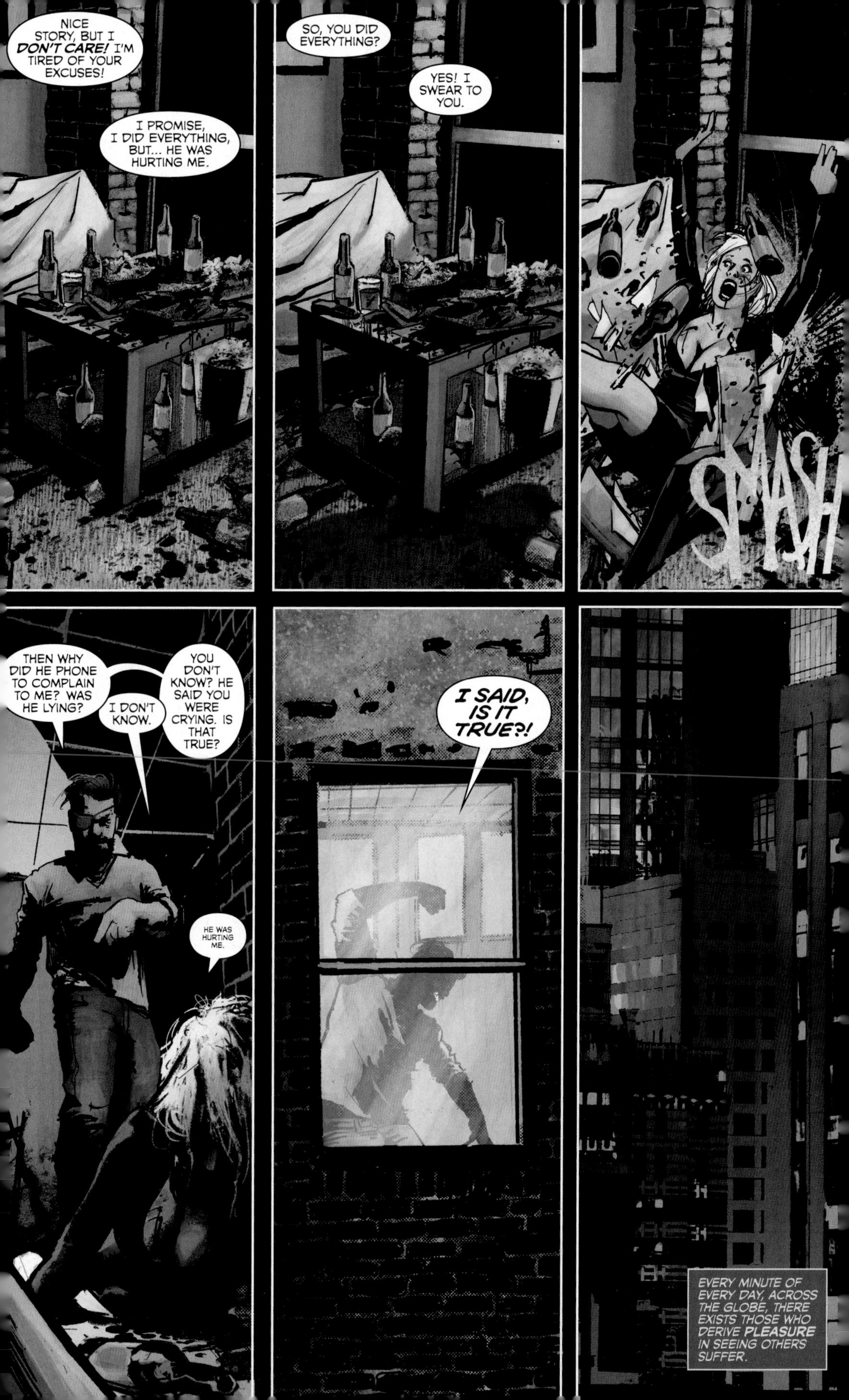
NICE STORY, BUT I DON'T CARE! I'M TIRED OF YOUR EXCUSES!
I PROMISE, I DID EVERYTHING, BUT... HE WAS HURTING ME.
SO, YOU DID EVERYTHING?
YES! I SWEAR TO YOU.
SMASH
THEN WHY DID HE PHONE TO COMPLAIN TO ME? WAS HE LYING?
I DON'T KNOW.
YOU DON'T KNOW? HE SAID YOU WERE CRYING. IS THAT TRUE?
HE WAS HURTING ME.
I SAID, IS IT TRUE?!
EVERY MINUTE OF EVERY DAY, ACROSS THE GLOBE, THERE EXISTS THOSE WHO DERIVE PLEASURE IN SEEING OTHERS SUFFER.

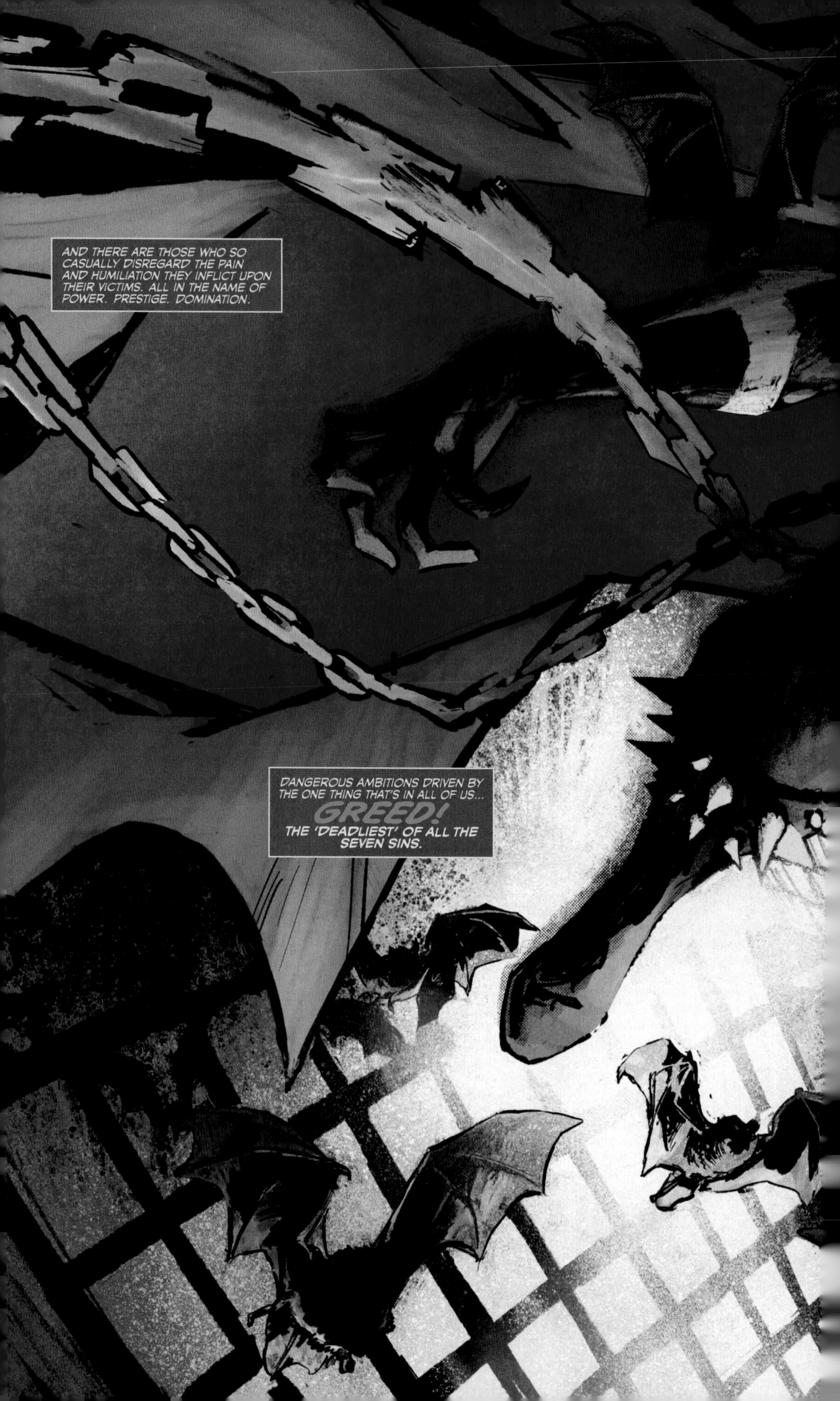
AND THERE ARE THOSE WHO SO CASUALLY DISREGARD THE PAIN AND HUMILIATION THEY INFLICT UPON THEIR VICTIMS. ALL IN THE NAME OF POWER. PRESTIGE. DOMINATION.
DANGEROUS AMBITIONS DRIVEN BY THE ONE THING THAT'S IN ALL OF US... GREED! THE 'DEADLIEST' OF ALL THE SEVEN SINS.

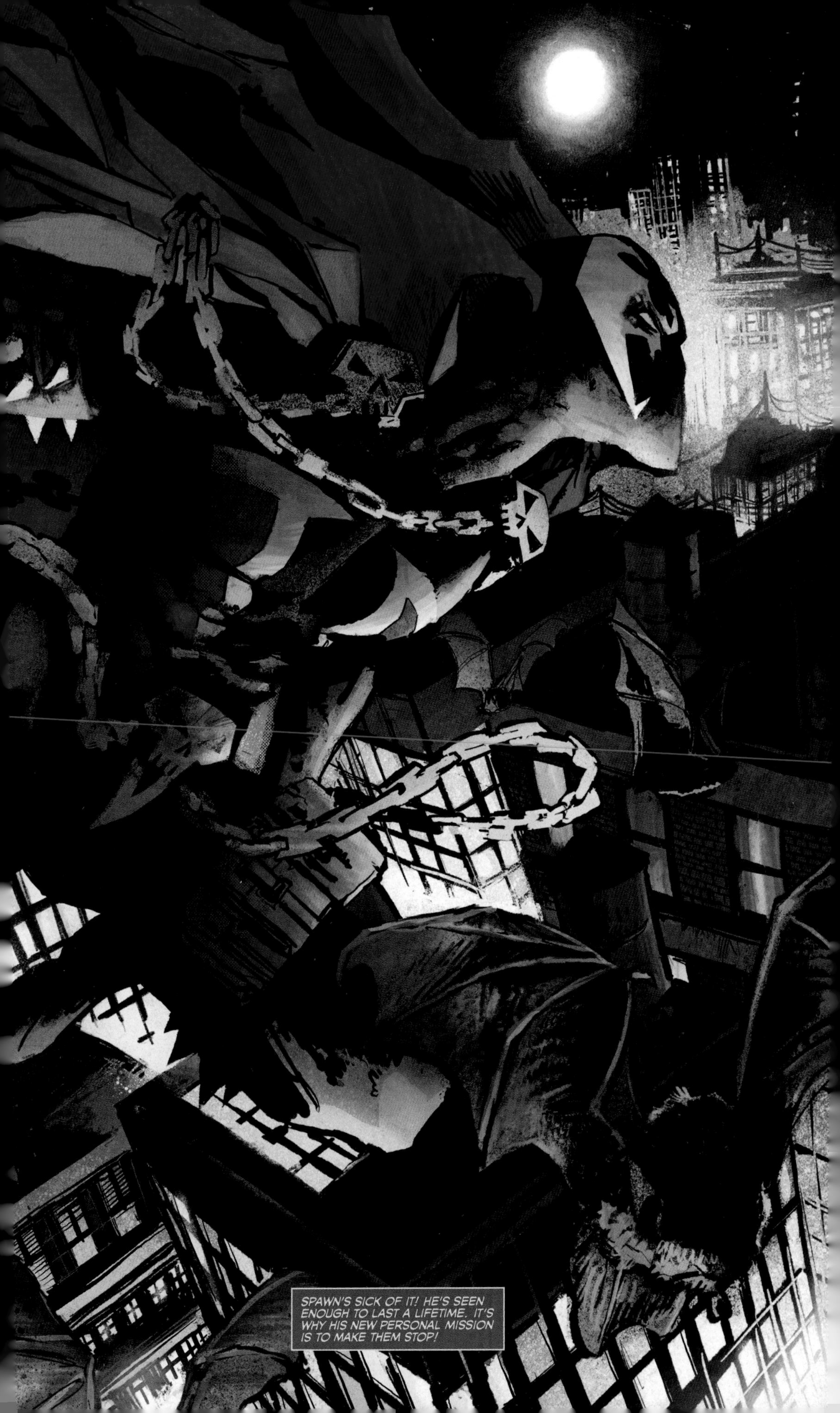
SPAWN'S SICK OF IT! HE'S SEEN ENOUGH TO LAST A LIFETIME. IT'S WHY HIS NEW PERSONAL MISSION IS TO MAKE THEM STOP!

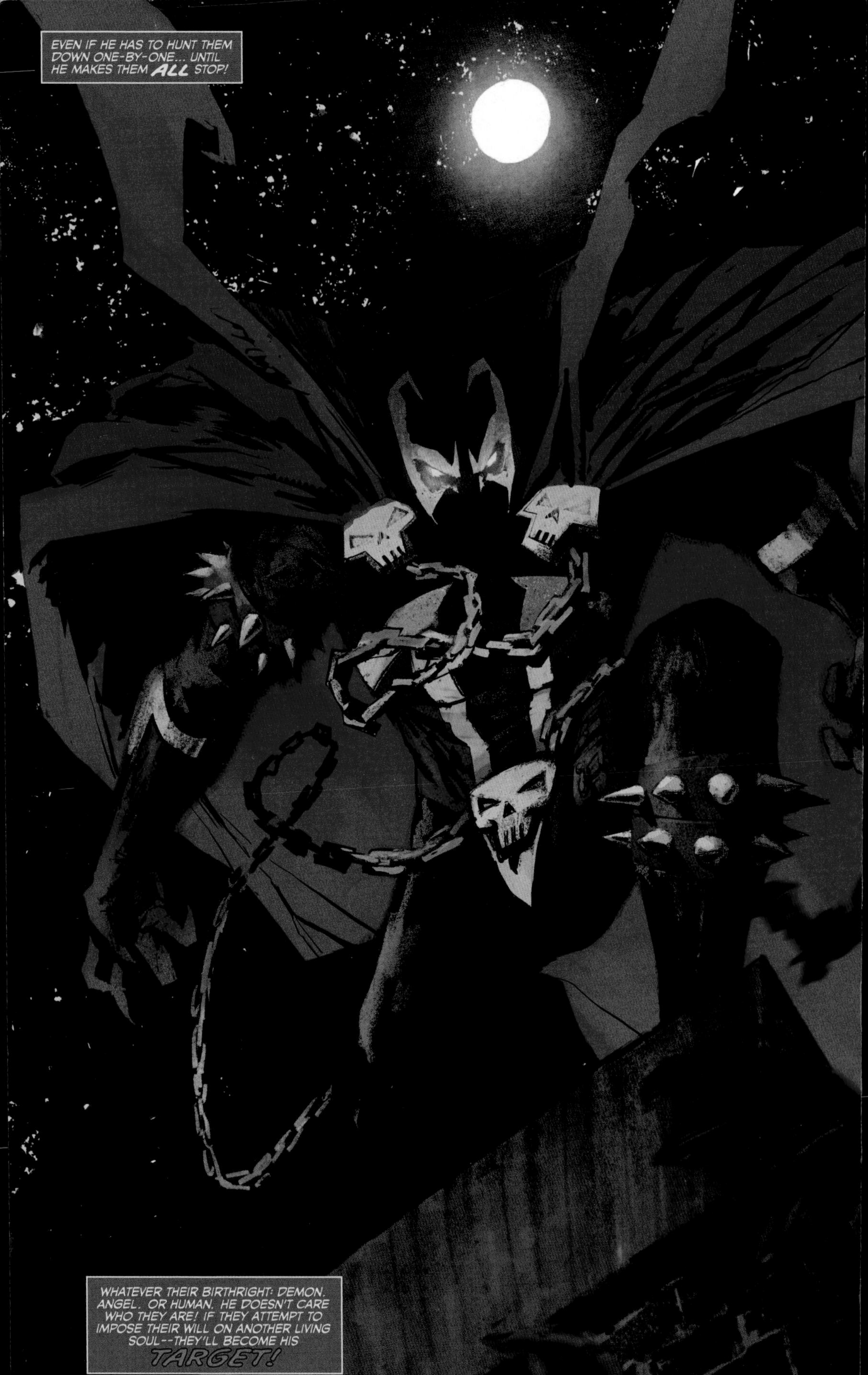
EVEN IF HE HAS TO HUNT THEM DOWN ONE-BY-ONE... UNTIL HE MAKES THEM ALL STOP!
WHATEVER THEIR BIRTHRIGHT: DEMON, ANGEL, OR HUMAN, HE DOESN'T CARE WHO THEY ARE! IF THEY ATTEMPT TO IMPOSE THEIR WILL ON ANOTHER LIVING SOUL--THEY'LL BECOME HIS TARGET!

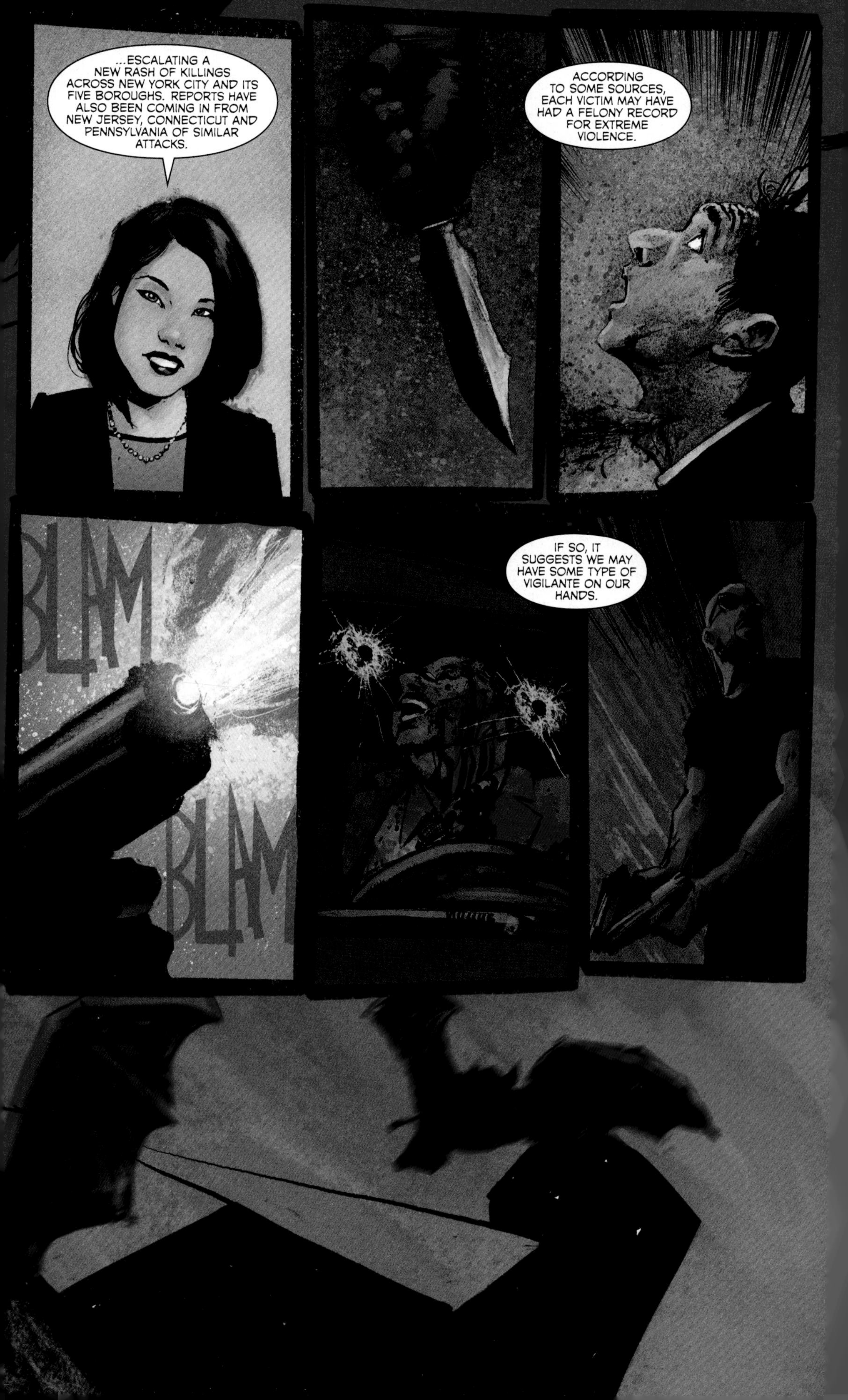
...ESCALATING A NEW RASH OF KILLINGS ACROSS NEW YORK CITY AND ITS FIVE BOROUGHS. REPORTS HAVE ALSO BEEN COMING IN FROM NEW JERSEY, CONNECTICUT AND PENNSYLVANIA OF SIMILAR ATTACKS.
ACCORDING TO SOME SOURCES, EACH VICTIM MAY HAVE HAD A FELONY RECORD FOR EXTREME VIOLENCE.
BLAM
BLAM
IF SO, IT SUGGESTS WE MAY HAVE SOME TYPE OF VIGILANTE ON OUR HANDS.

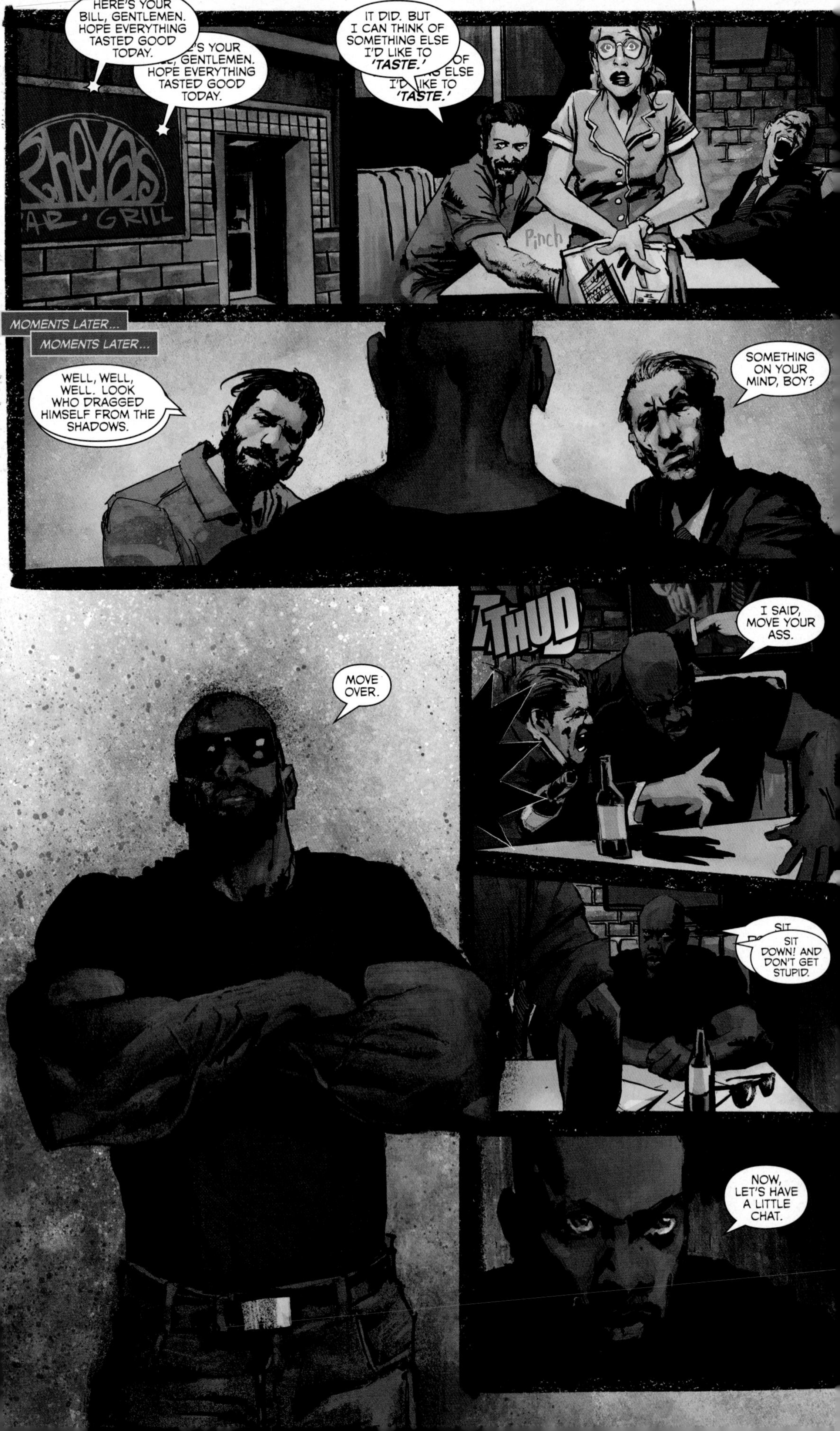
HERE'S YOUR BILL, GENTLEMEN. HOPE EVERYTHING TASTED GOOD TODAY.
E'S YOUR , GENTLEMEN. HOPE EVERYTHING TASTED GOOD TODAY.
Rheya's BAR · GRILL
IT DID. BUT I CAN THINK OF SOMETHING ELSE I'D LIKE TO *'TASTE.'*
ELSE I'D LIKE TO *'TASTE.'*
Pinch
MOMENTS LATER...
MOMENTS LATER...
WELL, WELL, WELL. LOOK WHO DRAGGED HIMSELF FROM THE SHADOWS.
SOMETHING ON YOUR MIND, BOY?
MOVE OVER.
THUD
I SAID, MOVE YOUR ASS.
SIT DOWN! AND DON'T GET STUPID.
NOW, LET'S HAVE A LITTLE CHAT.

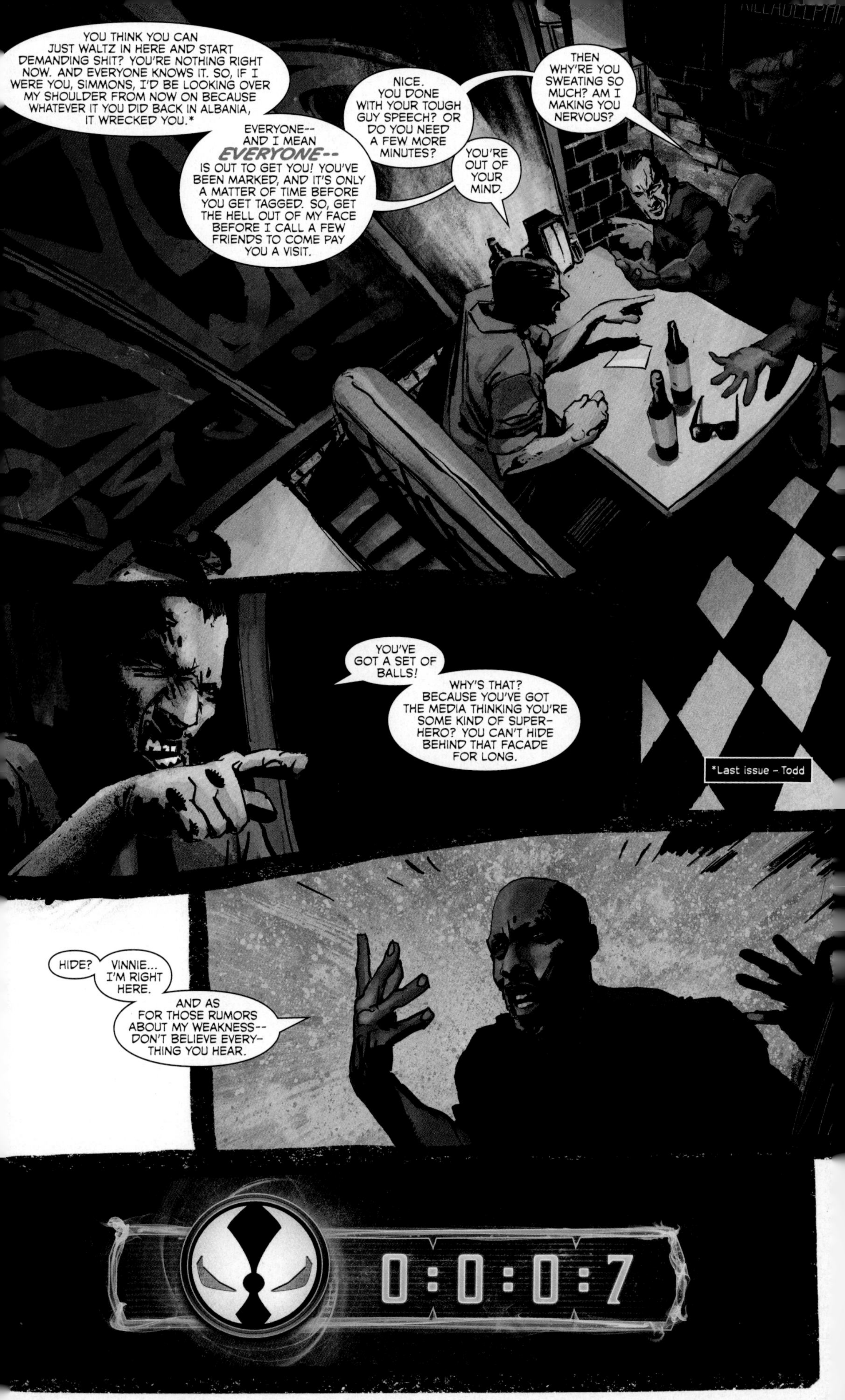

YOU THINK YOU CAN JUST WALTZ IN HERE AND START DEMANDING SHIT? YOU'RE NOTHING RIGHT NOW. AND EVERYONE KNOWS IT. SO, IF I WERE YOU, SIMMONS, I'D BE LOOKING OVER MY SHOULDER FROM NOW ON BECAUSE WHATEVER IT YOU DID BACK IN ALBANIA, IT WRECKED YOU.*
EVERYONE-- AND I MEAN EVERYONE-- IS OUT TO GET YOU! YOU'VE BEEN MARKED, AND IT'S ONLY A MATTER OF TIME BEFORE YOU GET TAGGED. SO, GET THE HELL OUT OF MY FACE BEFORE I CALL A FEW FRIENDS TO COME PAY YOU A VISIT.
NICE. YOU DONE WITH YOUR TOUGH GUY SPEECH? OR DO YOU NEED A FEW MORE MINUTES?
THEN WHY'RE YOU SWEATING SO MUCH? AM I MAKING YOU NERVOUS?
YOU'RE OUT OF YOUR MIND.
YOU'VE GOT A SET OF BALLS!
WHY'S THAT? BECAUSE YOU'VE GOT THE MEDIA THINKING YOU'RE SOME KIND OF SUPER-HERO? YOU CAN'T HIDE BEHIND THAT FACADE FOR LONG.
*Last issue - Todd
HIDE?
VINNIE... I'M RIGHT HERE.
AND AS FOR THOSE RUMORS ABOUT MY WEAKNESS-- DON'T BELIEVE EVERY-THING YOU HEAR.
0:0:0:7

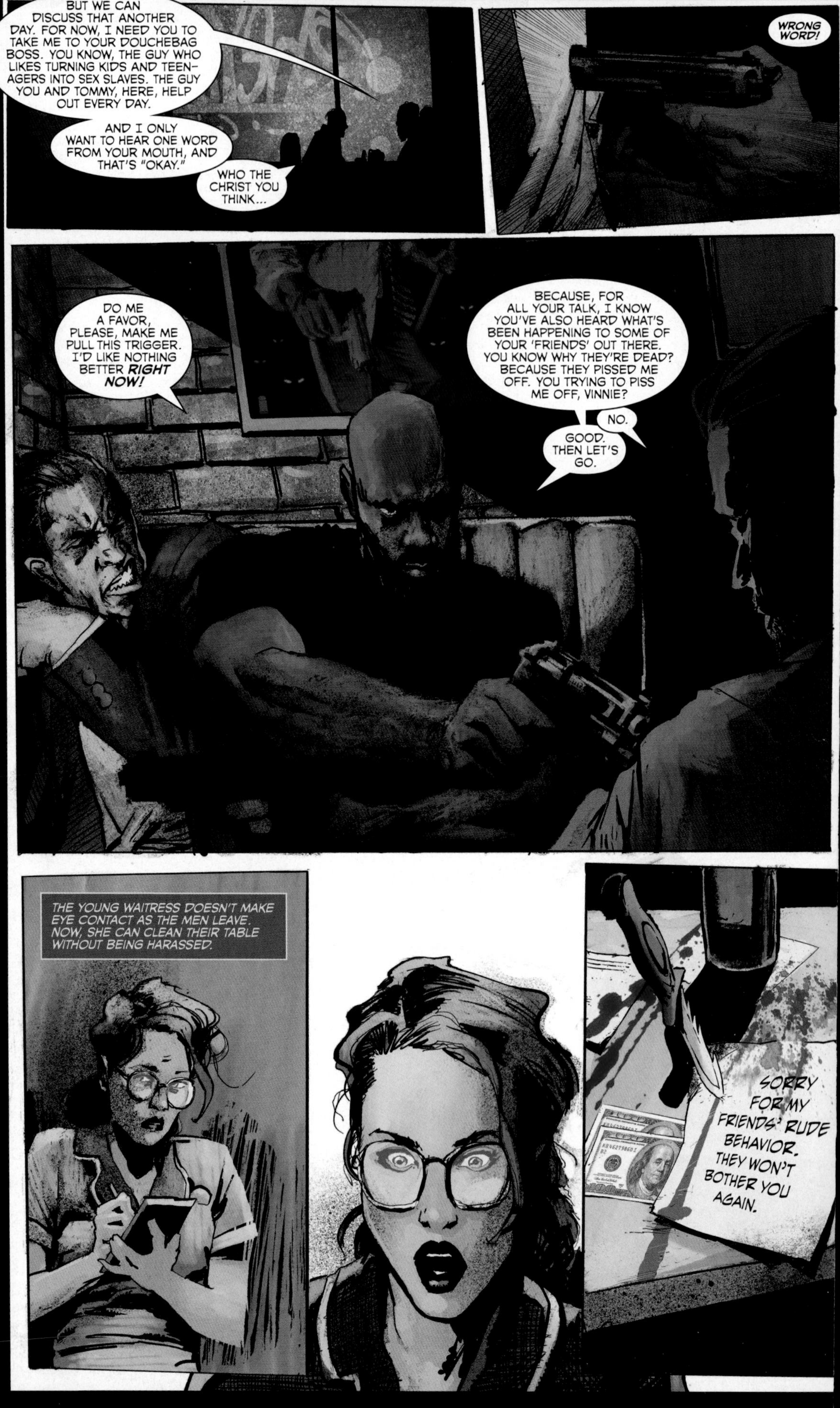

BUT WE CAN DISCUSS THAT ANOTHER DAY. FOR NOW, I NEED YOU TO TAKE ME TO YOUR DOUCHEBAG BOSS. YOU KNOW, THE GUY WHO LIKES TURNING KIDS AND TEEN-AGERS INTO SEX SLAVES. THE GUY YOU AND TOMMY, HERE, HELP OUT EVERY DAY.
AND I ONLY WANT TO HEAR ONE WORD FROM YOUR MOUTH, AND THAT'S "OKAY."
WHO THE CHRIST YOU THINK...
WRONG WORD!
DO ME A FAVOR, PLEASE, MAKE ME PULL THIS TRIGGER. I'D LIKE NOTHING BETTER RIGHT NOW!
BECAUSE, FOR ALL YOUR TALK, I KNOW YOU'VE ALSO HEARD WHAT'S BEEN HAPPENING TO SOME OF YOUR 'FRIENDS' OUT THERE. YOU KNOW WHY THEY'RE DEAD? BECAUSE THEY PISSED ME OFF. YOU TRYING TO PISS ME OFF, VINNIE?
NO.
GOOD. THEN LET'S GO.
THE YOUNG WAITRESS DOESN'T MAKE EYE CONTACT AS THE MEN LEAVE. NOW, SHE CAN CLEAN THEIR TABLE WITHOUT BEING HARASSED.
SORRY FOR MY FRIENDS' RUDE BEHAVIOR. THEY WON'T BOTHER YOU AGAIN.

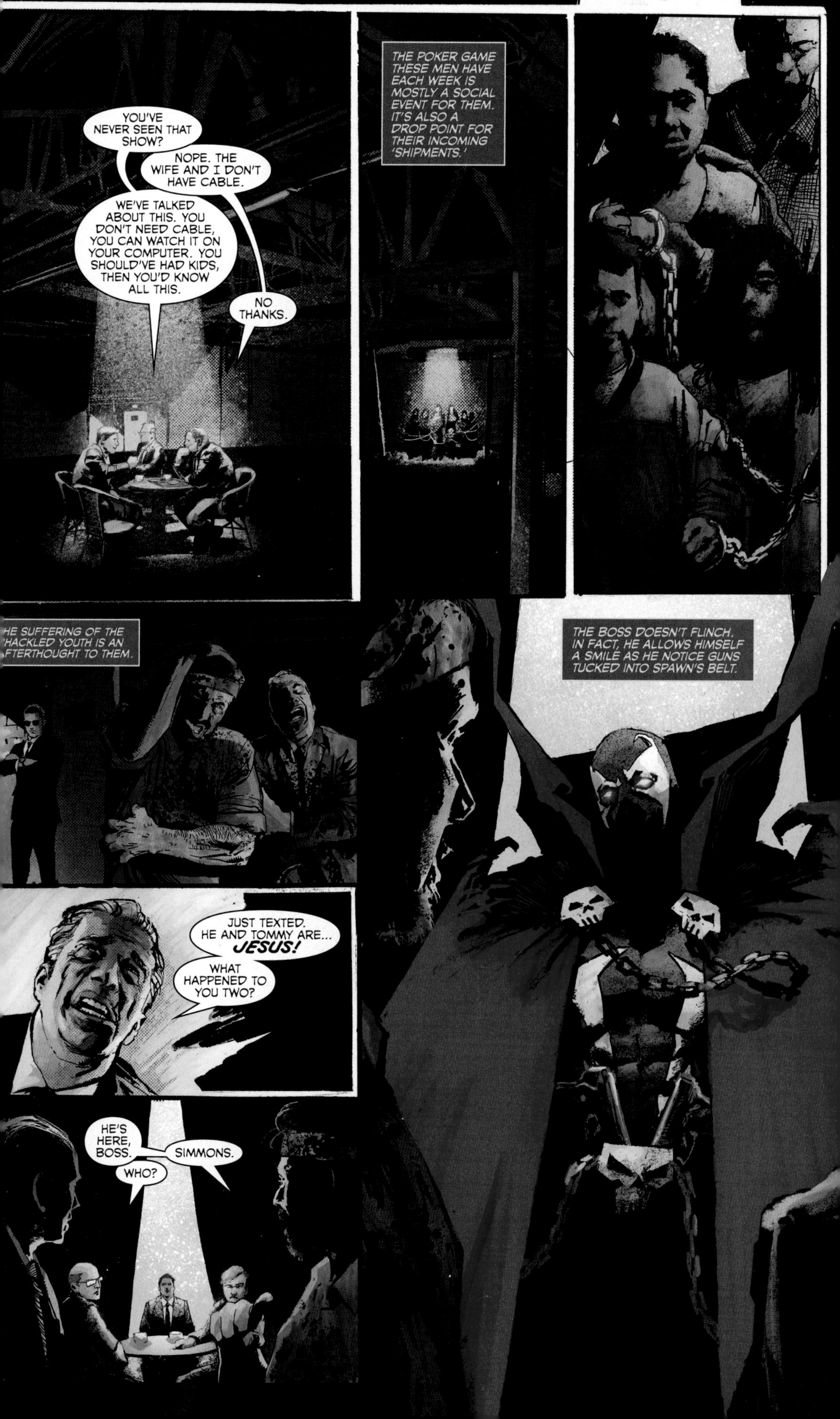
YOU'VE NEVER SEEN THAT SHOW?
NOPE. THE WIFE AND I DON'T HAVE CABLE.
WE'VE TALKED ABOUT THIS. YOU DON'T NEED CABLE, YOU CAN WATCH IT ON YOUR COMPUTER. YOU SHOULD'VE HAD KIDS, THEN YOU'D KNOW ALL THIS.
NO THANKS.
THE POKER GAME THESE MEN HAVE EACH WEEK IS MOSTLY A SOCIAL EVENT FOR THEM. IT'S ALSO A DROP POINT FOR THEIR INCOMING 'SHIPMENTS.'
HE SUFFERING OF THE HACKLED YOUTH IS AN FTERTHOUGHT TO THEM.
JUST TEXTED. HE AND TOMMY ARE... JESUS!
WHAT HAPPENED TO YOU TWO?
HE'S HERE, BOSS.
WHO?
SIMMONS.
THE BOSS DOESN'T FLINCH. IN FACT, HE ALLOWS HIMSELF A SMILE AS HE NOTICE GUNS TUCKED INTO SPAWN'S BELT.

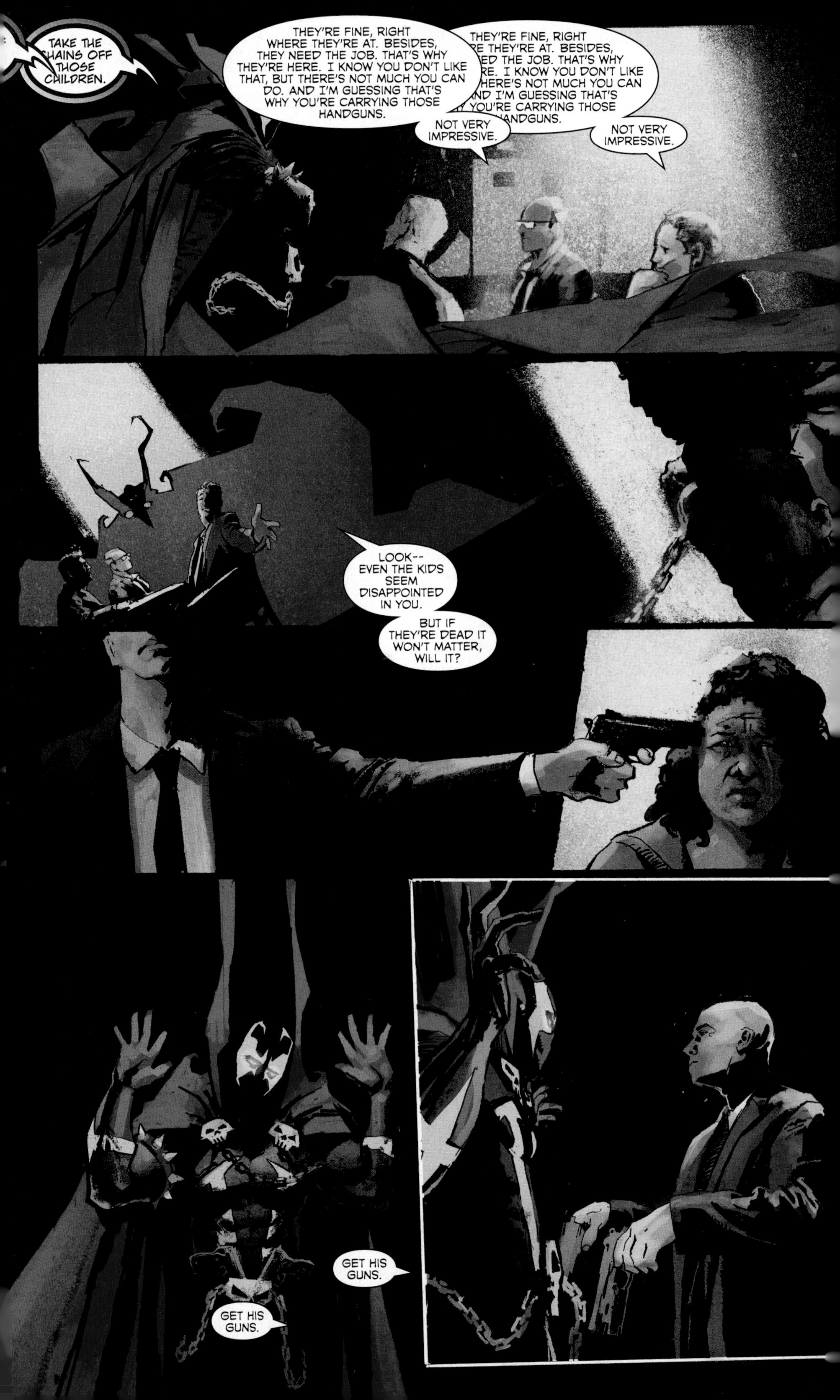
TAKE THE CHAINS OFF THOSE CHILDREN.
THEY'RE FINE, RIGHT WHERE THEY'RE AT. BESIDES, THEY NEED THE JOB. THAT'S WHY THEY'RE HERE. I KNOW YOU DON'T LIKE THAT, BUT THERE'S NOT MUCH YOU CAN DO. AND I'M GUESSING THAT'S WHY YOU'RE CARRYING THOSE HANDGUNS.
NOT VERY IMPRESSIVE.
THEY'RE FINE, RIGHT
E THEY'RE AT. BESIDES,
ED THE JOB. THAT'S WHY
RE. I KNOW YOU DON'T LIKE
HERE'S NOT MUCH YOU CAN
ND I'M GUESSING THAT'S
Y YOU'RE CARRYING THOSE
ANDGUNS.
NOT VERY IMPRESSIVE.
LOOK-- EVEN THE KIDS SEEM DISAPPOINTED IN YOU.
BUT IF THEY'RE DEAD IT WON'T MATTER, WILL IT?
GET HIS GUNS.
GET HIS GUNS.

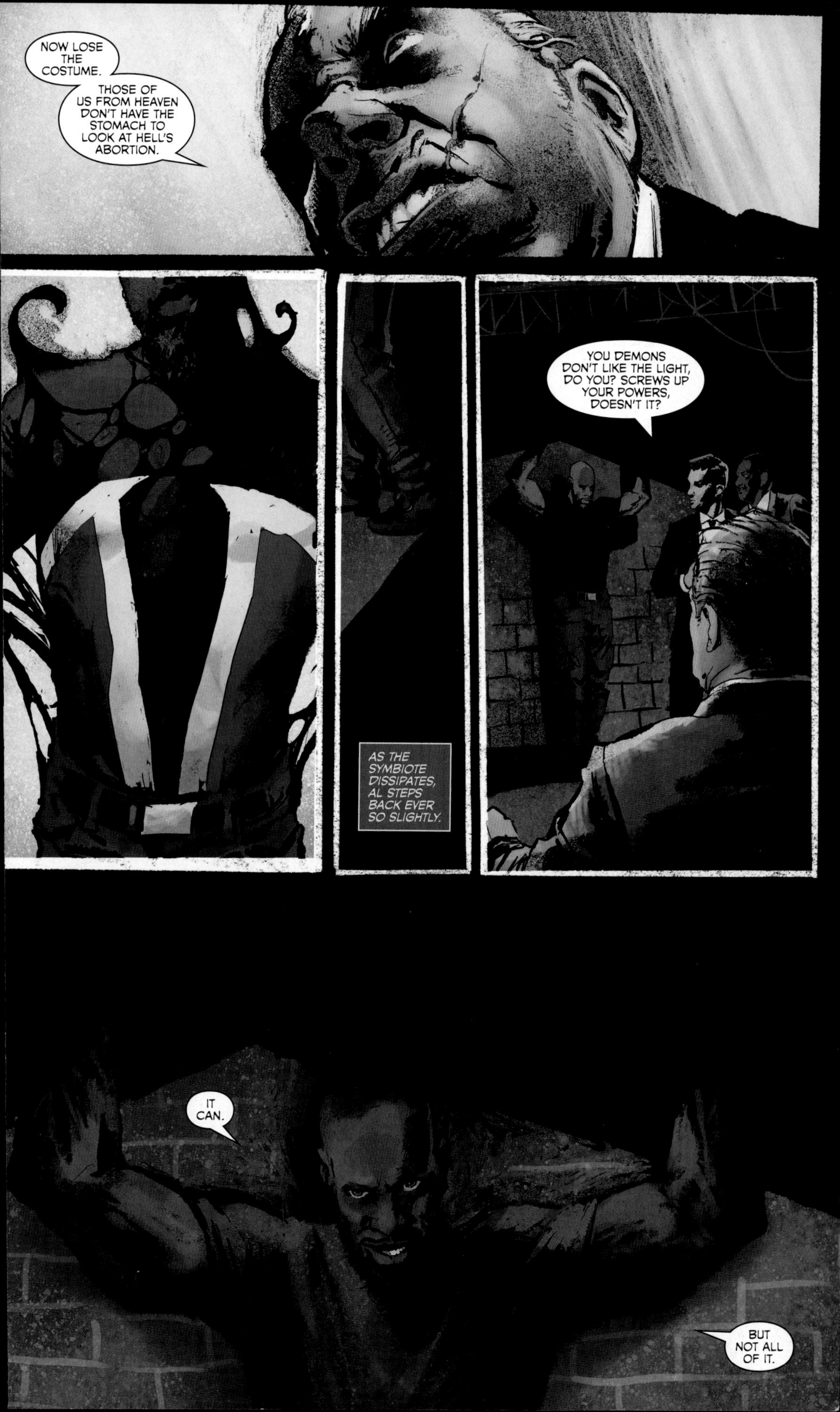
NOW LOSE THE COSTUME.
THOSE OF US FROM HEAVEN DON'T HAVE THE STOMACH TO LOOK AT HELL'S ABORTION.
AS THE SYMBIOTE DISSIPATES, AL STEPS BACK EVER SO SLIGHTLY.
YOU DEMONS DON'T LIKE THE LIGHT, DO YOU? SCREWS UP YOUR POWERS, DOESN'T IT?
IT CAN.
BUT NOT ALL OF IT.

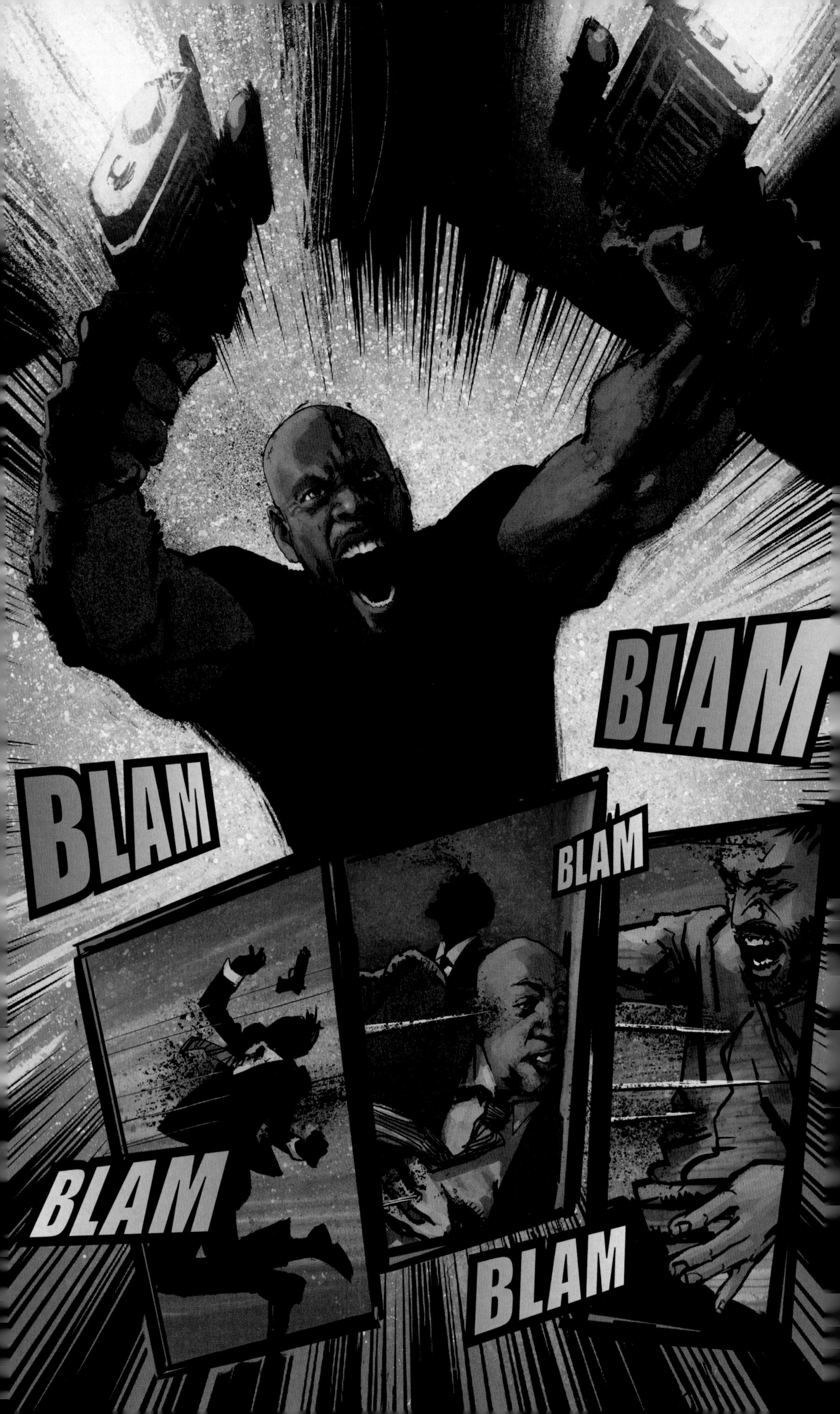
BLAM
BLAM
BLAM
BLAM
BLAM

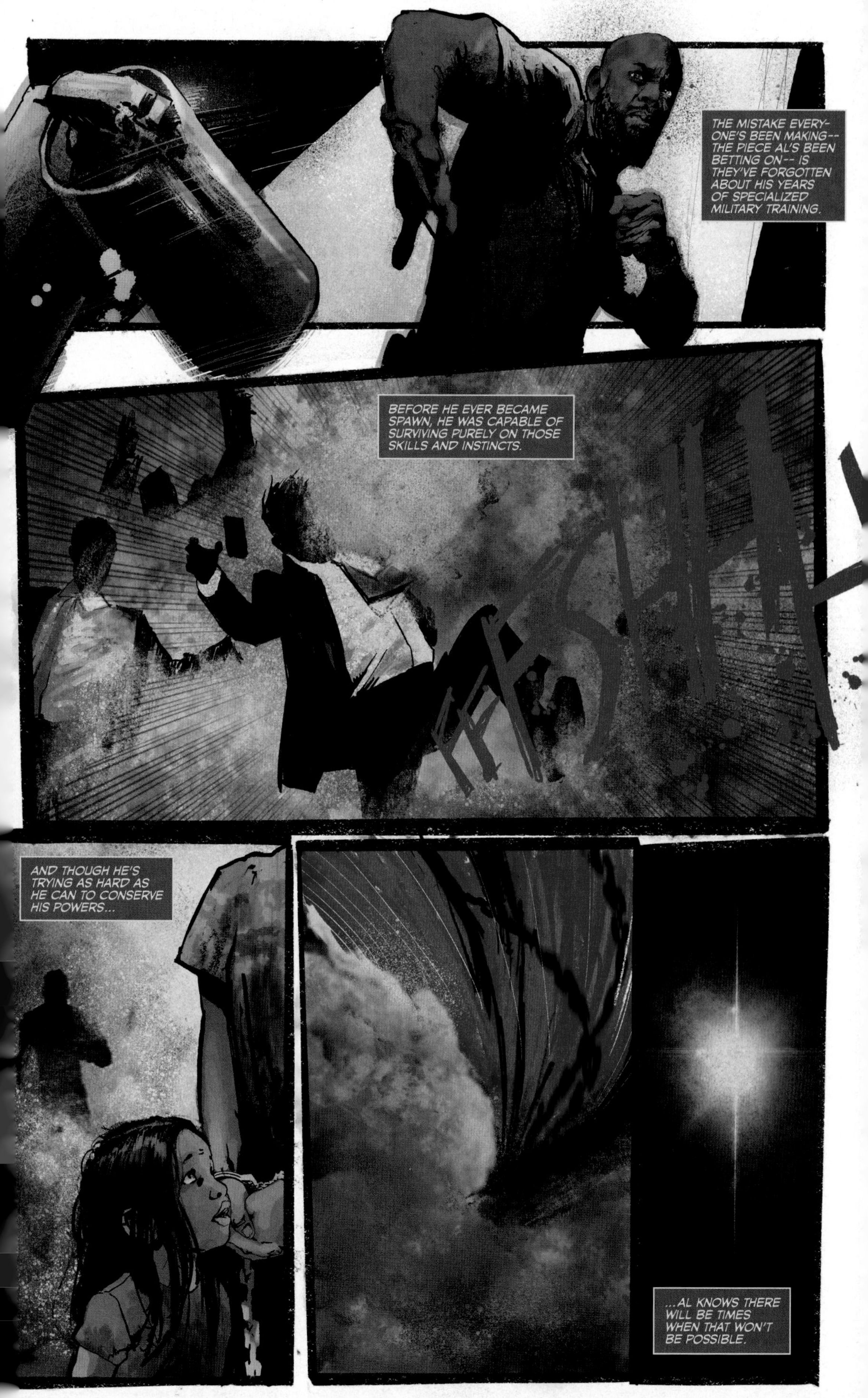

THE MISTAKE EVERY-ONE'S BEEN MAKING-- THE PIECE AL'S BEEN BETTING ON-- IS THEY'VE FORGOTTEN ABOUT HIS YEARS OF SPECIALIZED MILITARY TRAINING.
BEFORE HE EVER BECAME SPAWN, HE WAS CAPABLE OF SURVIVING PURELY ON THOSE SKILLS AND INSTINCTS.
SHHK
AND THOUGH HE'S TRYING AS HARD AS HE CAN TO CONSERVE HIS POWERS...
...AL KNOWS THERE WILL BE TIMES WHEN THAT WON'T BE POSSIBLE.

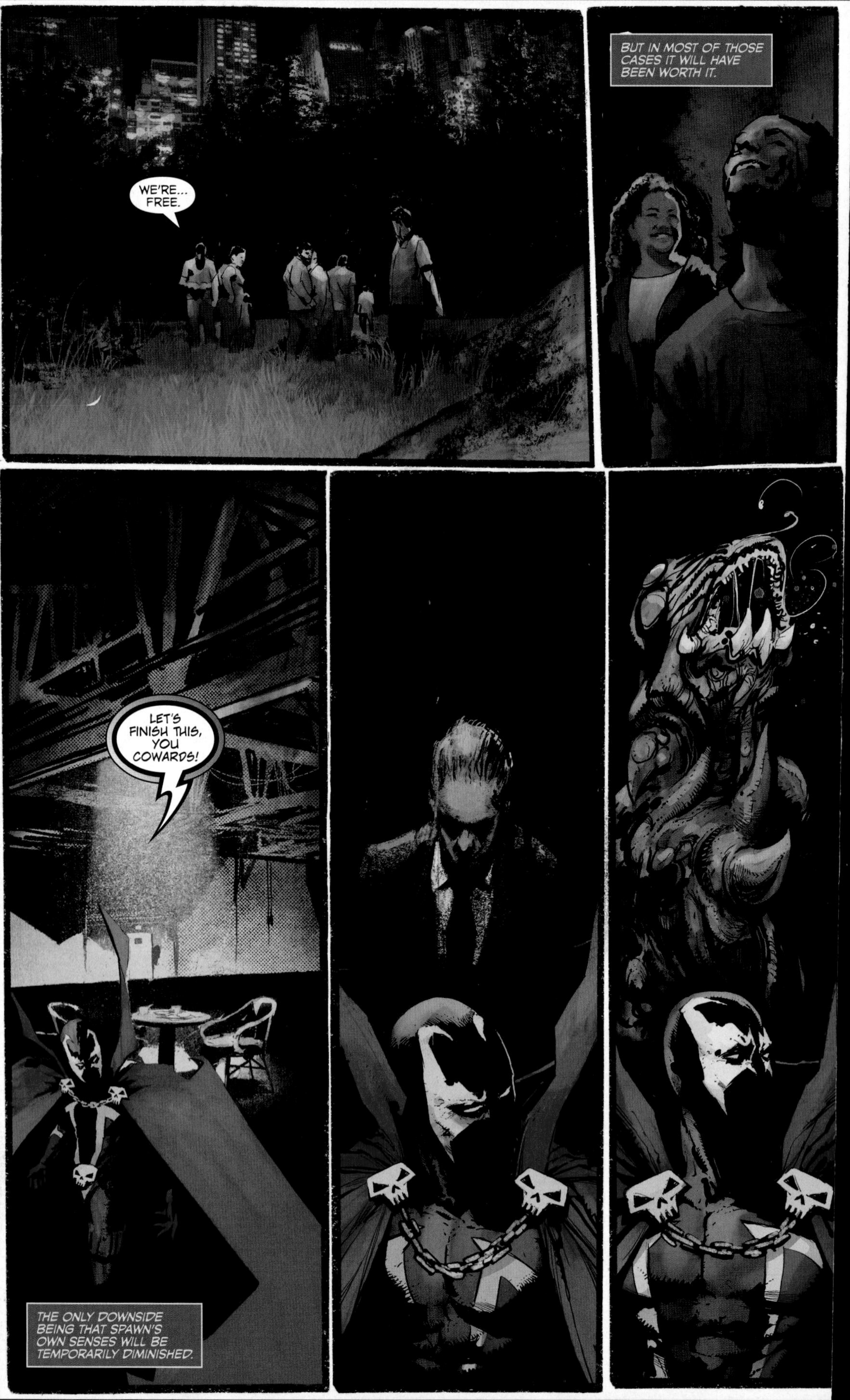
WE'RE... FREE.
BUT IN MOST OF THOSE CASES IT WILL HAVE BEEN WORTH IT.
LET'S FINISH THIS, YOU COWARDS!
THE ONLY DOWNSIDE BEING THAT SPAWN'S OWN SENSES WILL BE TEMPORARILY DIMINISHED.

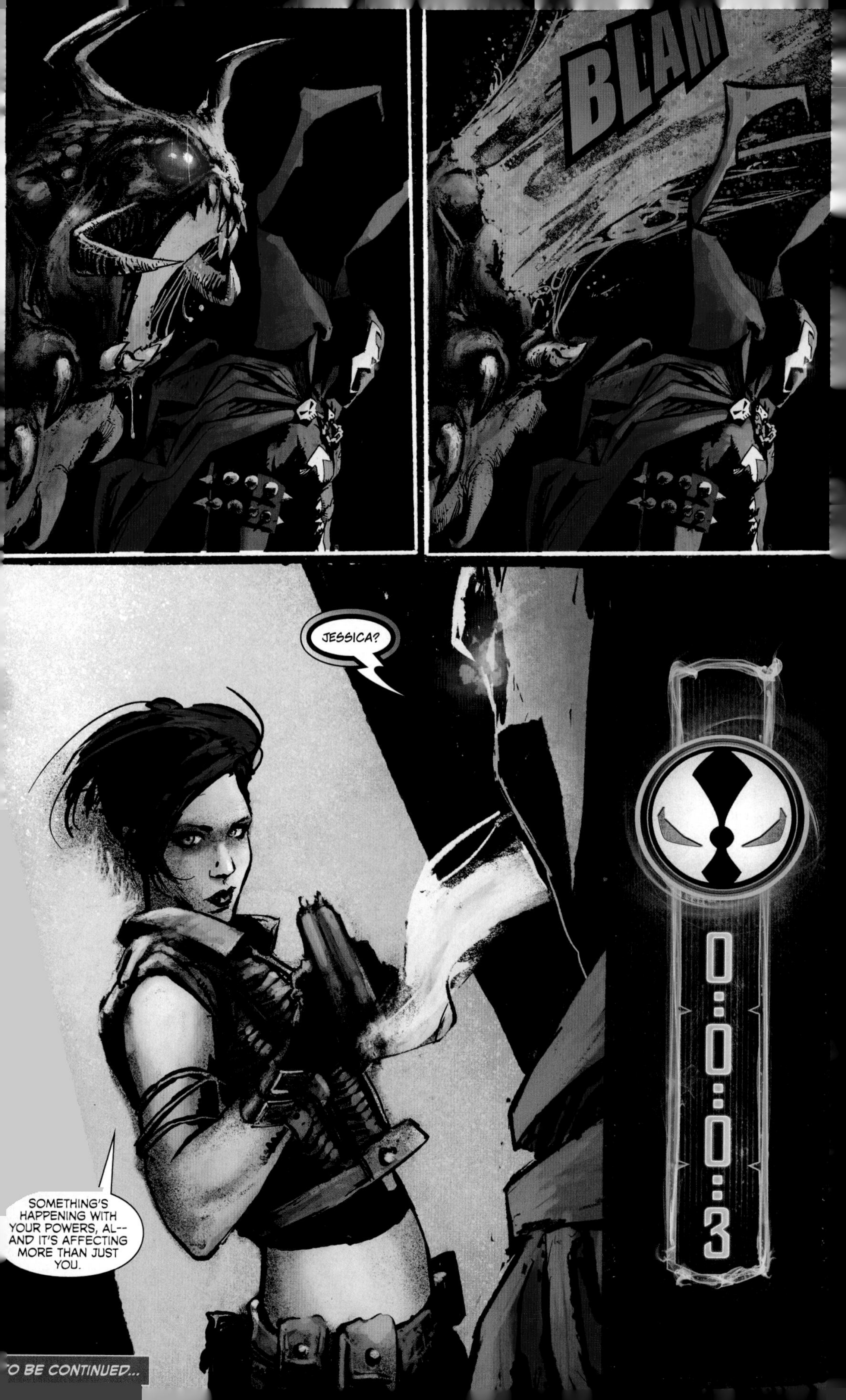
BLAM
JESSICA?
SOMETHING'S HAPPENING WITH YOUR POWERS, AL-- AND IT'S AFFECTING MORE THAN JUST YOU.
0:0:0:3
TO BE CONTINUED...

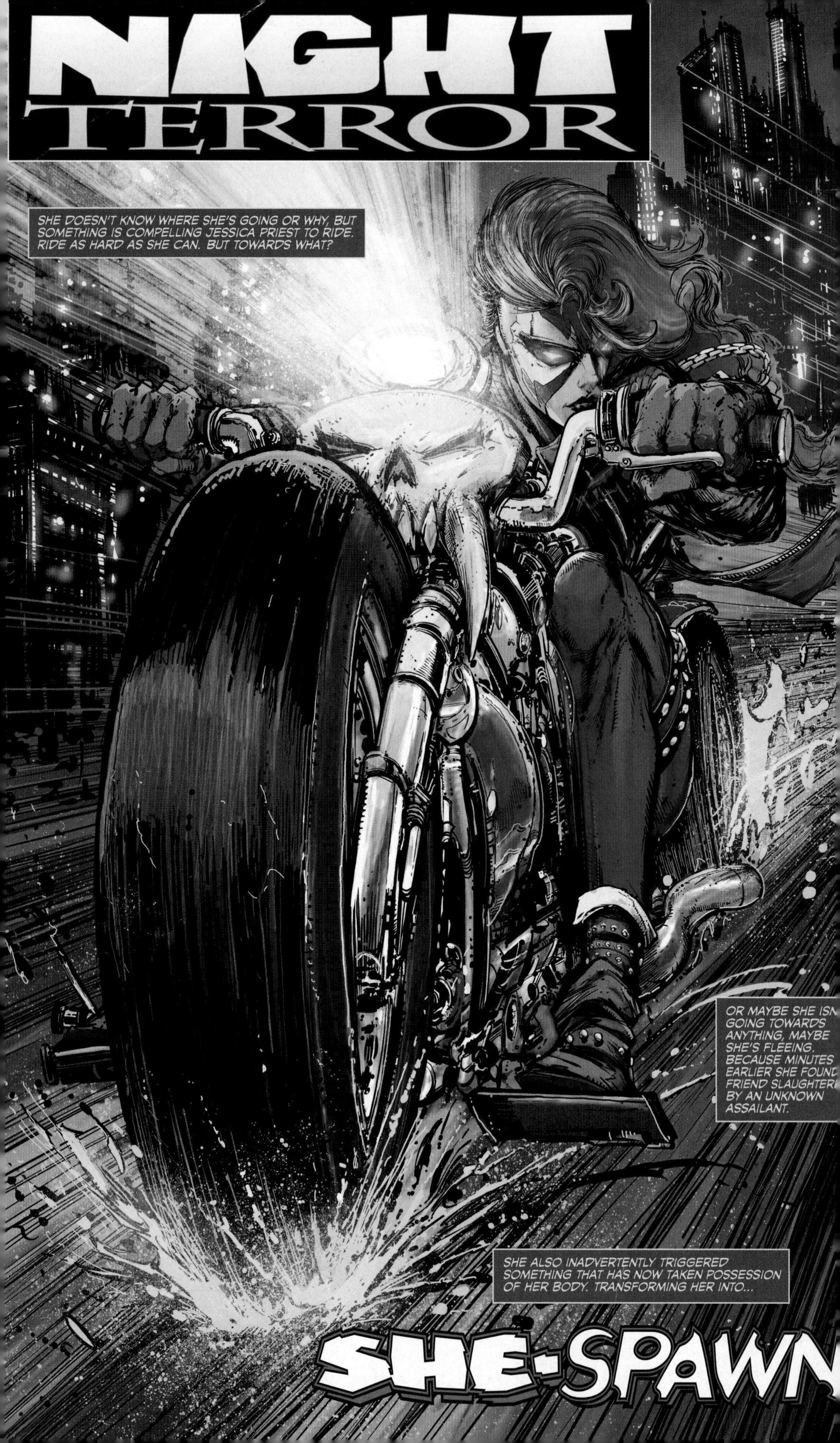
NIGHT TERROR
SHE DOESN'T KNOW WHERE SHE'S GOING OR WHY, BUT SOMETHING IS COMPELLING JESSICA PRIEST TO RIDE. RIDE AS HARD AS SHE CAN. BUT TOWARDS WHAT?
OR MAYBE SHE ISN GOING TOWARDS ANYTHING, MAYBE SHE'S FLEEING. BECAUSE MINUTES EARLIER SHE FOUND FRIEND SLAUGHTER BY AN UNKNOWN ASSAILANT.
SHE ALSO INADVERTENTLY TRIGGERED SOMETHING THAT HAS NOW TAKEN POSSESSION OF HER BODY. TRANSFORMING HER INTO...
SHE-SPAWN

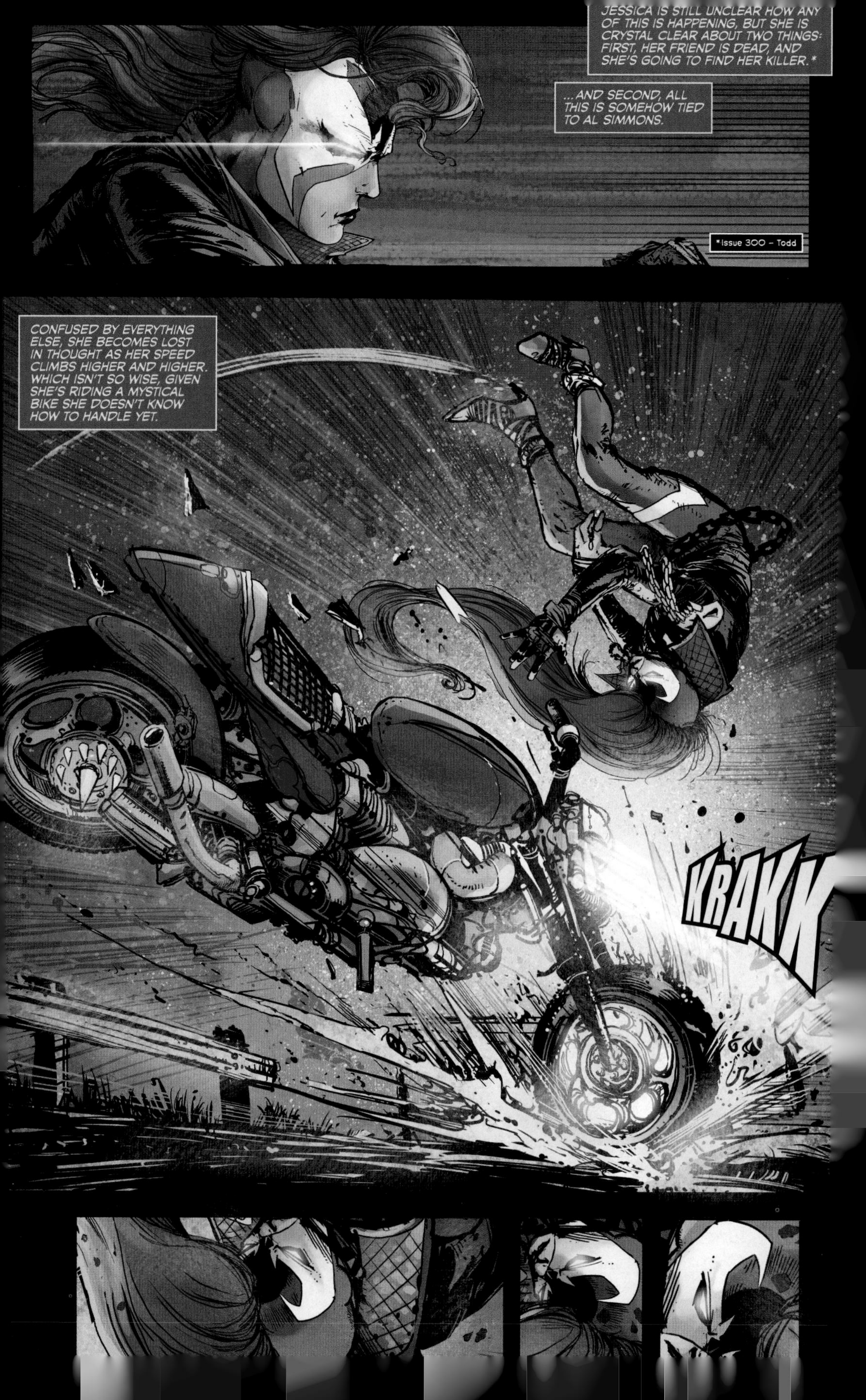
JESSICA IS STILL UNCLEAR HOW ANY OF THIS IS HAPPENING, BUT SHE IS CRYSTAL CLEAR ABOUT TWO THINGS: FIRST, HER FRIEND IS DEAD, AND SHE'S GOING TO FIND HER KILLER.*
...AND SECOND, ALL THIS IS SOMEHOW TIED TO AL SIMMONS.
*Issue 300 – Todd
CONFUSED BY EVERYTHING ELSE, SHE BECOMES LOST IN THOUGHT AS HER SPEED CLIMBS HIGHER AND HIGHER. WHICH ISN'T SO WISE, GIVEN SHE'S RIDING A MYSTICAL BIKE SHE DOESN'T KNOW HOW TO HANDLE YET.
KRAKK

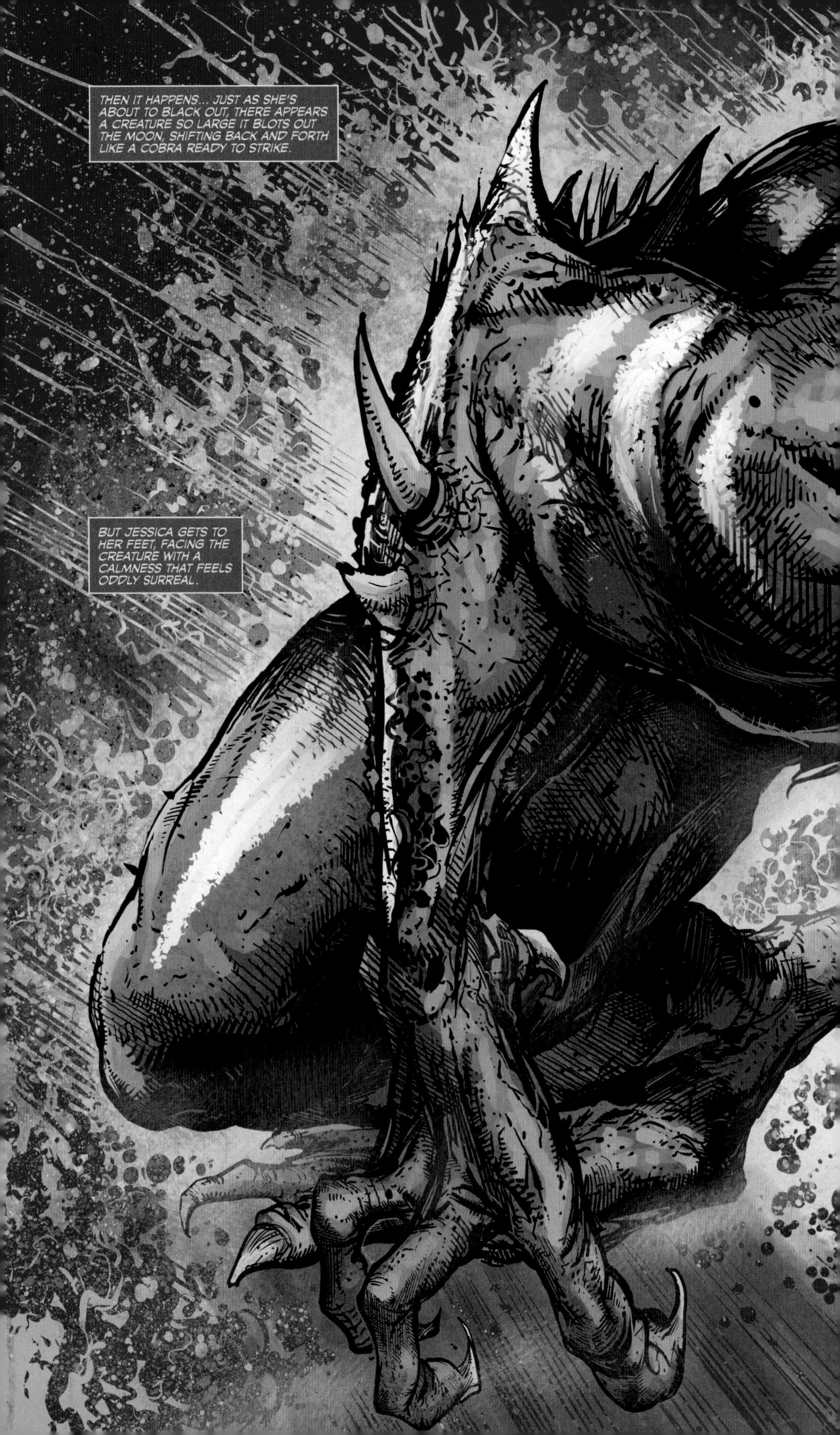
THEN IT HAPPENS... JUST AS SHE'S ABOUT TO BLACK OUT, THERE APPEARS A CREATURE SO LARGE IT BLOTS OUT THE MOON, SHIFTING BACK AND FORTH LIKE A COBRA READY TO STRIKE.
BUT JESSICA GETS TO HER FEET, FACING THE CREATURE WITH A CALMNESS THAT FEELS ODDLY SURREAL.

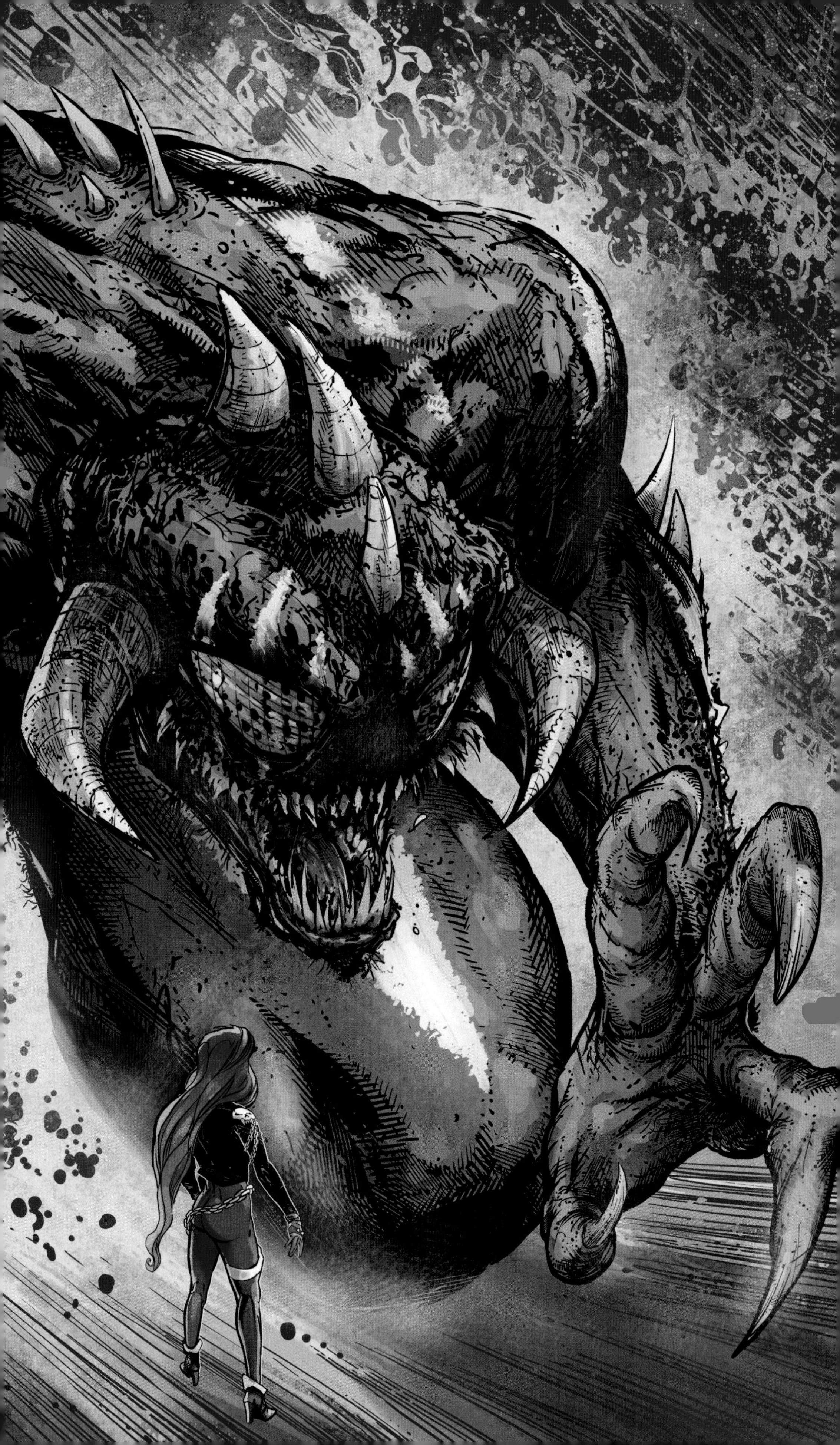

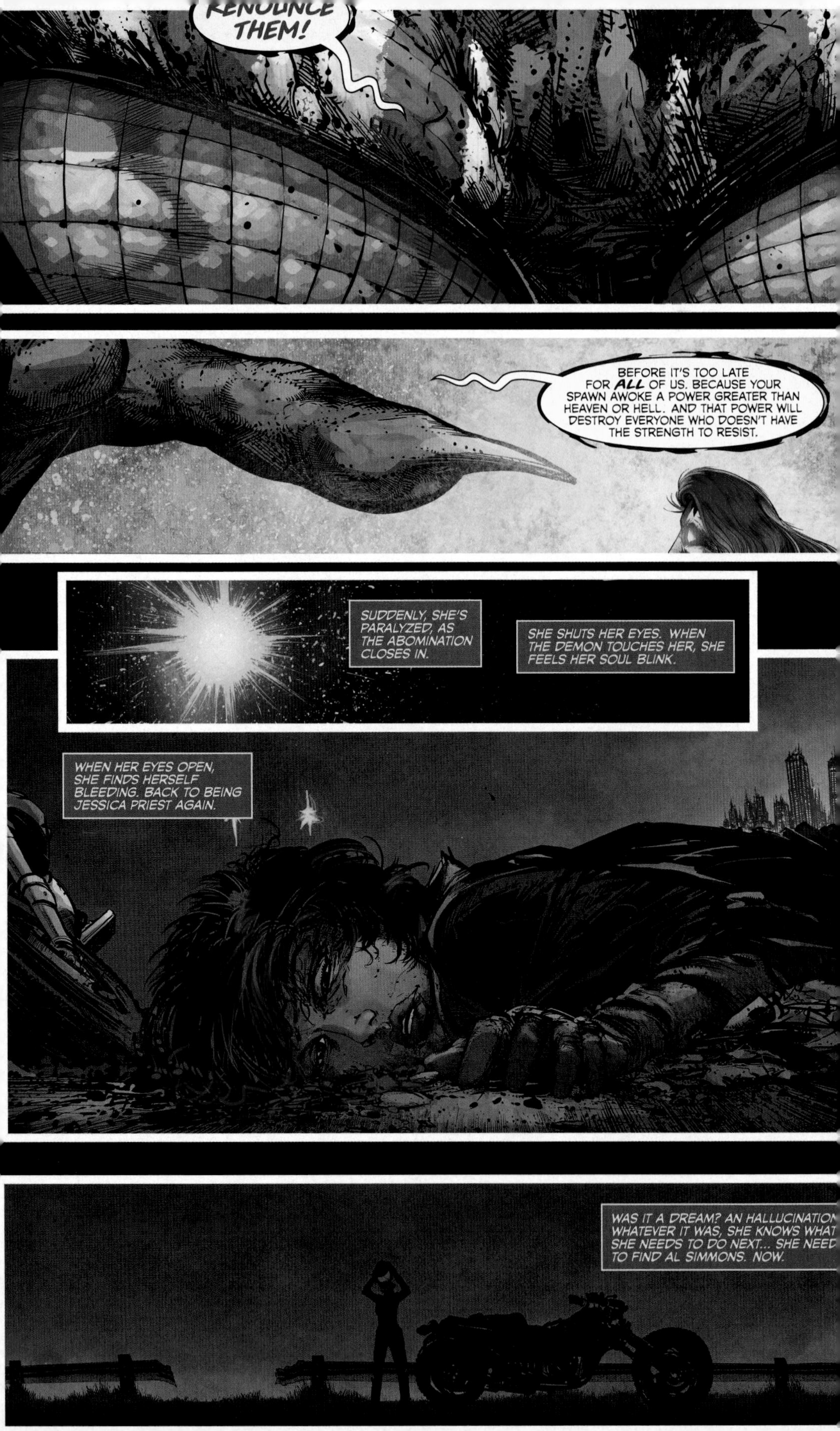
THEM!
BEFORE IT'S TOO LATE FOR ALL OF US. BECAUSE YOUR SPAWN AWOKE A POWER GREATER THAN HEAVEN OR HELL. AND THAT POWER WILL DESTROY EVERYONE WHO DOESN'T HAVE THE STRENGTH TO RESIST.
SUDDENLY, SHE'S PARALYZED, AS THE ABOMINATION CLOSES IN.
SHE SHUTS HER EYES. WHEN THE DEMON TOUCHES HER, SHE FEELS HER SOUL BLINK.
WHEN HER EYES OPEN, SHE FINDS HERSELF BLEEDING. BACK TO BEING JESSICA PRIEST AGAIN.
WAS IT A DREAM? AN HALLUCINATION WHATEVER IT WAS, SHE KNOWS WHAT SHE NEEDS TO DO NEXT... SHE NEED TO FIND AL SIMMONS. NOW.

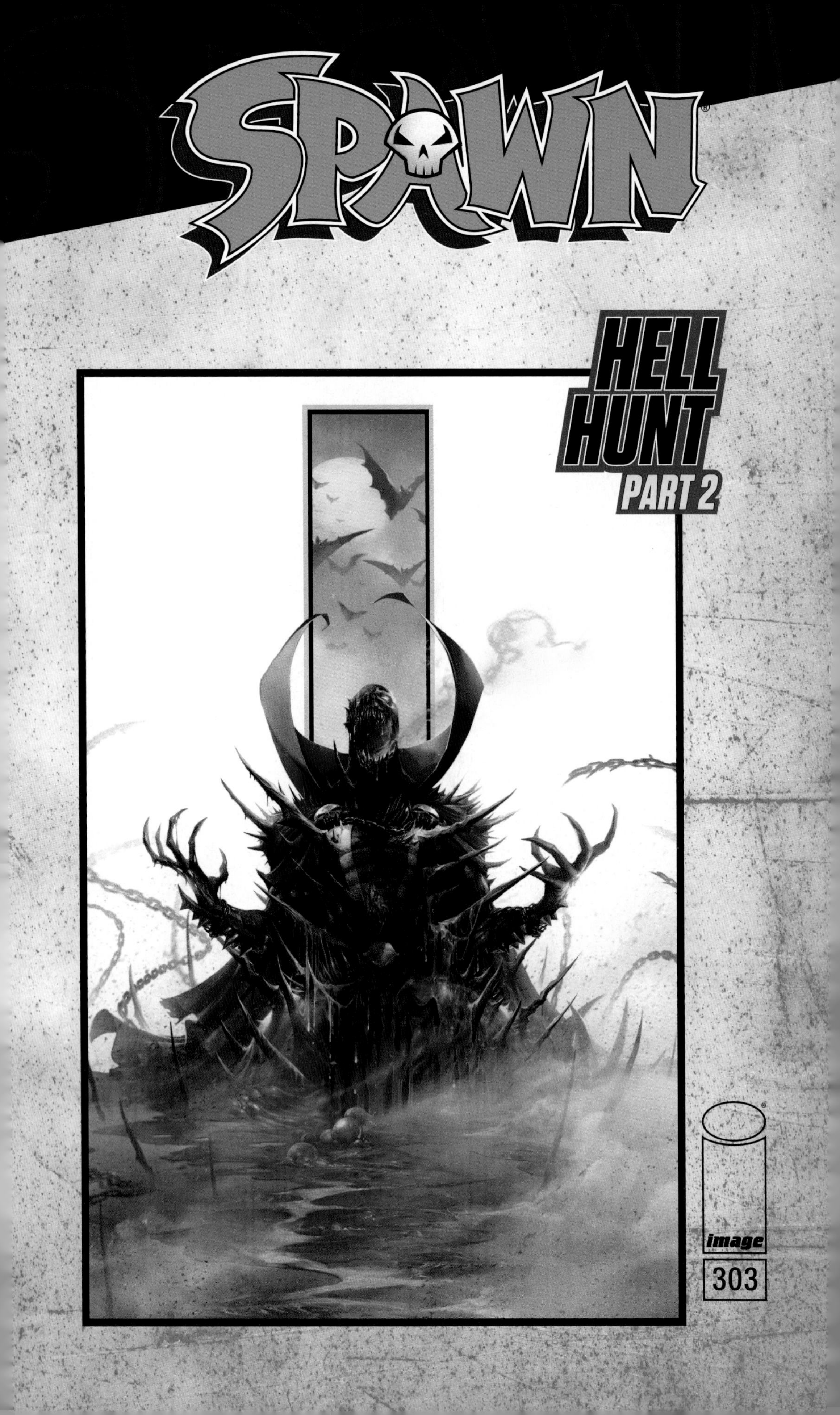
SPAWN
HELL HUNT
PART 2
image
303

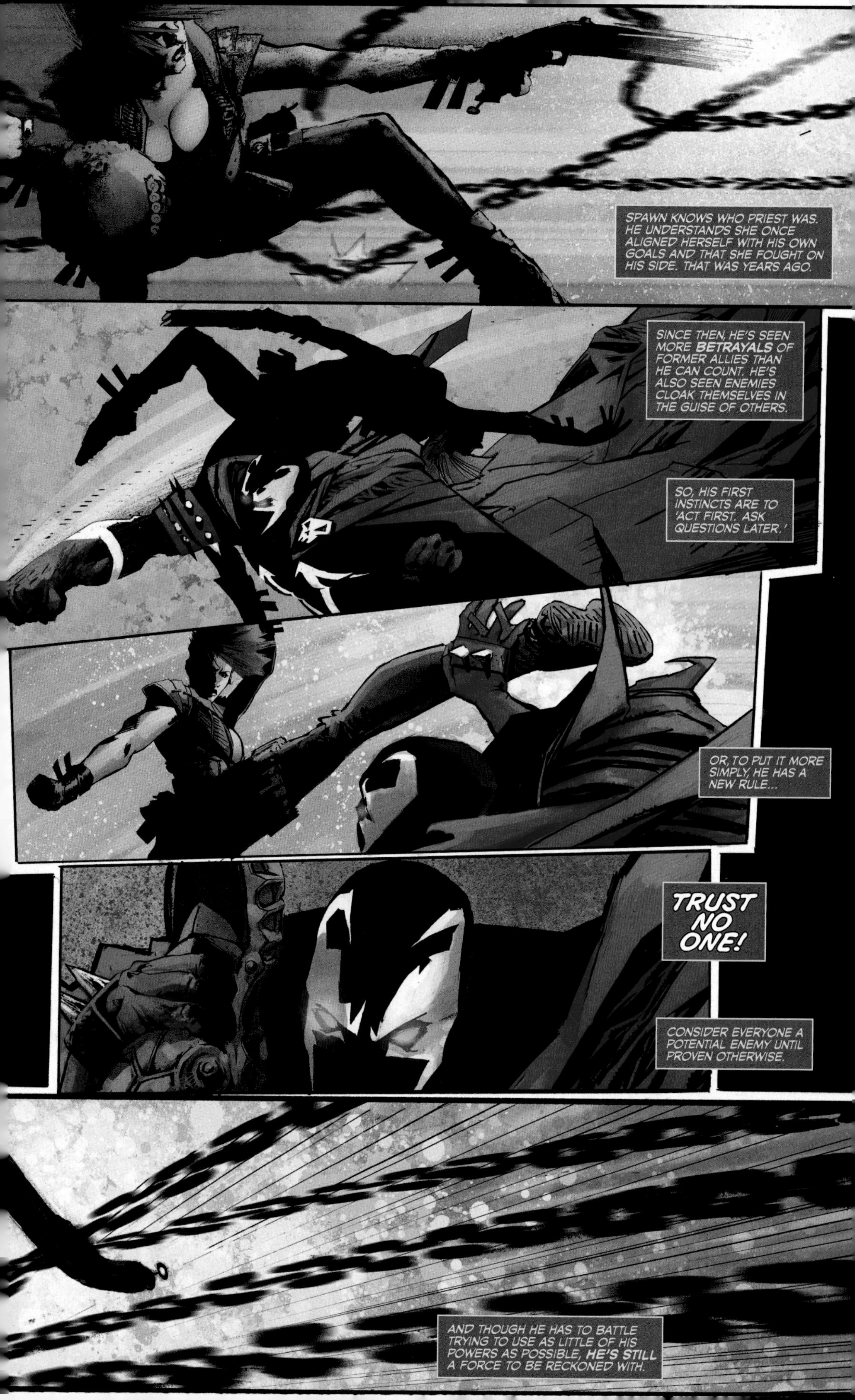
SPAWN KNOWS WHO PRIEST WAS. HE UNDERSTANDS SHE ONCE ALIGNED HERSELF WITH HIS OWN GOALS AND THAT SHE FOUGHT ON HIS SIDE. THAT WAS YEARS AGO.
SINCE THEN, HE'S SEEN MORE BETRAYALS OF FORMER ALLIES THAN HE CAN COUNT. HE'S ALSO SEEN ENEMIES CLOAK THEMSELVES IN THE GUISE OF OTHERS.
SO, HIS FIRST INSTINCTS ARE TO 'ACT FIRST. ASK QUESTIONS LATER.'
OR, TO PUT IT MORE SIMPLY, HE HAS A NEW RULE...
TRUST NO ONE!
CONSIDER EVERYONE A POTENTIAL ENEMY UNTIL PROVEN OTHERWISE.
AND THOUGH HE HAS TO BATTLE TRYING TO USE AS LITTLE OF HIS POWERS AS POSSIBLE, HE'S STILL A FORCE TO BE RECKONED WITH.

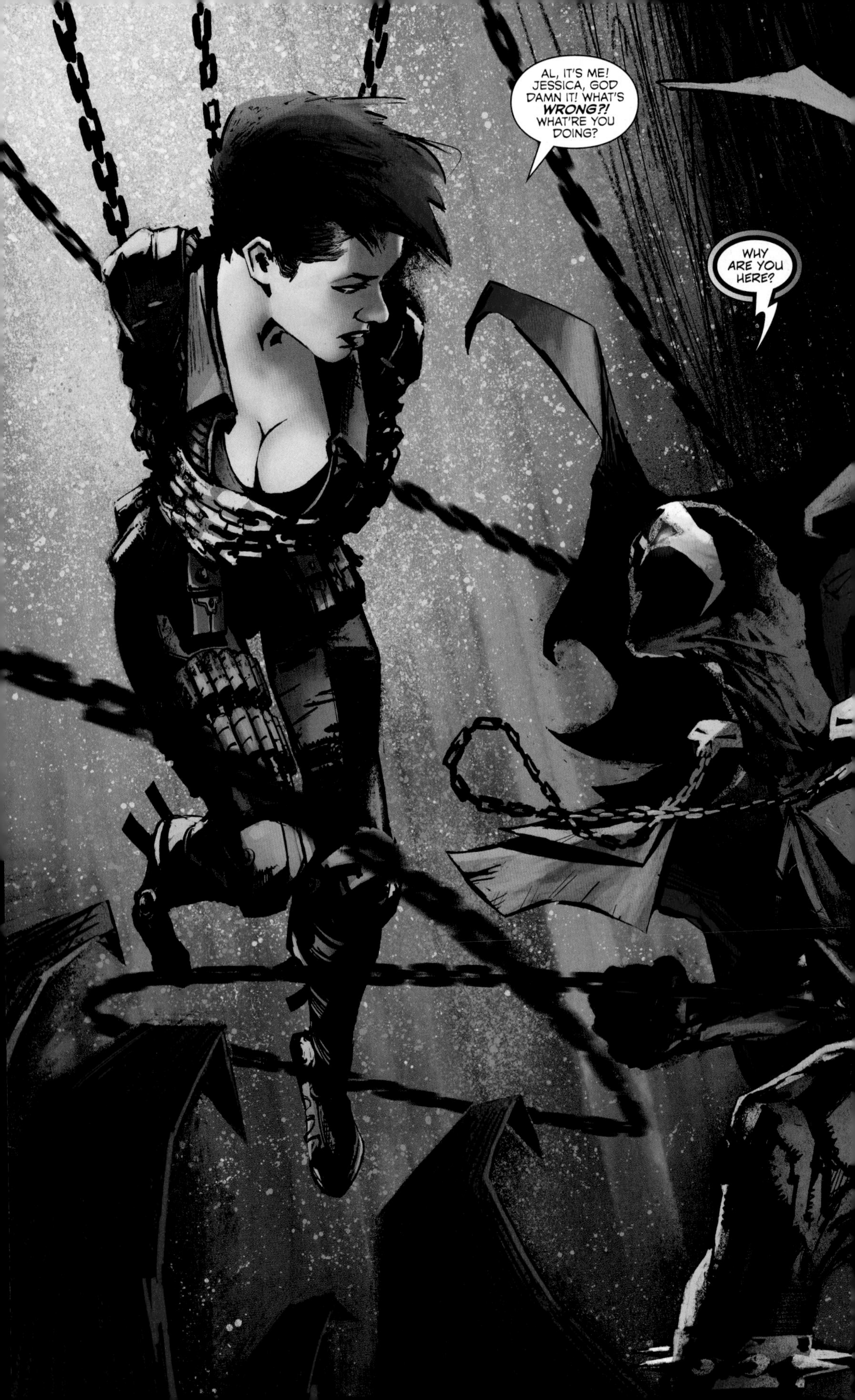
AL, IT'S ME! JESSICA, GOD DAMN IT! WHAT'S ***WRONG?!*** WHAT'RE YOU DOING?
WHY ARE YOU HERE?

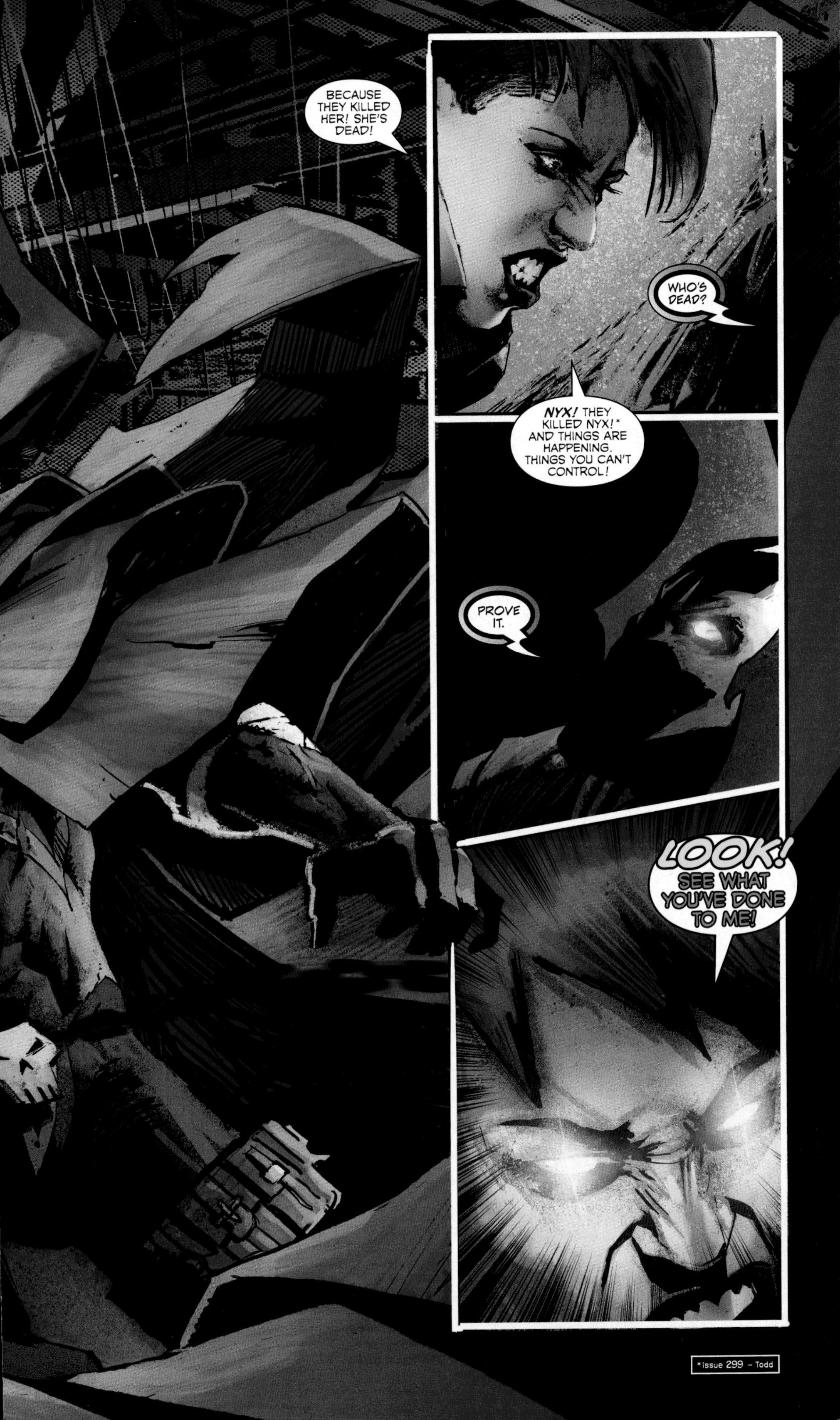
BECAUSE THEY KILLED HER! SHE'S DEAD!
WHO'S DEAD?
NYX! THEY KILLED NYX!* AND THINGS ARE HAPPENING. THINGS YOU CAN'T CONTROL!
PROVE IT.
LOOK! SEE WHAT YOU'VE DONE TO ME!
*Issue 299 - Todd

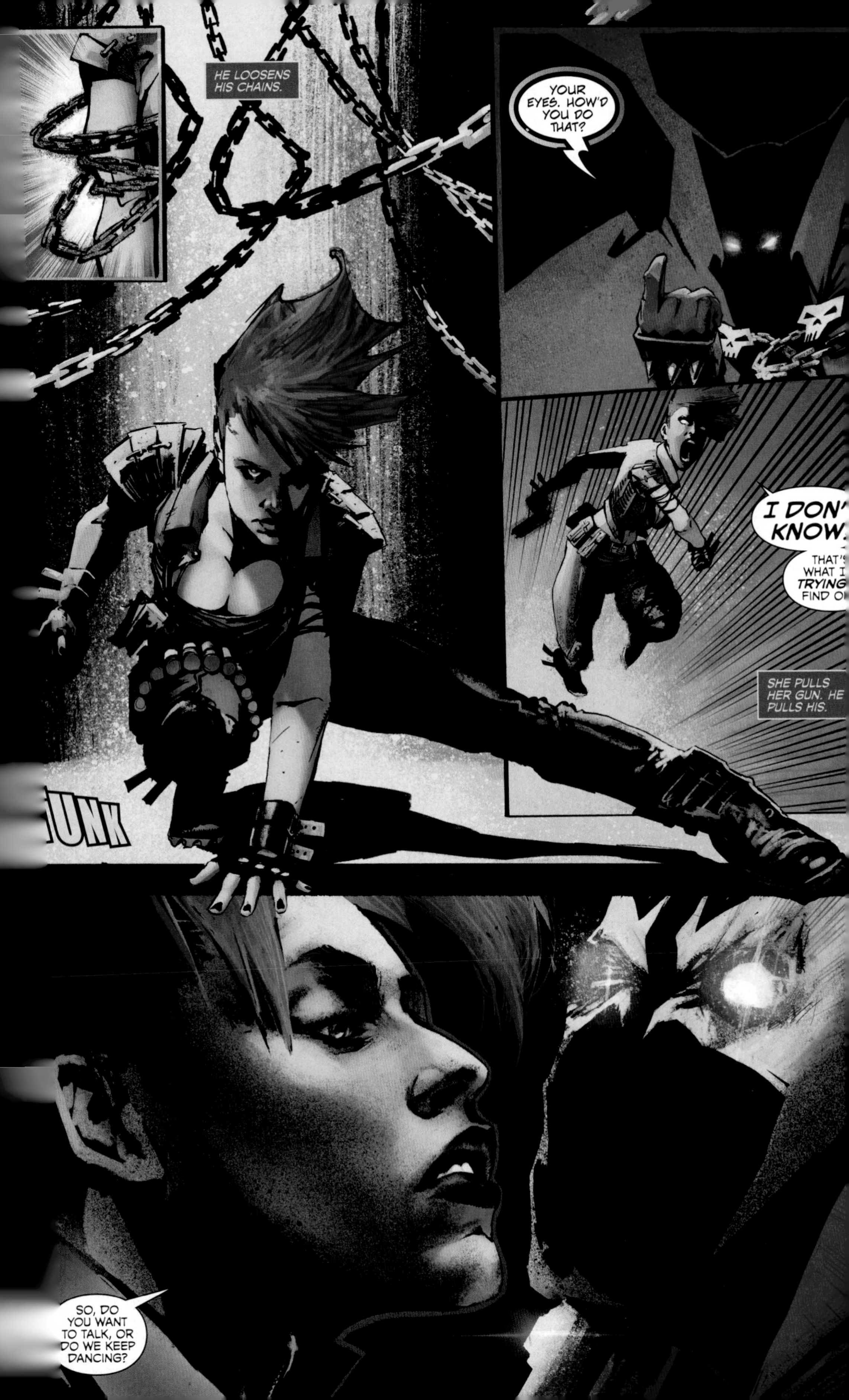
HE LOOSENS HIS CHAINS.
YOUR EYES. HOW'D YOU DO THAT?
I DON' KNOW.
THAT'S WHAT I TRYING FIND O
SHE PULLS HER GUN. HE PULLS HIS.
UNK
SO, DO YOU WANT TO TALK, OR DO WE KEEP DANCING?

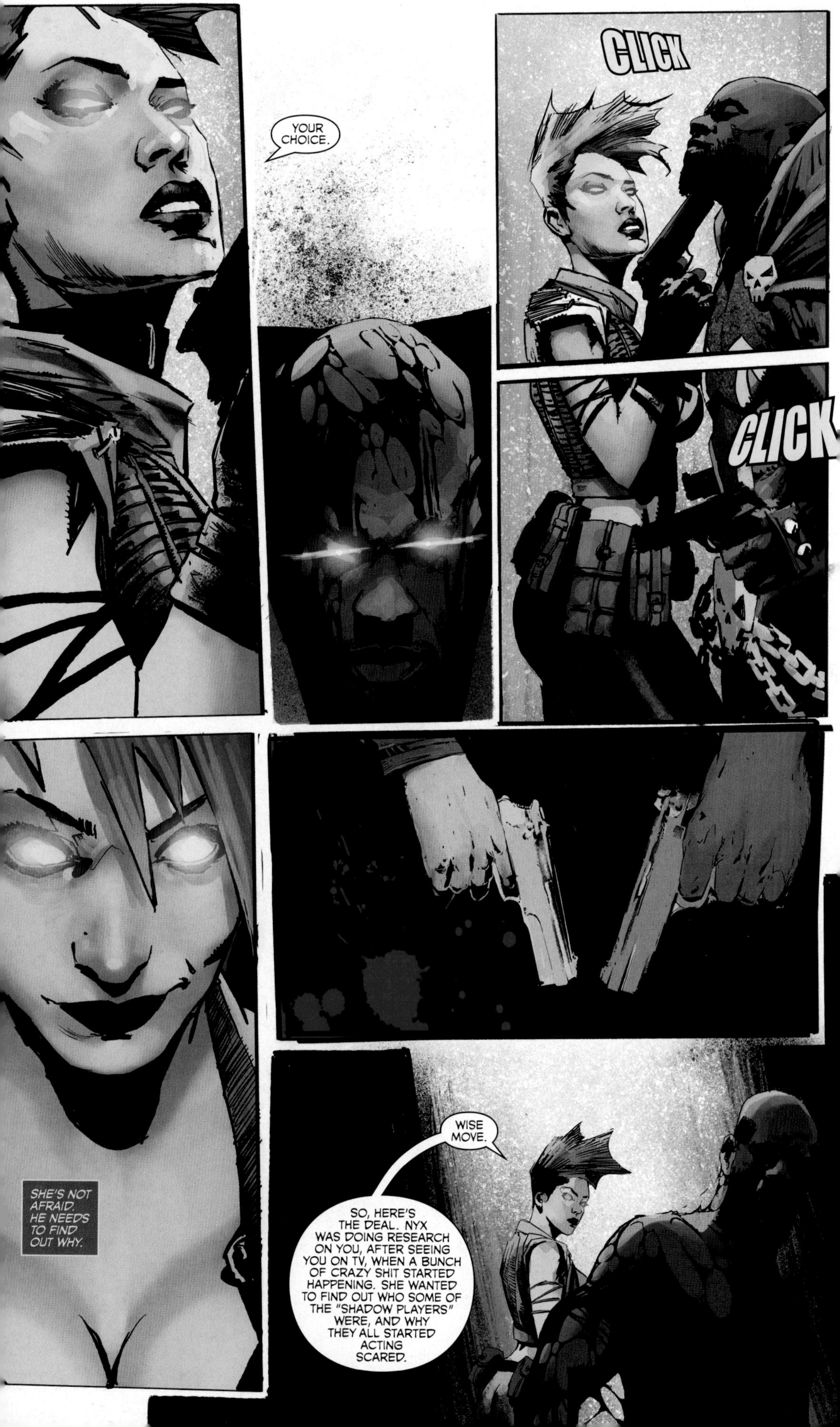
YOUR CHOICE.
CLICK
CLICK
SHE'S NOT AFRAID. HE NEEDS TO FIND OUT WHY.
WISE MOVE.
SO, HERE'S THE DEAL. NYX WAS DOING RESEARCH ON YOU, AFTER SEEING YOU ON TV, WHEN A BUNCH OF CRAZY SHIT STARTED HAPPENING. SHE WANTED TO FIND OUT WHO SOME OF THE "SHADOW PLAYERS" WERE, AND WHY THEY ALL STARTED ACTING SCARED.

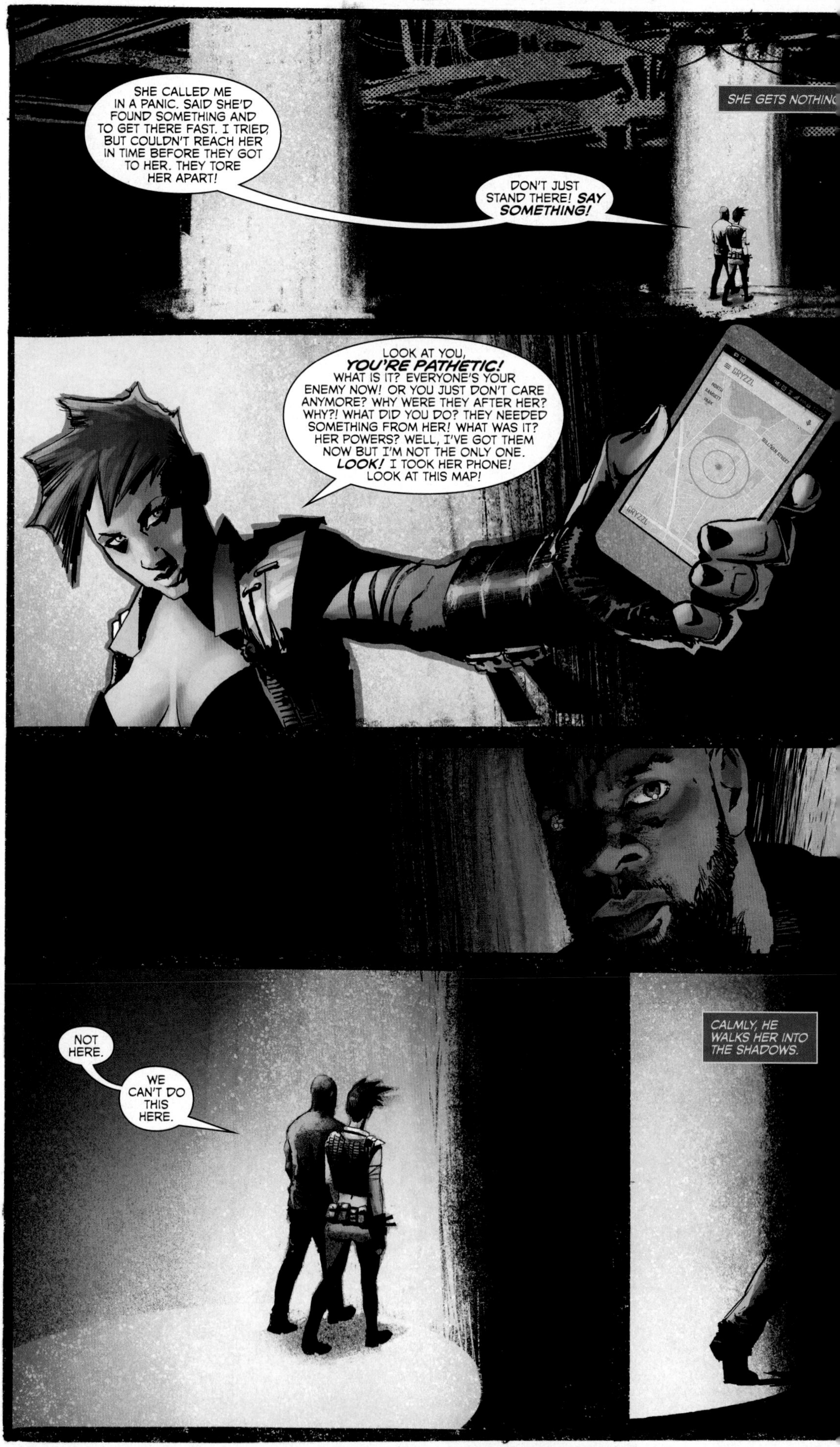
SHE CALLED ME IN A PANIC. SAID SHE'D FOUND SOMETHING AND TO GET THERE FAST. I TRIED, BUT COULDN'T REACH HER IN TIME BEFORE THEY GOT TO HER. THEY TORE HER APART!
SHE GETS NOTHING
DON'T JUST STAND THERE! SAY SOMETHING!
LOOK AT YOU, YOU'RE PATHETIC! WHAT IS IT? EVERYONE'S YOUR ENEMY NOW! OR YOU JUST DON'T CARE ANYMORE? WHY WERE THEY AFTER HER? WHY?! WHAT DID YOU DO? THEY NEEDED SOMETHING FROM HER! WHAT WAS IT? HER POWERS? WELL, I'VE GOT THEM NOW BUT I'M NOT THE ONLY ONE. LOOK! I TOOK HER PHONE! LOOK AT THIS MAP!
GRYZZL
NOT HERE.
WE CAN'T DO THIS HERE.
CALMLY, HE WALKS HER INTO THE SHADOWS.

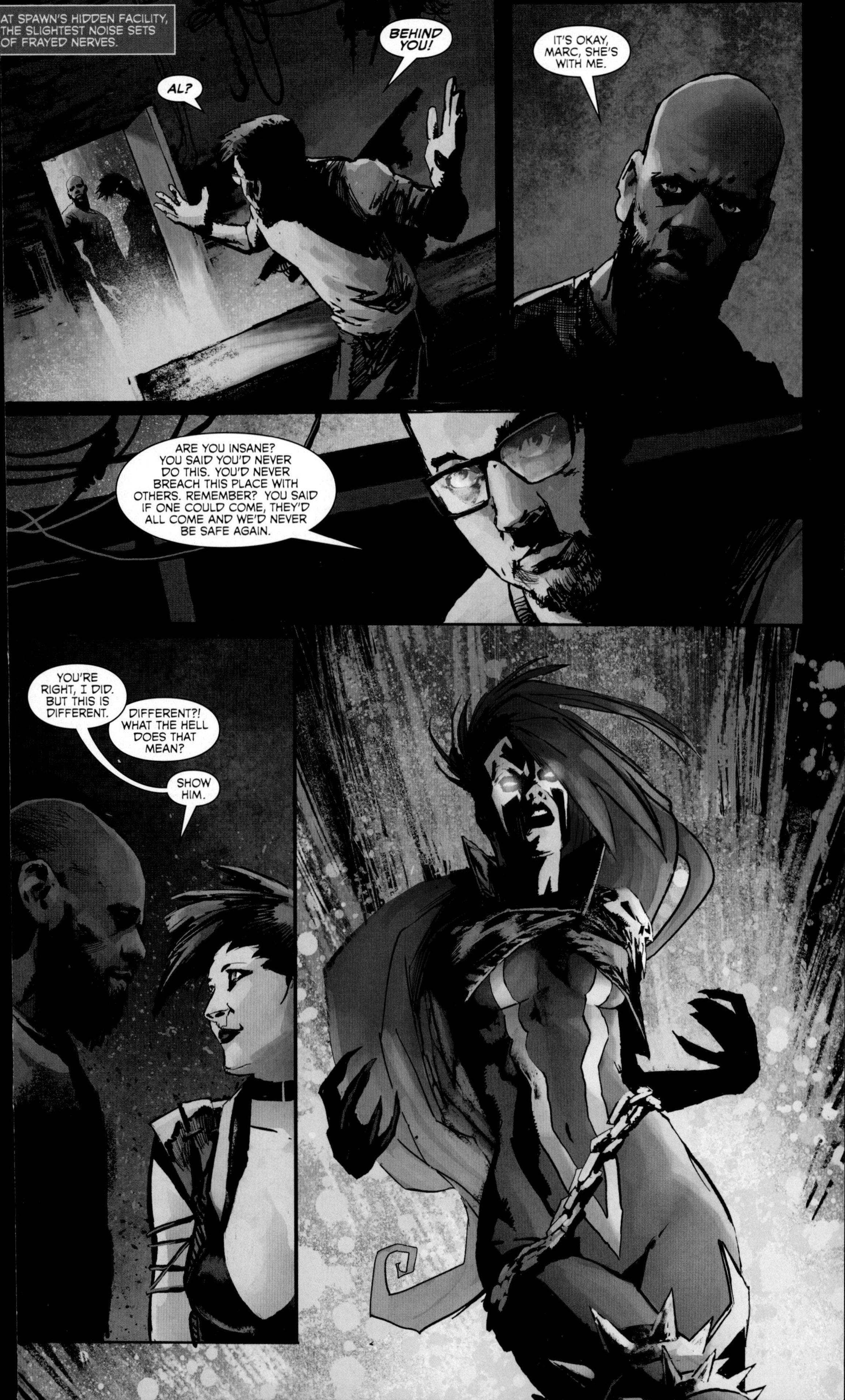
AT SPAWN'S HIDDEN FACILITY, THE SLIGHTEST NOISE SETS OF FRAYED NERVES.
AL?
BEHIND YOU!
IT'S OKAY, MARC, SHE'S WITH ME.
ARE YOU INSANE? YOU SAID YOU'D NEVER DO THIS. YOU'D NEVER BREACH THIS PLACE WITH OTHERS. REMEMBER? YOU SAID IF ONE COULD COME, THEY'D ALL COME AND WE'D NEVER BE SAFE AGAIN.
YOU'RE RIGHT, I DID. BUT THIS IS DIFFERENT.
DIFFERENT?! WHAT THE HELL DOES THAT MEAN?
SHOW HIM.

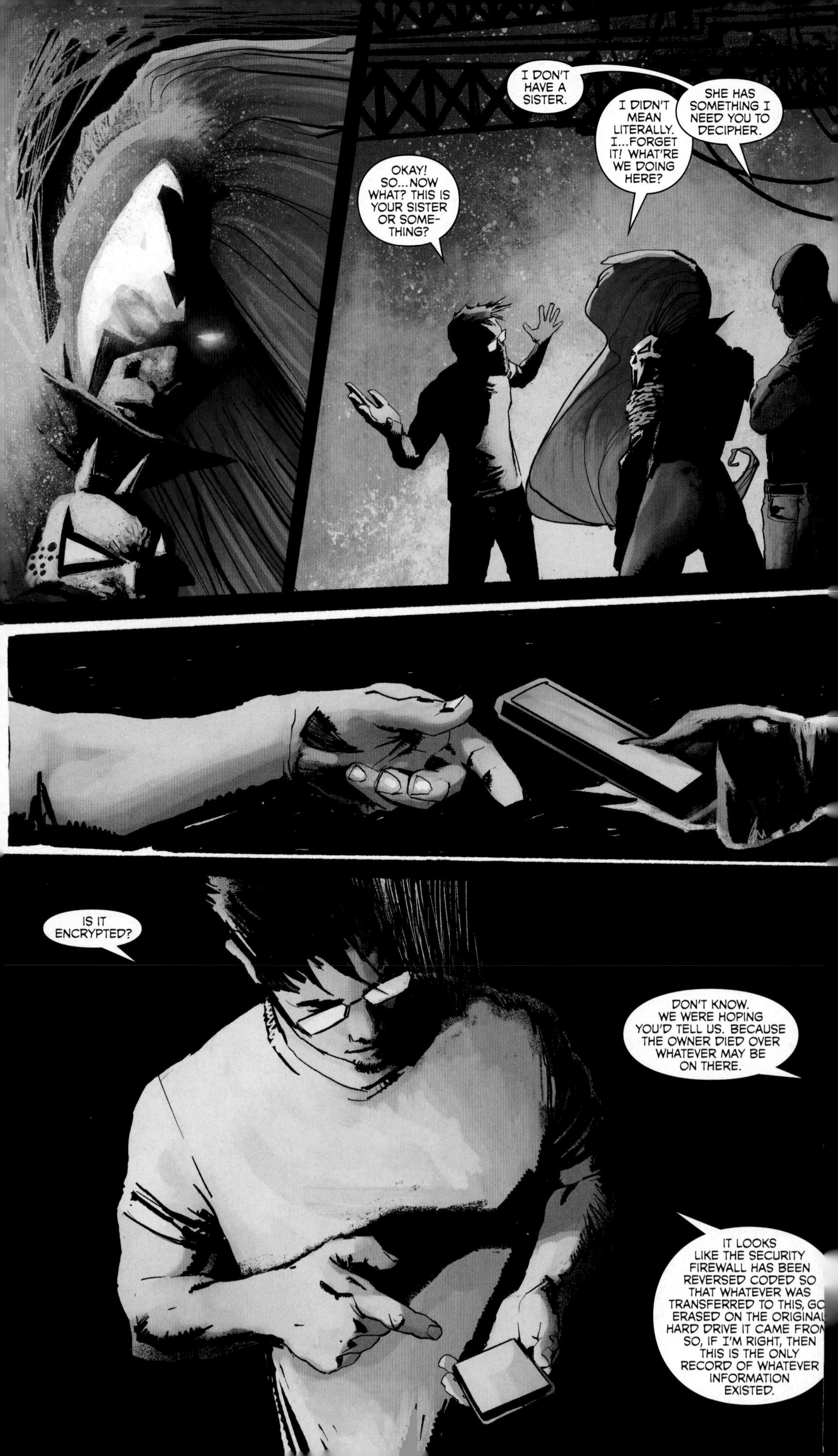
OKAY! SO...NOW WHAT? THIS IS YOUR SISTER OR SOME-THING?
I DON'T HAVE A SISTER.
I DIDN'T MEAN LITERALLY. I...FORGET IT! WHAT'RE WE DOING HERE?
SHE HAS SOMETHING I NEED YOU TO DECIPHER.
IS IT ENCRYPTED?
DON'T KNOW. WE WERE HOPING YOU'D TELL US. BECAUSE THE OWNER DIED OVER WHATEVER MAY BE ON THERE.
IT LOOKS LIKE THE SECURITY FIREWALL HAS BEEN REVERSED CODED SO THAT WHATEVER WAS TRANSFERRED TO THIS, GO ERASED ON THE ORIGINAL HARD DRIVE IT CAME FROM SO, IF I'M RIGHT, THEN THIS IS THE ONLY RECORD OF WHATEVER INFORMATION EXISTED.

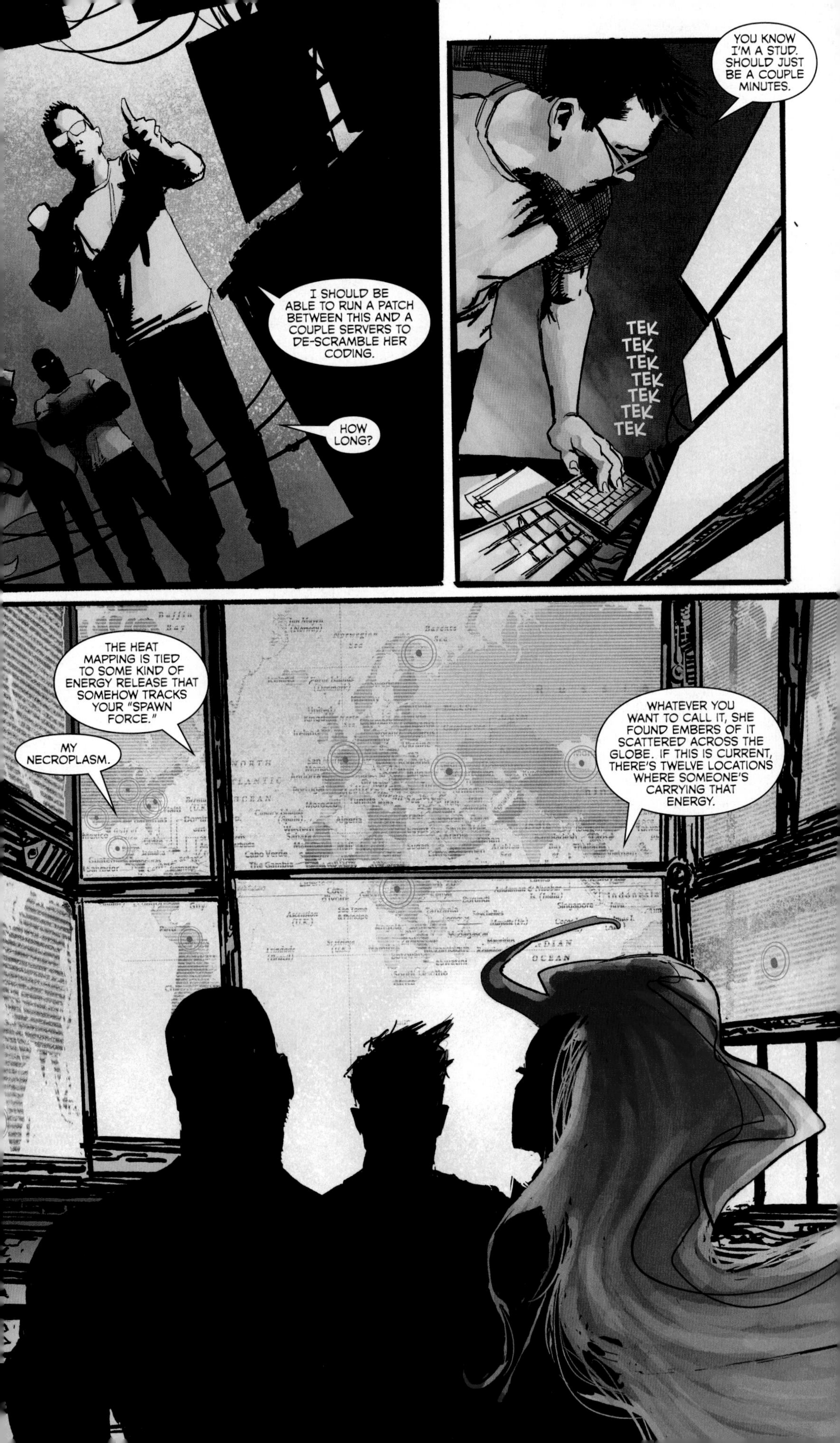
I SHOULD BE ABLE TO RUN A PATCH BETWEEN THIS AND A COUPLE SERVERS TO DE-SCRAMBLE HER CODING.
HOW LONG?
YOU KNOW I'M A STUD. SHOULD JUST BE A COUPLE MINUTES.
TEK TEK TEK TEK TEK TEK TEK
THE HEAT MAPPING IS TIED TO SOME KIND OF ENERGY RELEASE THAT SOMEHOW TRACKS YOUR "SPAWN FORCE."
MY NECROPLASM.
WHATEVER YOU WANT TO CALL IT, SHE FOUND EMBERS OF IT SCATTERED ACROSS THE GLOBE. IF THIS IS CURRENT, THERE'S TWELVE LOCATIONS WHERE SOMEONE'S CARRYING THAT ENERGY.

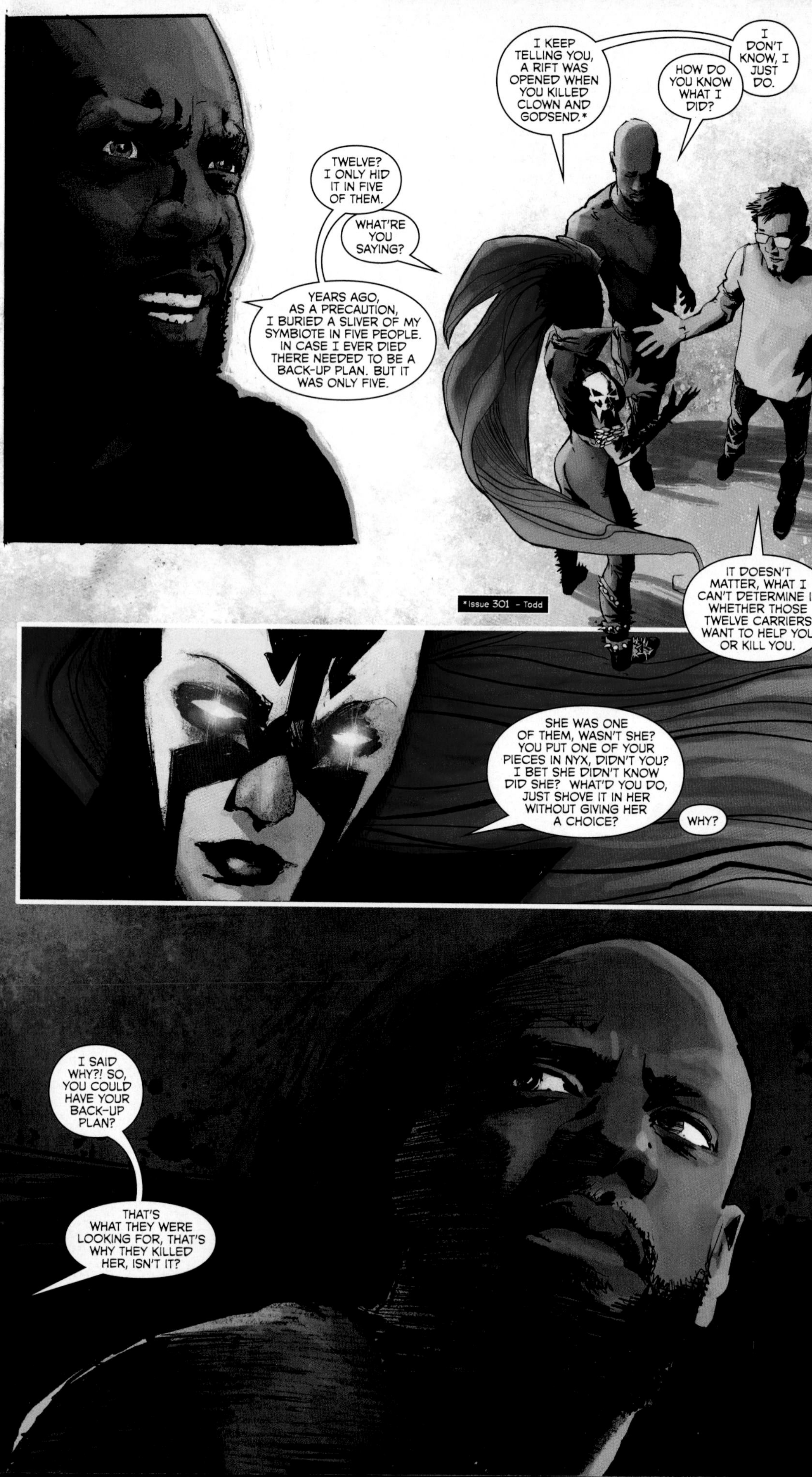
I KEEP TELLING YOU, A RIFT WAS OPENED WHEN YOU KILLED CLOWN AND GODSEND.*
HOW DO YOU KNOW WHAT I DID?
I DON'T KNOW, I JUST DO.
TWELVE? I ONLY HID IT IN FIVE OF THEM.
WHAT'RE YOU SAYING?
YEARS AGO, AS A PRECAUTION, I BURIED A SLIVER OF MY SYMBIOTE IN FIVE PEOPLE. IN CASE I EVER DIED THERE NEEDED TO BE A BACK-UP PLAN. BUT IT WAS ONLY FIVE.
IT DOESN'T MATTER, WHAT I CAN'T DETERMINE I WHETHER THOSE TWELVE CARRIERS WANT TO HELP YOU OR KILL YOU.
*Issue 301 – Todd
SHE WAS ONE OF THEM, WASN'T SHE? YOU PUT ONE OF YOUR PIECES IN NYX, DIDN'T YOU? I BET SHE DIDN'T KNOW DID SHE? WHAT'D YOU DO, JUST SHOVE IT IN HER WITHOUT GIVING HER A CHOICE?
WHY?
I SAID WHY?! SO, YOU COULD HAVE YOUR BACK-UP PLAN?
THAT'S WHAT THEY WERE LOOKING FOR, THAT'S WHY THEY KILLED HER, ISN'T IT?

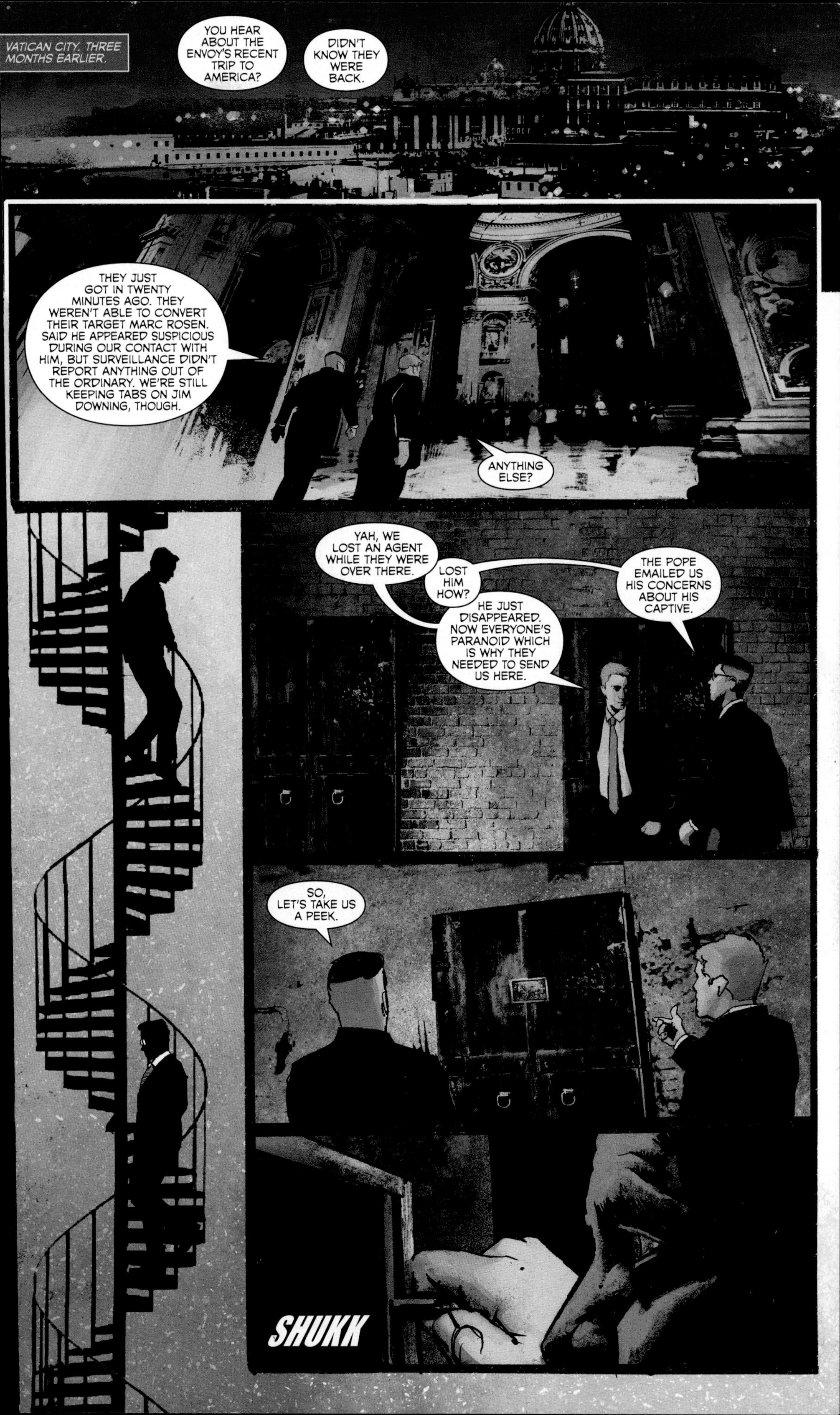
VATICAN CITY. THREE MONTHS EARLIER.
YOU HEAR ABOUT THE ENVOY'S RECENT TRIP TO AMERICA?
DIDN'T KNOW THEY WERE BACK.
THEY JUST GOT IN TWENTY MINUTES AGO. THEY WEREN'T ABLE TO CONVERT THEIR TARGET MARC ROSEN. SAID HE APPEARED SUSPICIOUS DURING OUR CONTACT WITH HIM, BUT SURVEILLANCE DIDN'T REPORT ANYTHING OUT OF THE ORDINARY. WE'RE STILL KEEPING TABS ON JIM DOWNING, THOUGH.
ANYTHING ELSE?
YAH, WE LOST AN AGENT WHILE THEY WERE OVER THERE.
LOST HIM HOW?
HE JUST DISAPPEARED. NOW EVERYONE'S PARANOID WHICH IS WHY THEY NEEDED TO SEND US HERE.
THE POPE EMAILED US HIS CONCERNS ABOUT HIS CAPTIVE.
SO, LET'S TAKE US A PEEK.
SHUKK

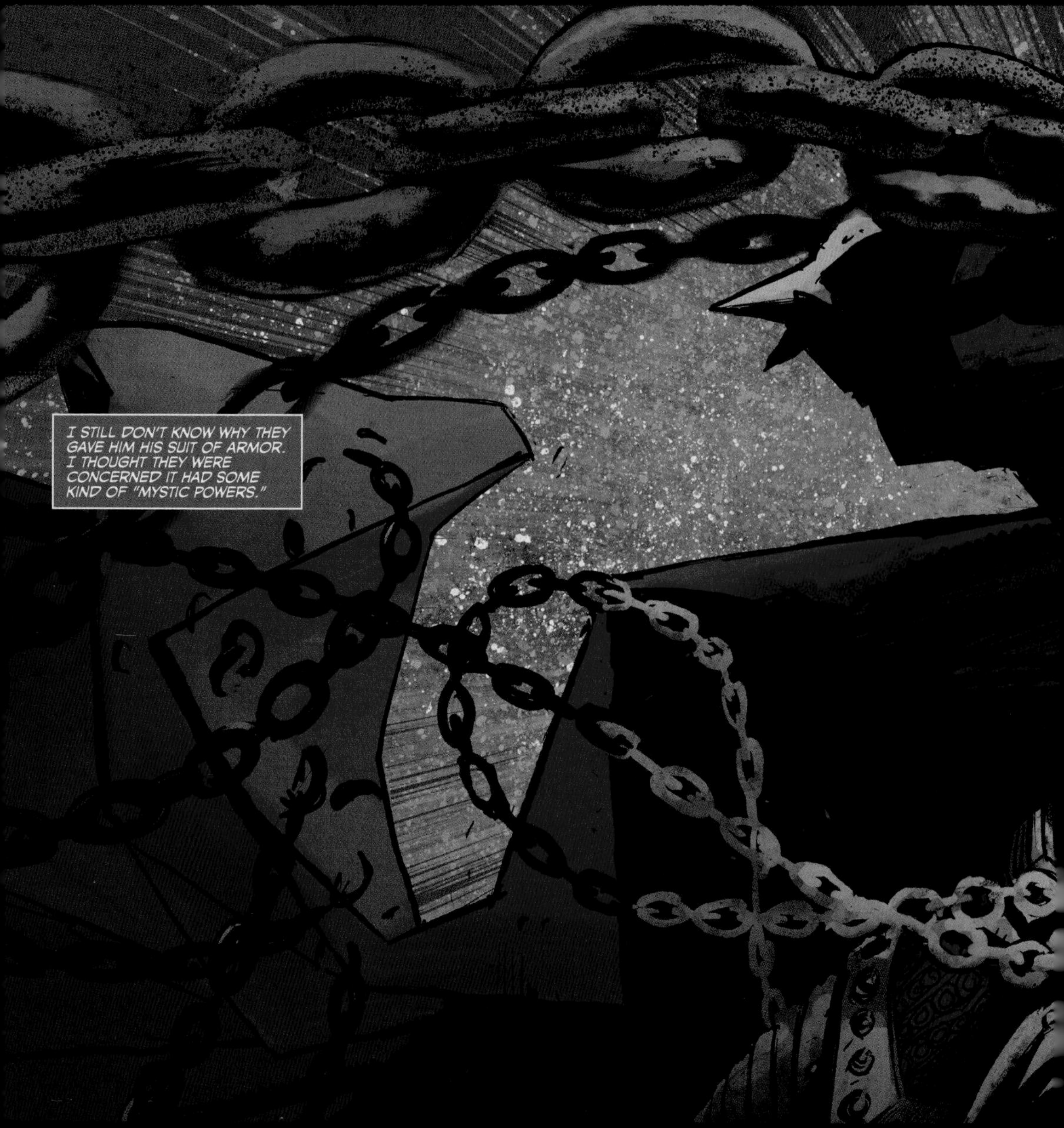
I STILL DON'T KNOW WHY THEY GAVE HIM HIS SUIT OF ARMOR. I THOUGHT THEY WERE CONCERNED IT HAD SOME KIND OF "MYSTIC POWERS."

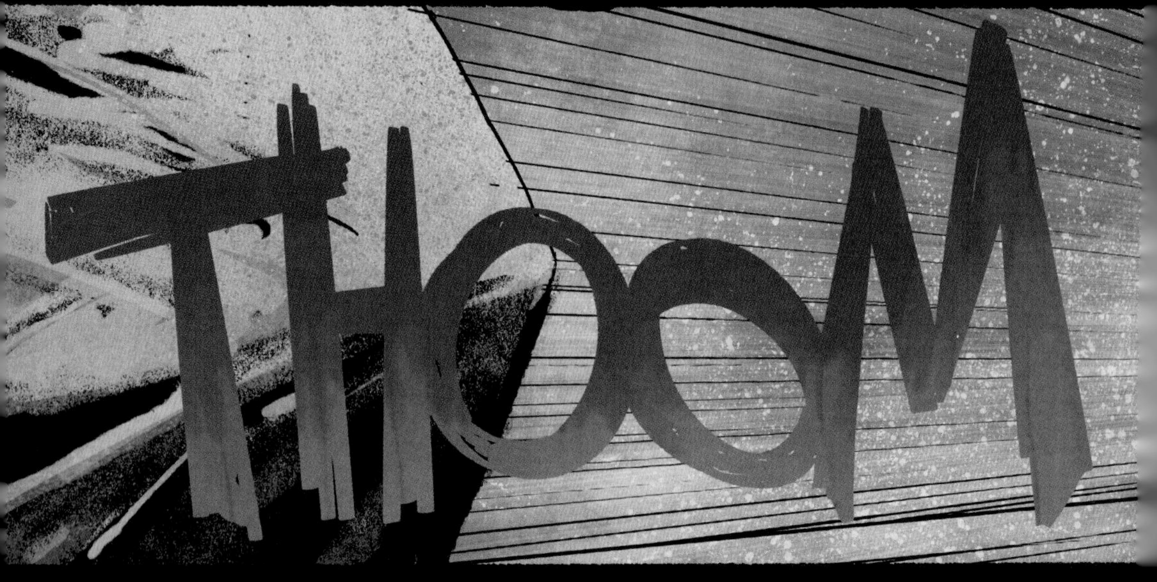
THOOM

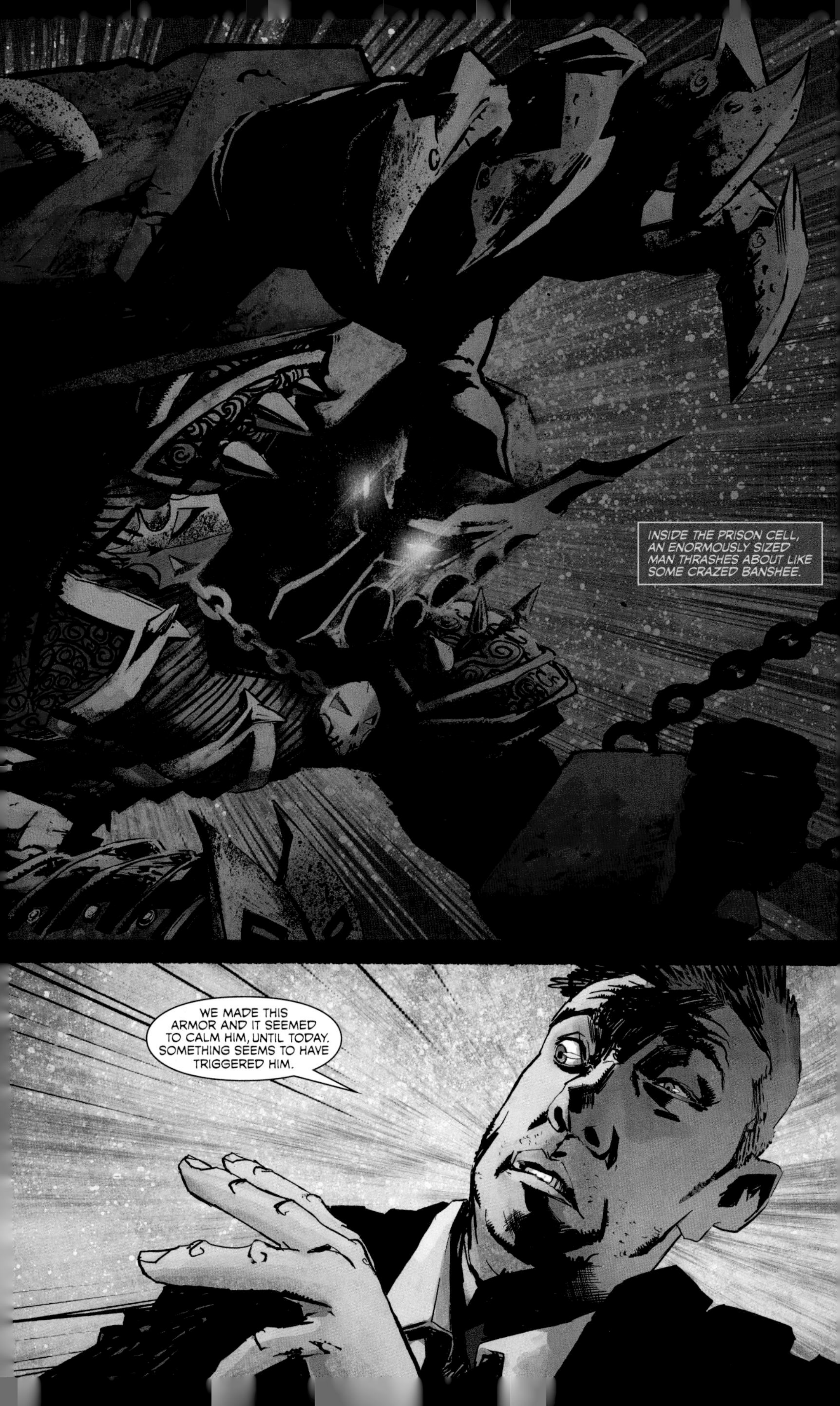
INSIDE THE PRISON CELL, AN ENORMOUSLY SIZED MAN THRASHES ABOUT LIKE SOME CRAZED BANSHEE.
WE MADE THIS ARMOR AND IT SEEMED TO CALM HIM, UNTIL TODAY. SOMETHING SEEMS TO HAVE TRIGGERED HIM.

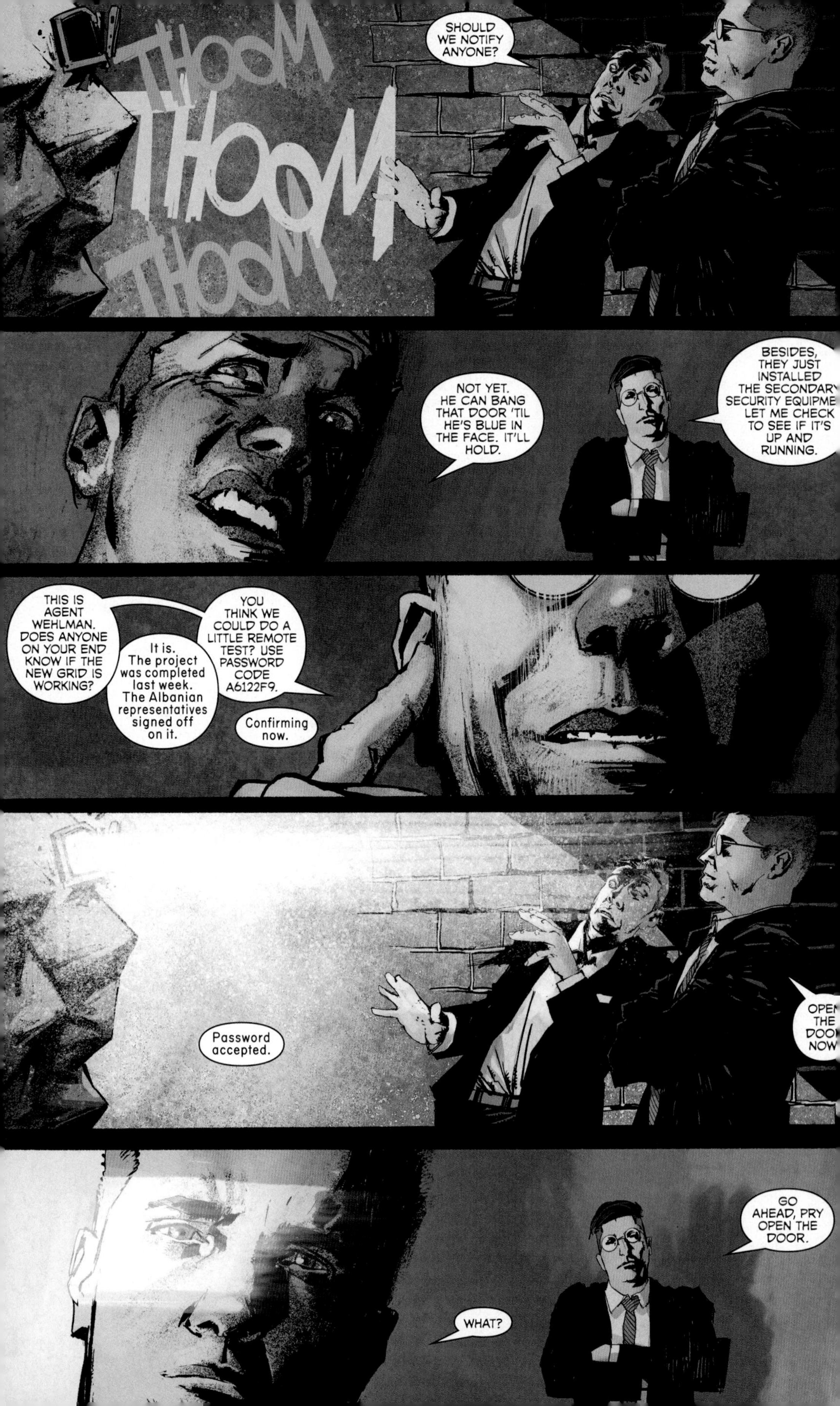
THOOM THOOM THOOM
SHOULD WE NOTIFY ANYONE?
NOT YET. HE CAN BANG THAT DOOR 'TIL HE'S BLUE IN THE FACE. IT'LL HOLD.
BESIDES, THEY JUST INSTALLED THE SECONDARY SECURITY EQUIPME LET ME CHECK TO SEE IF IT'S UP AND RUNNING.
THIS IS AGENT WEHLMAN. DOES ANYONE ON YOUR END KNOW IF THE NEW GRID IS WORKING?
It is. The project was completed last week. The Albanian representatives signed off on it.
YOU THINK WE COULD DO A LITTLE REMOTE TEST? USE PASSWORD CODE A6122F9.
Confirming now.
Password accepted.
OPEN THE DOO NOW
GO AHEAD, PRY OPEN THE DOOR.
WHAT?

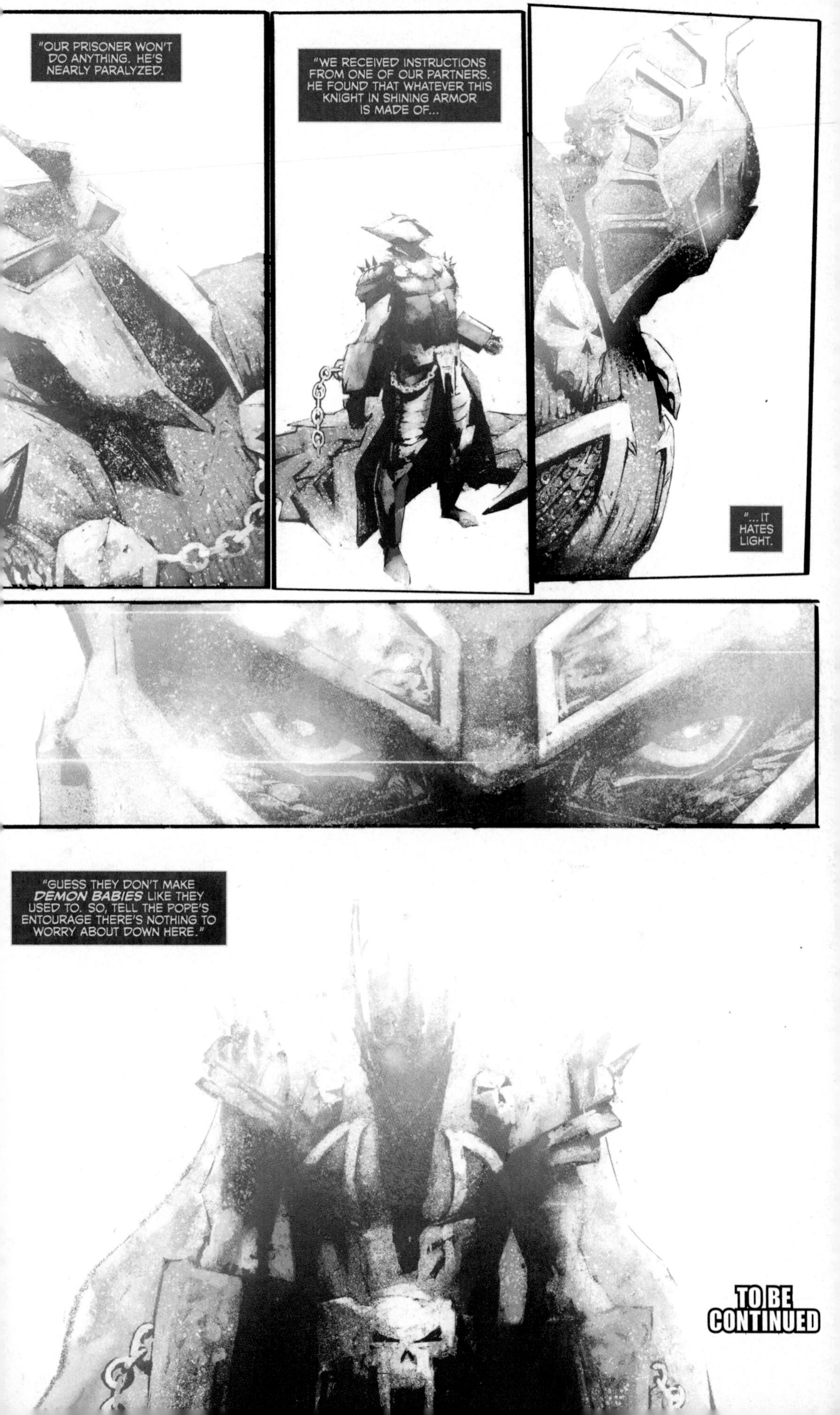
"OUR PRISONER WON'T DO ANYTHING. HE'S NEARLY PARALYZED.
"WE RECEIVED INSTRUCTIONS FROM ONE OF OUR PARTNERS. HE FOUND THAT WHATEVER THIS KNIGHT IN SHINING ARMOR IS MADE OF...
"... IT HATES LIGHT.
"GUESS THEY DON'T MAKE *DEMON BABIES* LIKE THEY USED TO. SO, TELL THE POPE'S ENTOURAGE THERE'S NOTHING TO WORRY ABOUT DOWN HERE."
TO BE CONTINUED

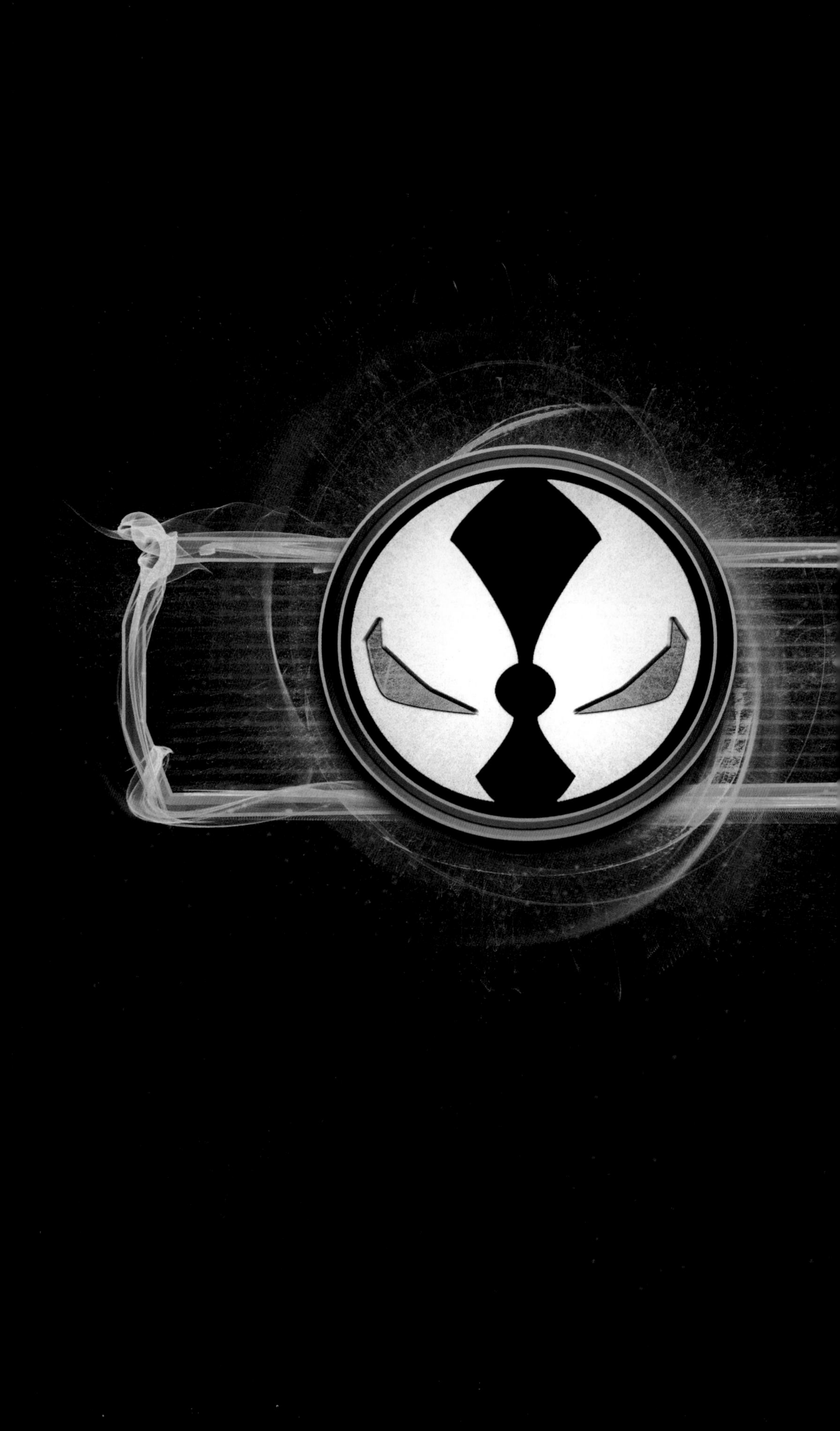

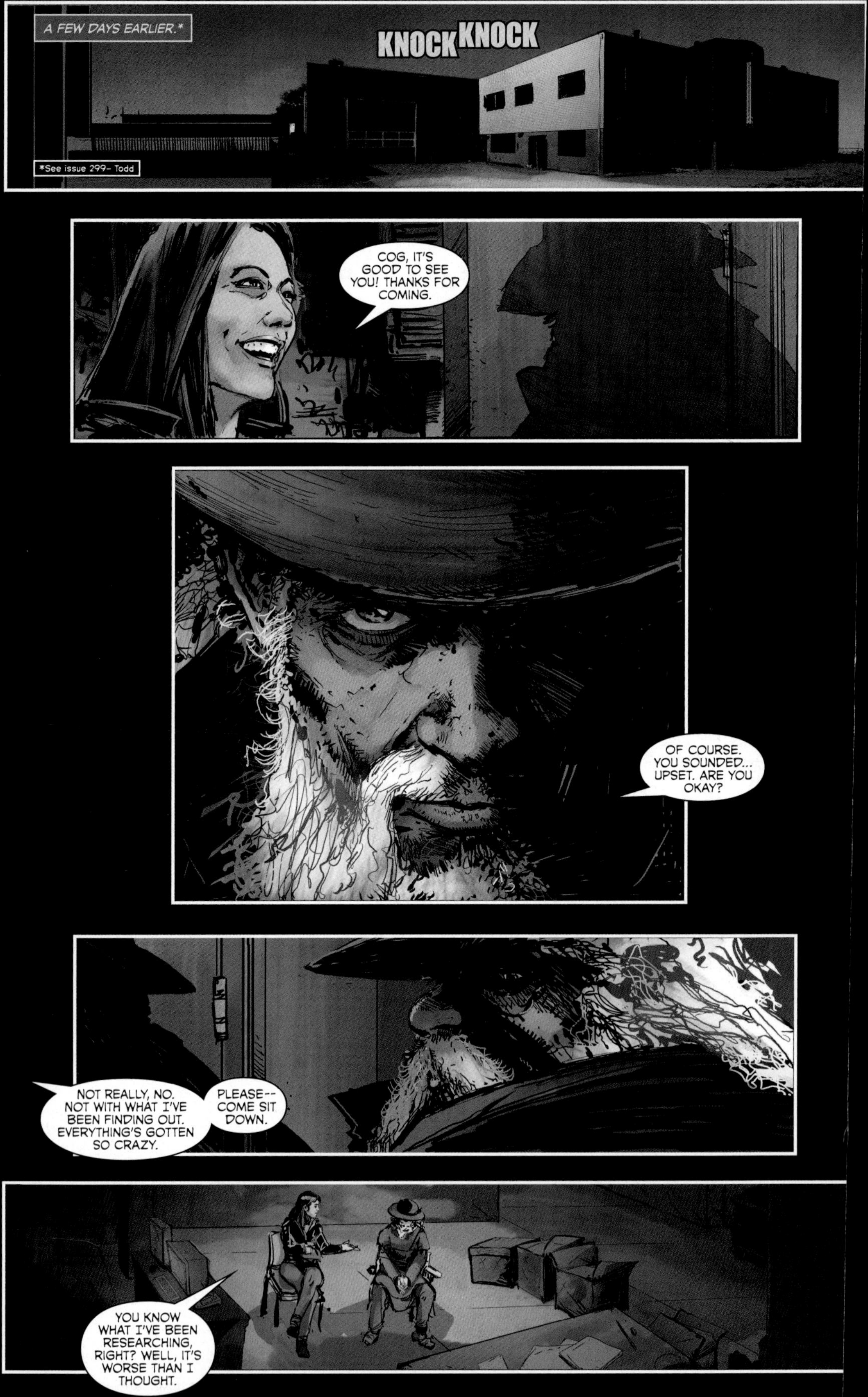
A FEW DAYS EARLIER.*
KNOCK KNOCK
*See issue 299– Todd
COG, IT'S GOOD TO SEE YOU! THANKS FOR COMING.
OF COURSE. YOU SOUNDED... UPSET. ARE YOU OKAY?
NOT REALLY, NO. NOT WITH WHAT I'VE BEEN FINDING OUT. EVERYTHING'S GOTTEN SO CRAZY.
PLEASE-- COME SIT DOWN.
YOU KNOW WHAT I'VE BEEN RESEARCHING, RIGHT? WELL, IT'S WORSE THAN I THOUGHT.

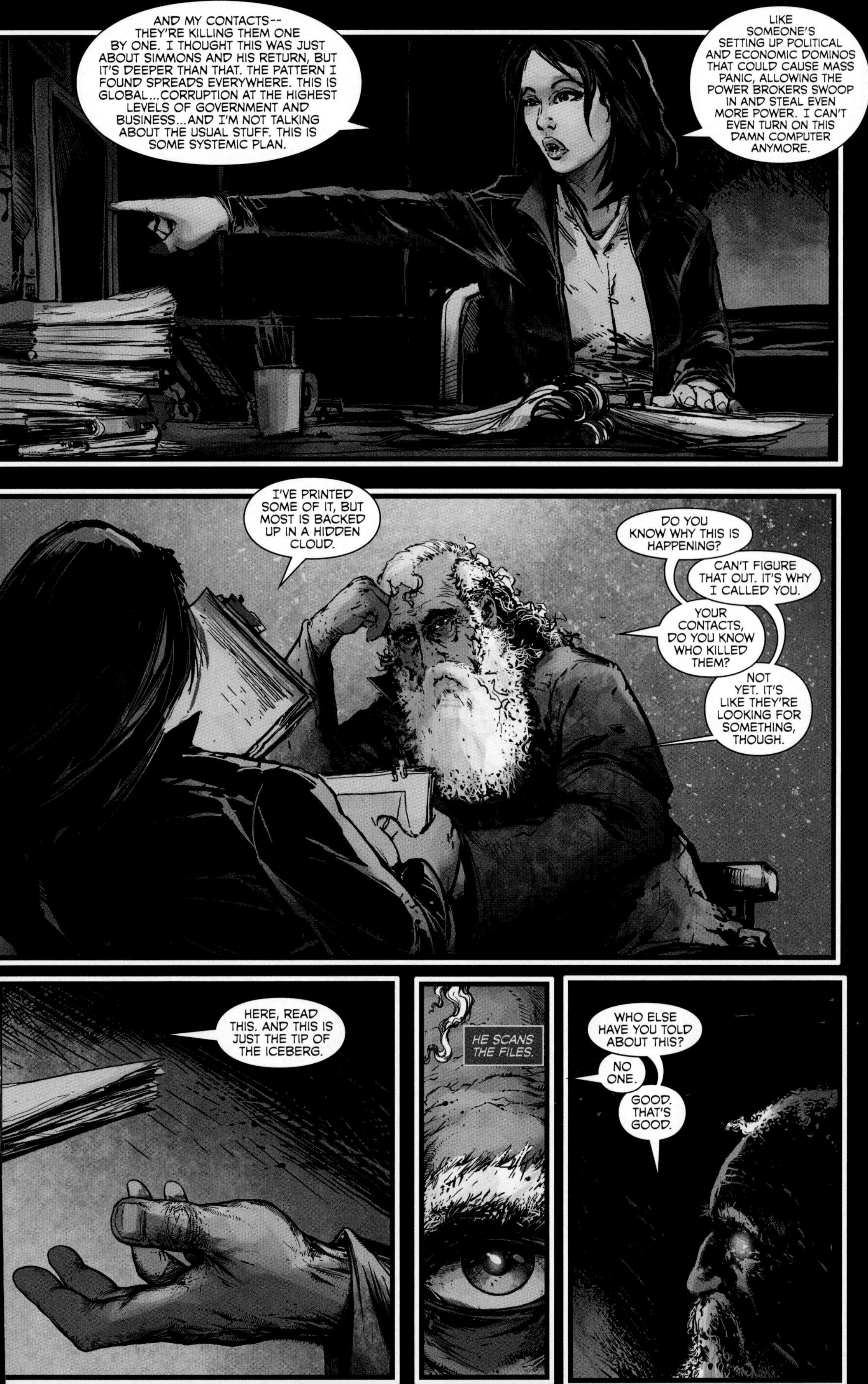
AND MY CONTACTS-- THEY'RE KILLING THEM ONE BY ONE. I THOUGHT THIS WAS JUST ABOUT SIMMONS AND HIS RETURN, BUT IT'S DEEPER THAN THAT. THE PATTERN I FOUND SPREADS EVERYWHERE. THIS IS GLOBAL...CORRUPTION AT THE HIGHEST LEVELS OF GOVERNMENT AND BUSINESS...AND I'M NOT TALKING ABOUT THE USUAL STUFF. THIS IS SOME SYSTEMIC PLAN.
LIKE SOMEONE'S SETTING UP POLITICAL AND ECONOMIC DOMINOS THAT COULD CAUSE MASS PANIC, ALLOWING THE POWER BROKERS SWOOP IN AND STEAL EVEN MORE POWER. I CAN'T EVEN TURN ON THIS DAMN COMPUTER ANYMORE.
I'VE PRINTED SOME OF IT, BUT MOST IS BACKED UP IN A HIDDEN CLOUD.
DO YOU KNOW WHY THIS IS HAPPENING?
CAN'T FIGURE THAT OUT. IT'S WHY I CALLED YOU.
YOUR CONTACTS, DO YOU KNOW WHO KILLED THEM?
NOT YET. IT'S LIKE THEY'RE LOOKING FOR SOMETHING, THOUGH.
HERE, READ THIS. AND THIS IS JUST THE TIP OF THE ICEBERG.
HE SCANS THE FILES.
WHO ELSE HAVE YOU TOLD ABOUT THIS?
NO ONE.
GOOD. THAT'S GOOD.

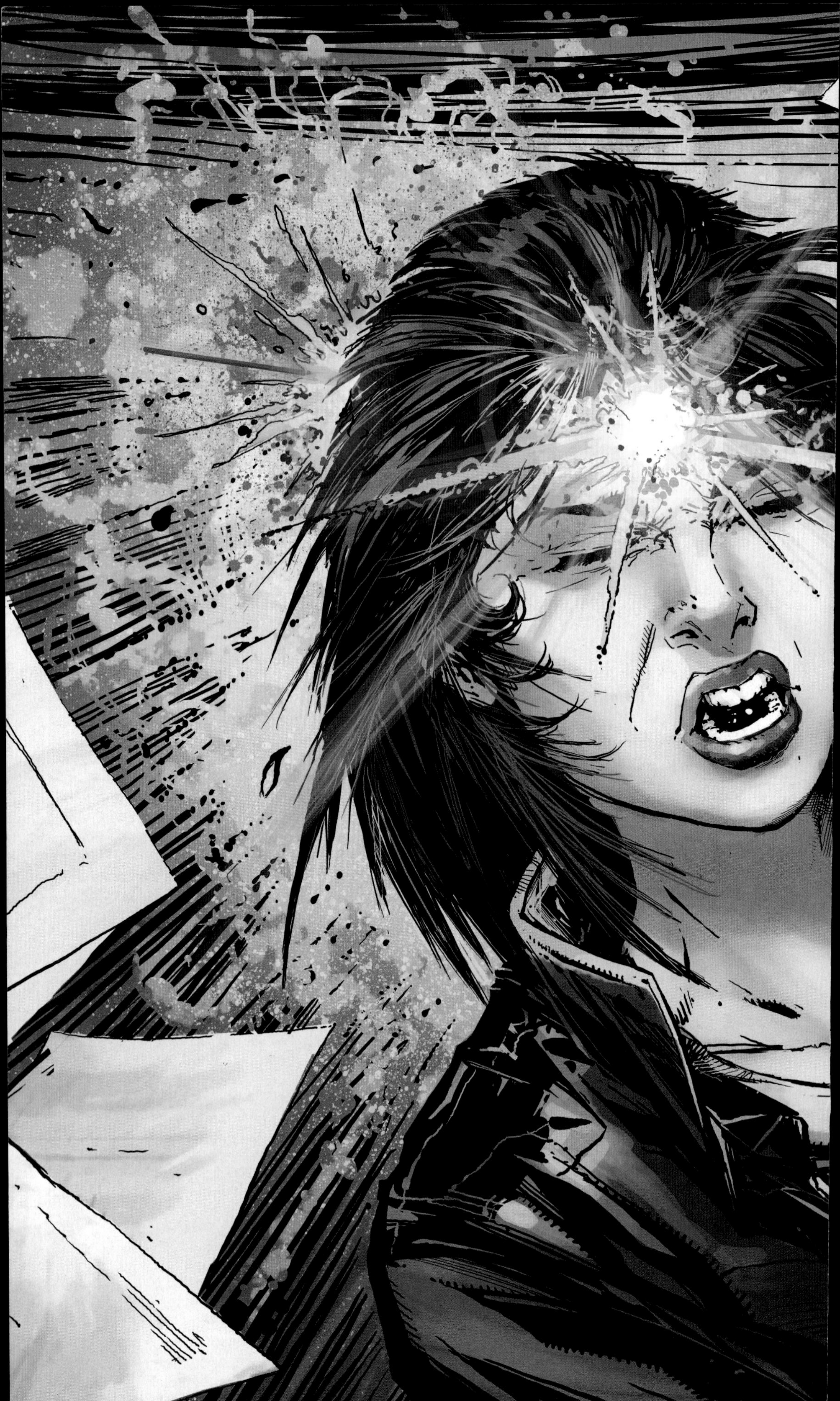

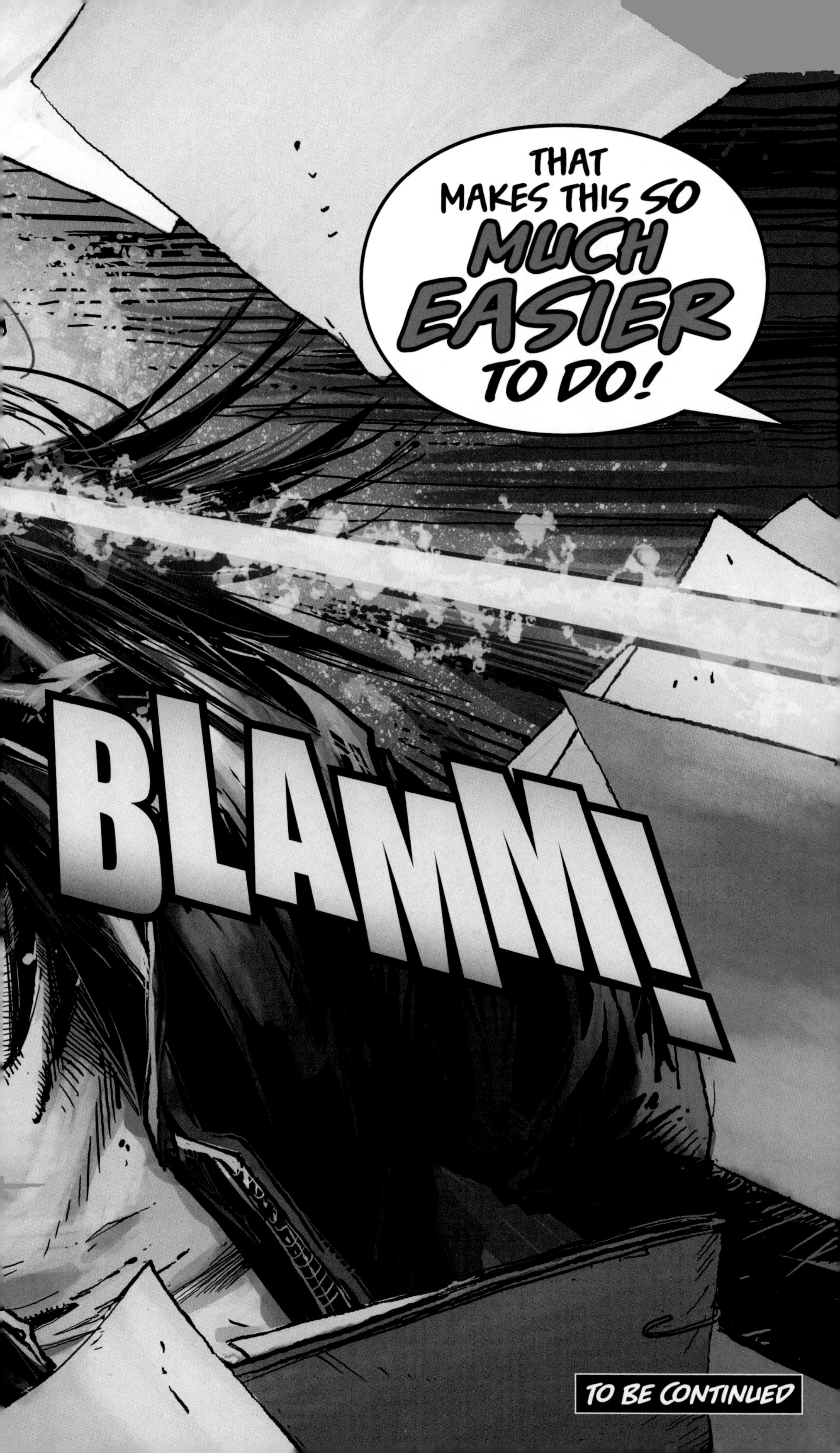
THAT MAKES THIS SO MUCH EASIER TO DO!
BLAMM!
TO BE CONTINUED

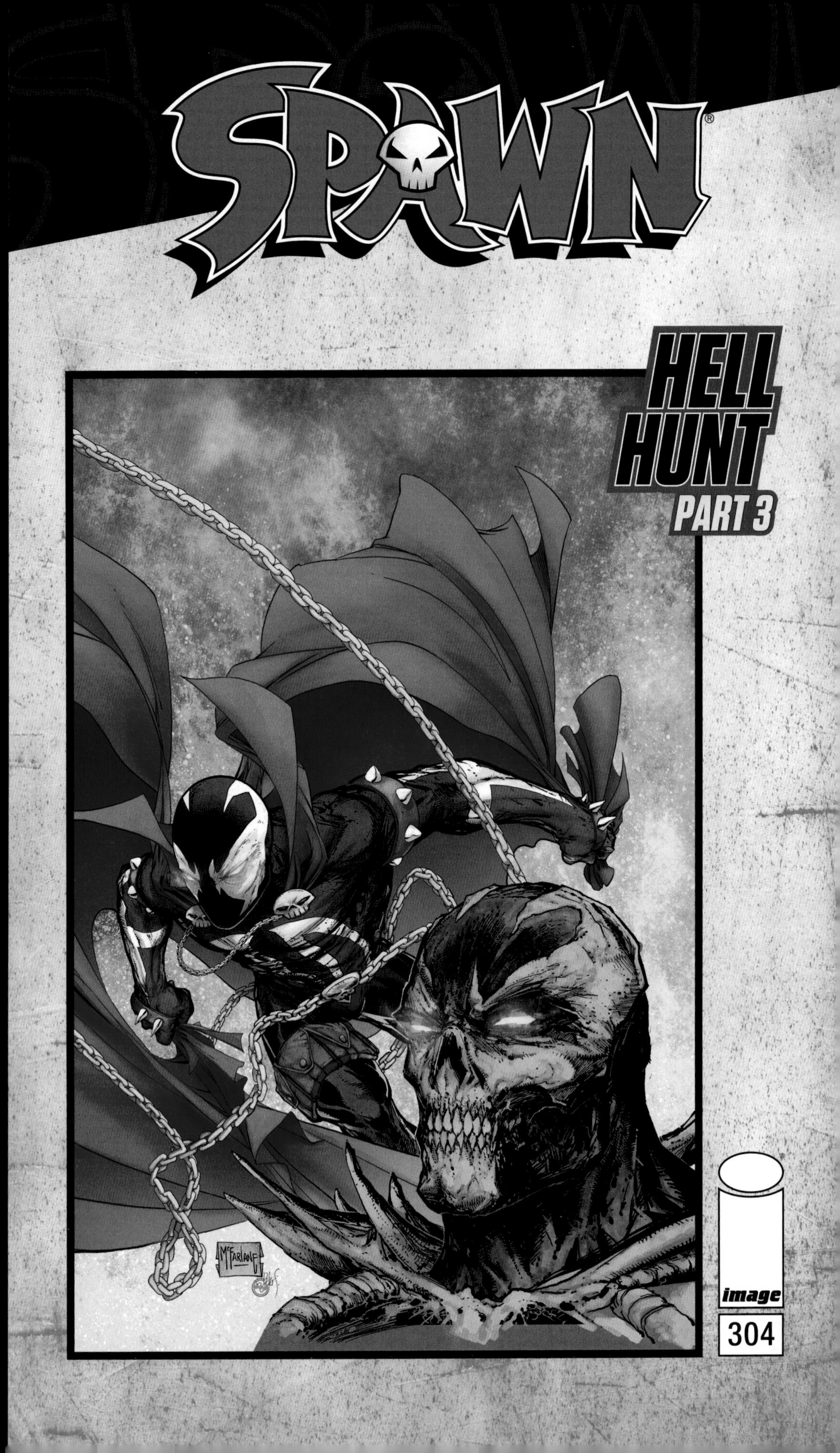
SPAWN®
HELL HUNT
PART 3
image
304
McFarlane

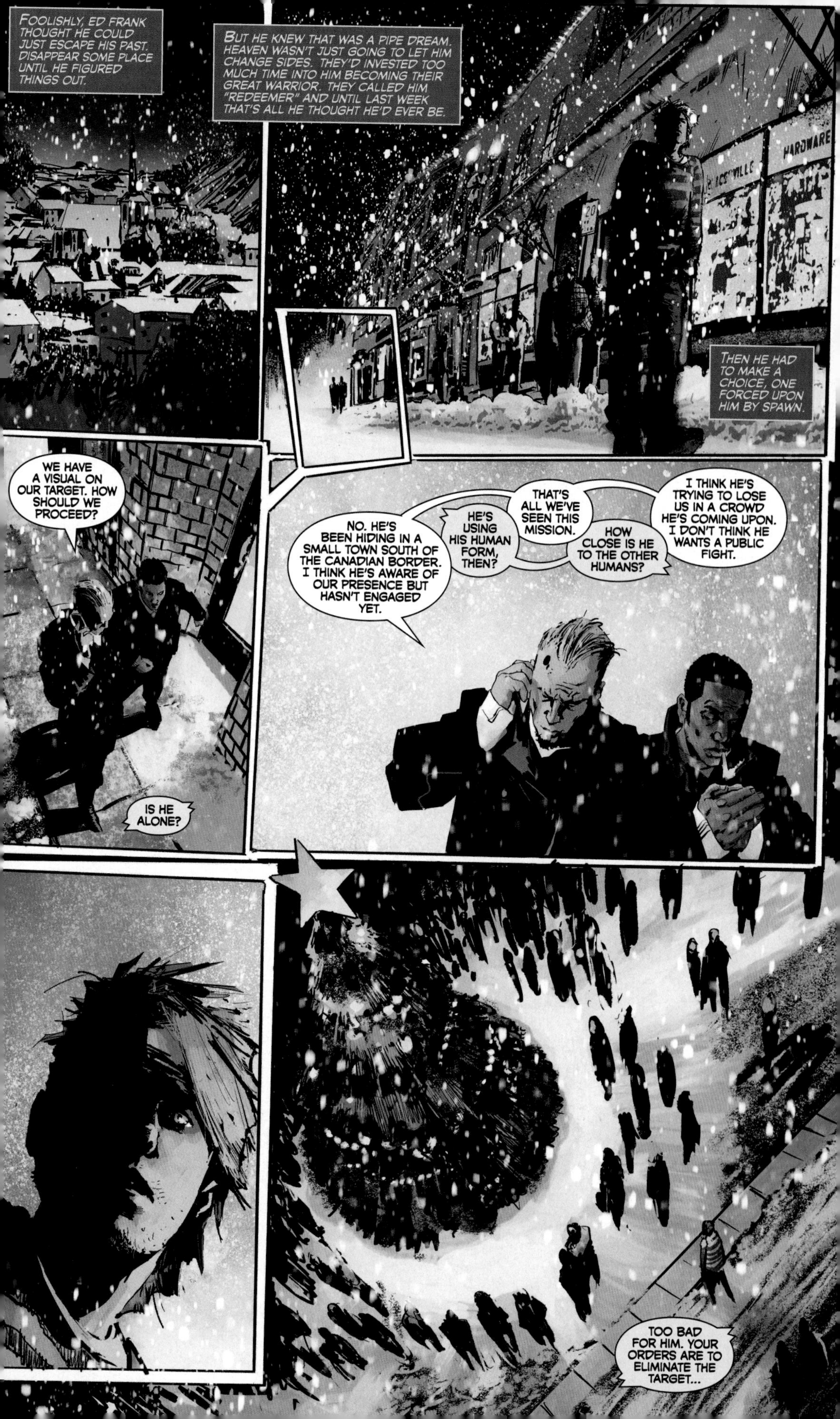
FOOLISHLY, ED FRANK THOUGHT HE COULD JUST ESCAPE HIS PAST. DISAPPEAR SOME PLACE UNTIL HE FIGURED THINGS OUT.
BUT HE KNEW THAT WAS A PIPE DREAM. HEAVEN WASN'T JUST GOING TO LET HIM CHANGE SIDES. THEY'D INVESTED TOO MUCH TIME INTO HIM BECOMING THEIR GREAT WARRIOR. THEY CALLED HIM "REDEEMER" AND UNTIL LAST WEEK THAT'S ALL HE THOUGHT HE'D EVER BE.
HARDWARE
20
THEN HE HAD TO MAKE A CHOICE, ONE FORCED UPON HIM BY SPAWN.
WE HAVE A VISUAL ON OUR TARGET. HOW SHOULD WE PROCEED?
IS HE ALONE?
NO. HE'S BEEN HIDING IN A SMALL TOWN SOUTH OF THE CANADIAN BORDER. I THINK HE'S AWARE OF OUR PRESENCE BUT HASN'T ENGAGED YET.
HE'S USING HIS HUMAN FORM, THEN?
THAT'S ALL WE'VE SEEN THIS MISSION.
HOW CLOSE IS HE TO THE OTHER HUMANS?
I THINK HE'S TRYING TO LOSE US IN A CROWD HE'S COMING UPON. I DON'T THINK HE WANTS A PUBLIC FIGHT.
TOO BAD FOR HIM. YOUR ORDERS ARE TO ELIMINATE THE TARGET...

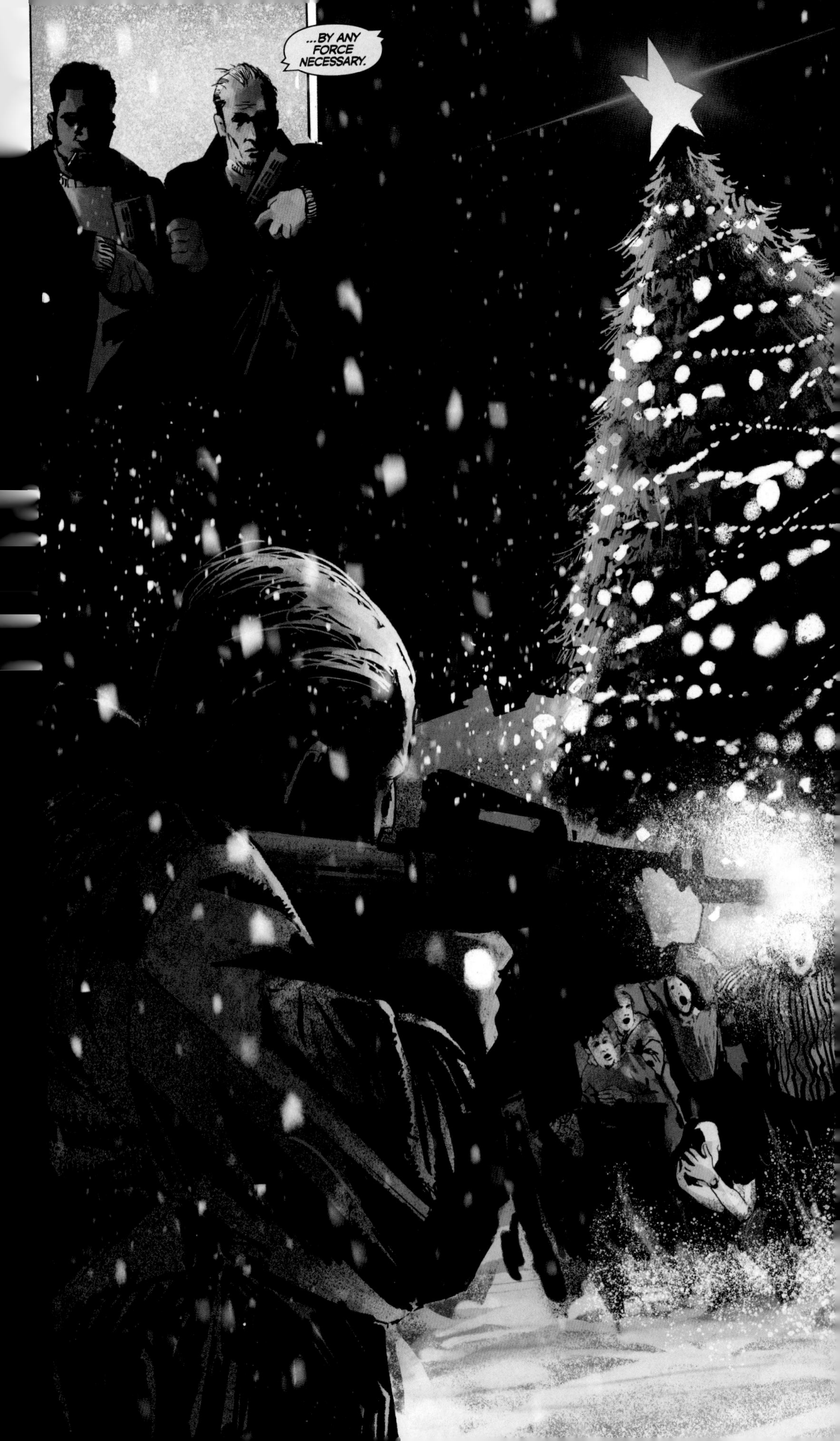
...BY ANY FORCE NECESSARY.

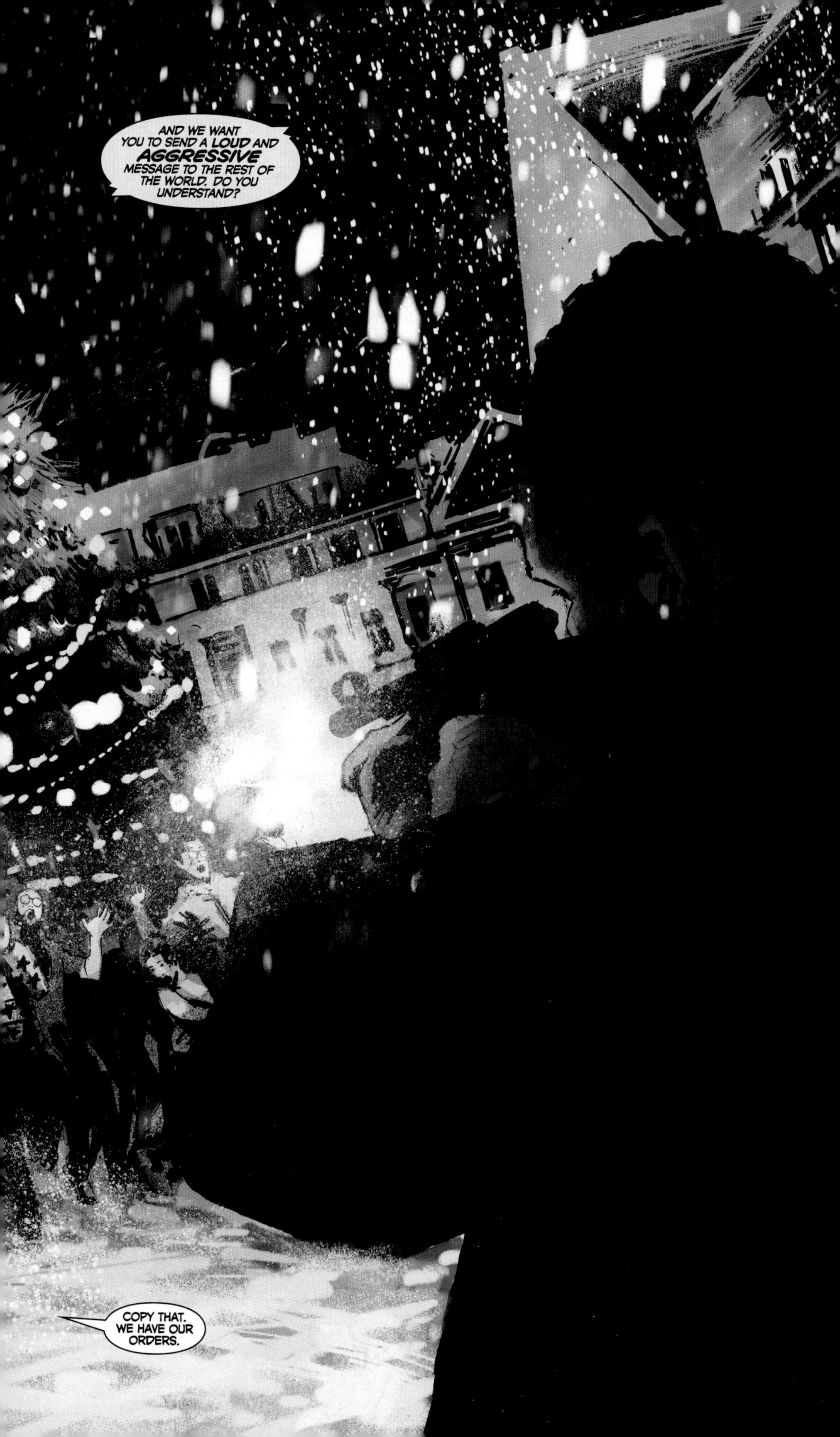
AND WE WANT YOU TO SEND A LOUD AND AGGRESSIVE MESSAGE TO THE REST OF THE WORLD. DO YOU UNDERSTAND?
COPY THAT. WE HAVE OUR ORDERS.

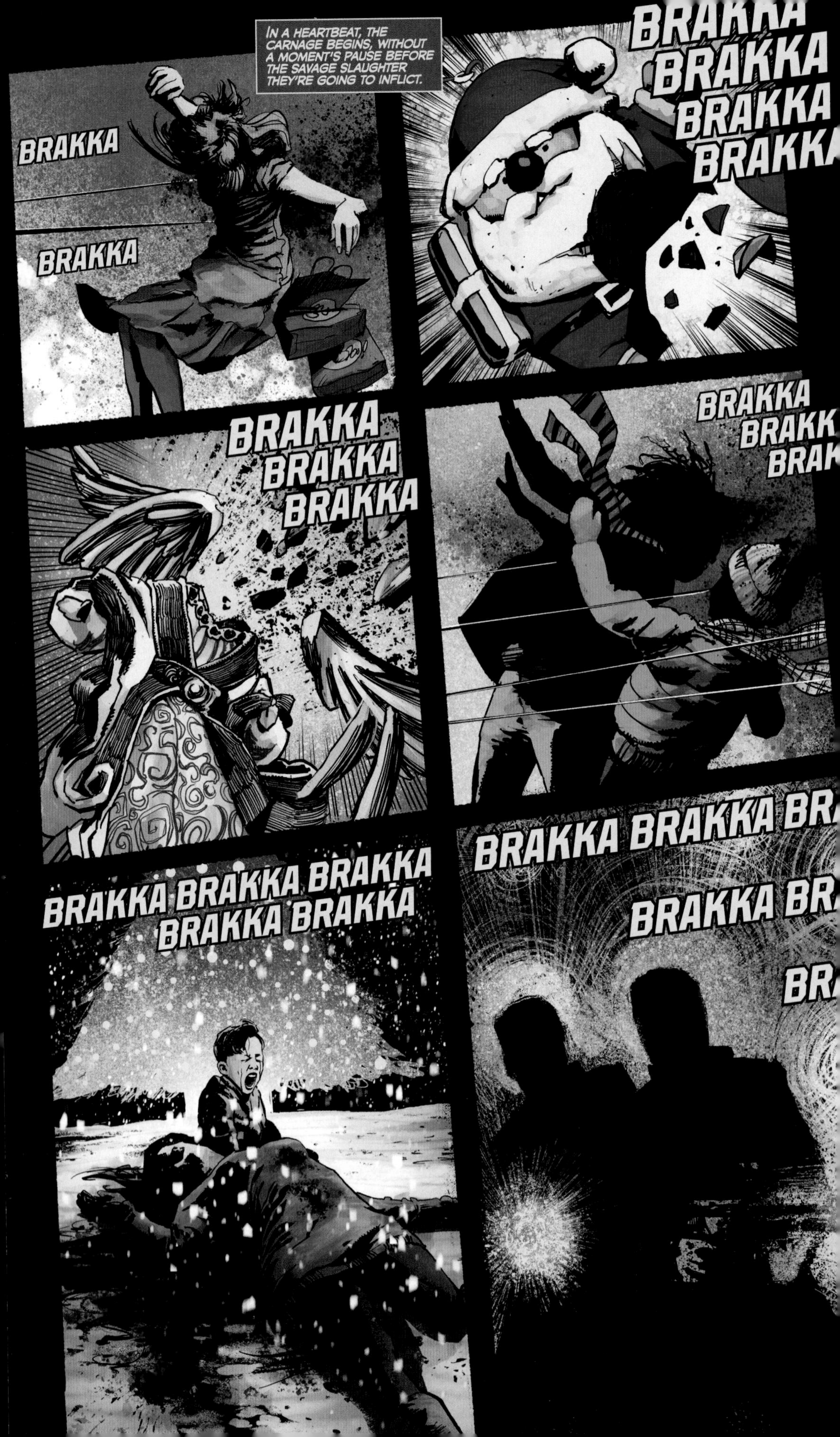

In a heartbeat, the carnage begins, without a moment's pause before the savage slaughter they're going to inflict.
BRAKKA
BRAKKA
BRAKKA
BRAKKA
BRAKKA
BRAKKA
BRAKKA
BRAKKA
BRAKKA
BRAKKA
BRAKKA BRAKKA BRAKKA
BRAKKA BRAKKA
BRAKKA BRAKKA
BRAKKA

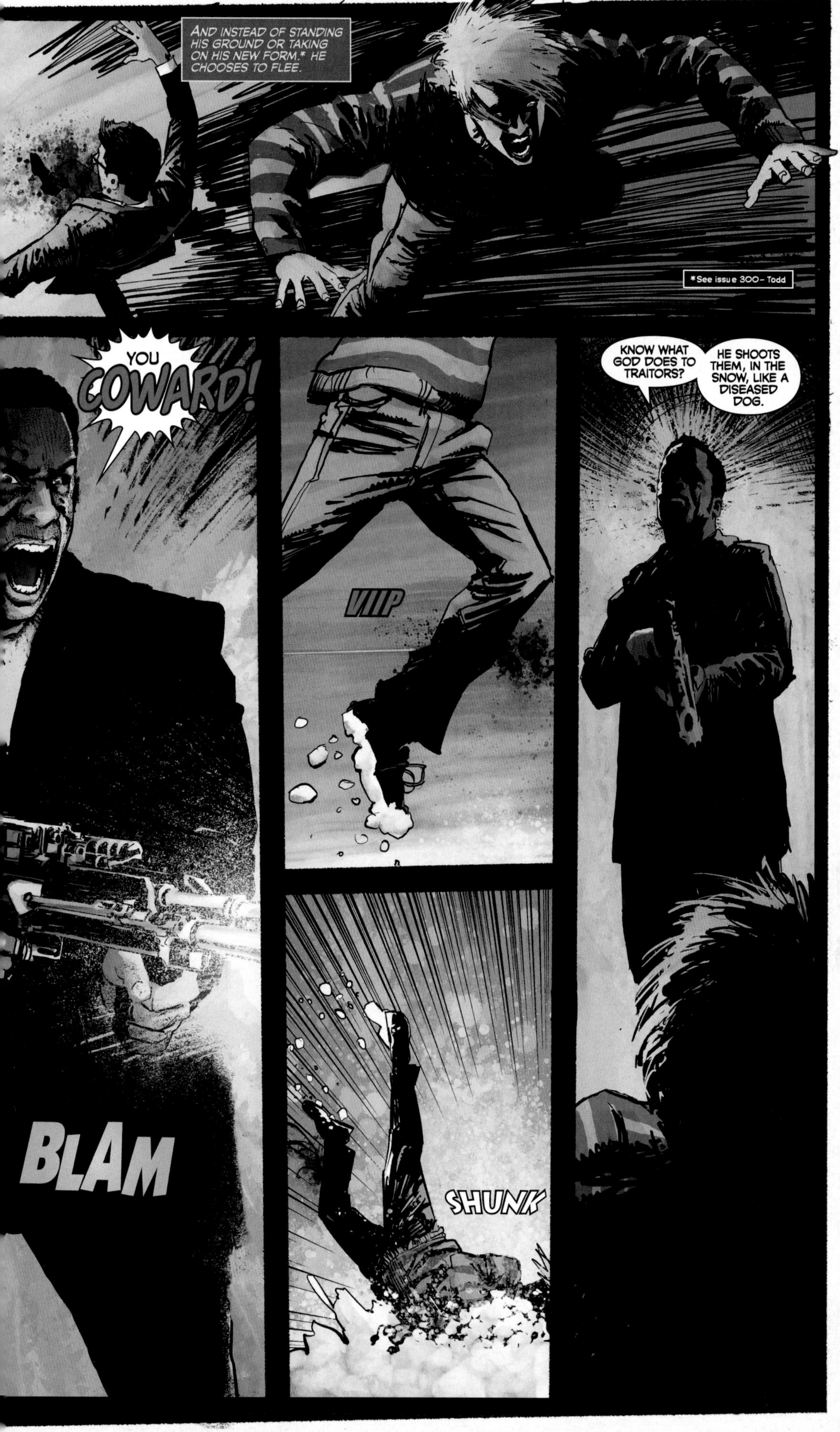
AND INSTEAD OF STANDING HIS GROUND OR TAKING ON HIS NEW FORM.* HE CHOOSES TO FLEE.
*See issue 300- Todd
YOU COWARD!
VIIP
KNOW WHAT GOD DOES TO TRAITORS?
HE SHOOTS THEM, IN THE SNOW, LIKE A DISEASED DOG.
BLAM
SHUNK

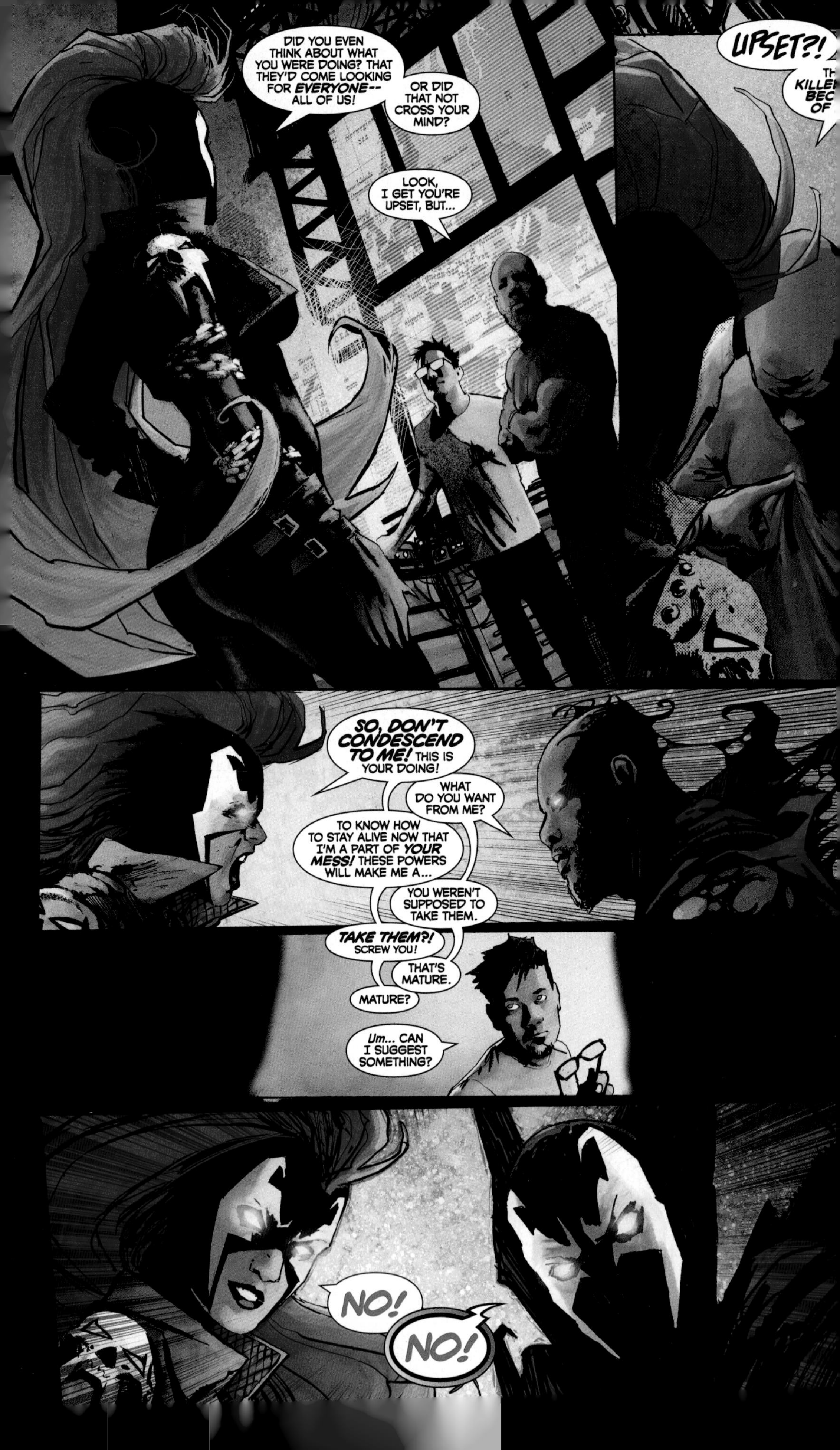
DID YOU EVEN THINK ABOUT WHAT YOU WERE DOING? THAT THEY'D COME LOOKING FOR *EVERYONE*-- ALL OF US!
OR DID THAT NOT CROSS YOUR MIND?
LOOK, I GET YOU'RE UPSET, BUT...
UPSET?!
SO, DON'T CONDESCEND TO ME! THIS IS YOUR DOING!
WHAT DO YOU WANT FROM ME?
TO KNOW HOW TO STAY ALIVE NOW THAT I'M A PART OF *YOUR MESS!* THESE POWERS WILL MAKE ME A...
YOU WEREN'T SUPPOSED TO TAKE THEM.
TAKE THEM?! SCREW YOU!
THAT'S MATURE.
MATURE?
Um... CAN I SUGGEST SOMETHING?
NO!
NO!

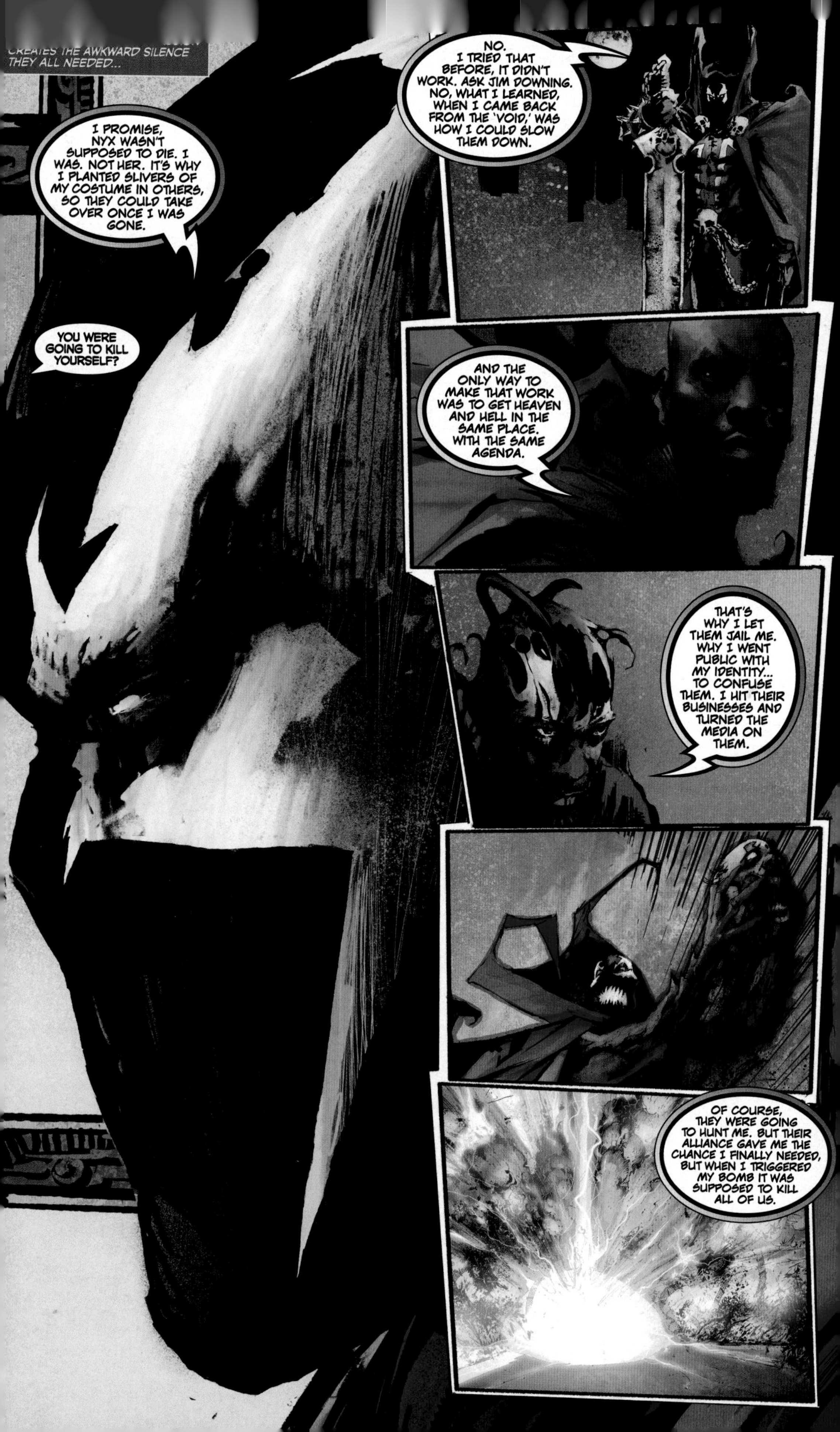
CREATES THE AWKWARD SILENCE THEY ALL NEEDED...
I PROMISE, NYX WASN'T SUPPOSED TO DIE. I WAS. NOT HER. IT'S WHY I PLANTED SLIVERS OF MY COSTUME IN OTHERS, SO THEY COULD TAKE OVER ONCE I WAS GONE.
YOU WERE GOING TO KILL YOURSELF?
NO. I TRIED THAT BEFORE, IT DIDN'T WORK. ASK JIM DOWNING. NO, WHAT I LEARNED, WHEN I CAME BACK FROM THE 'VOID,' WAS HOW I COULD SLOW THEM DOWN.
AND THE ONLY WAY TO MAKE THAT WORK WAS TO GET HEAVEN AND HELL IN THE SAME PLACE. WITH THE SAME AGENDA.
THAT'S WHY I LET THEM JAIL ME. WHY I WENT PUBLIC WITH MY IDENTITY... TO CONFUSE THEM. I HIT THEIR BUSINESSES AND TURNED THE MEDIA ON THEM.
OF COURSE, THEY WERE GOING TO HUNT ME. BUT THEIR ALLIANCE GAVE ME THE CHANCE I FINALLY NEEDED, BUT WHEN I TRIGGERED MY BOMB IT WAS SUPPOSED TO KILL ALL OF US.

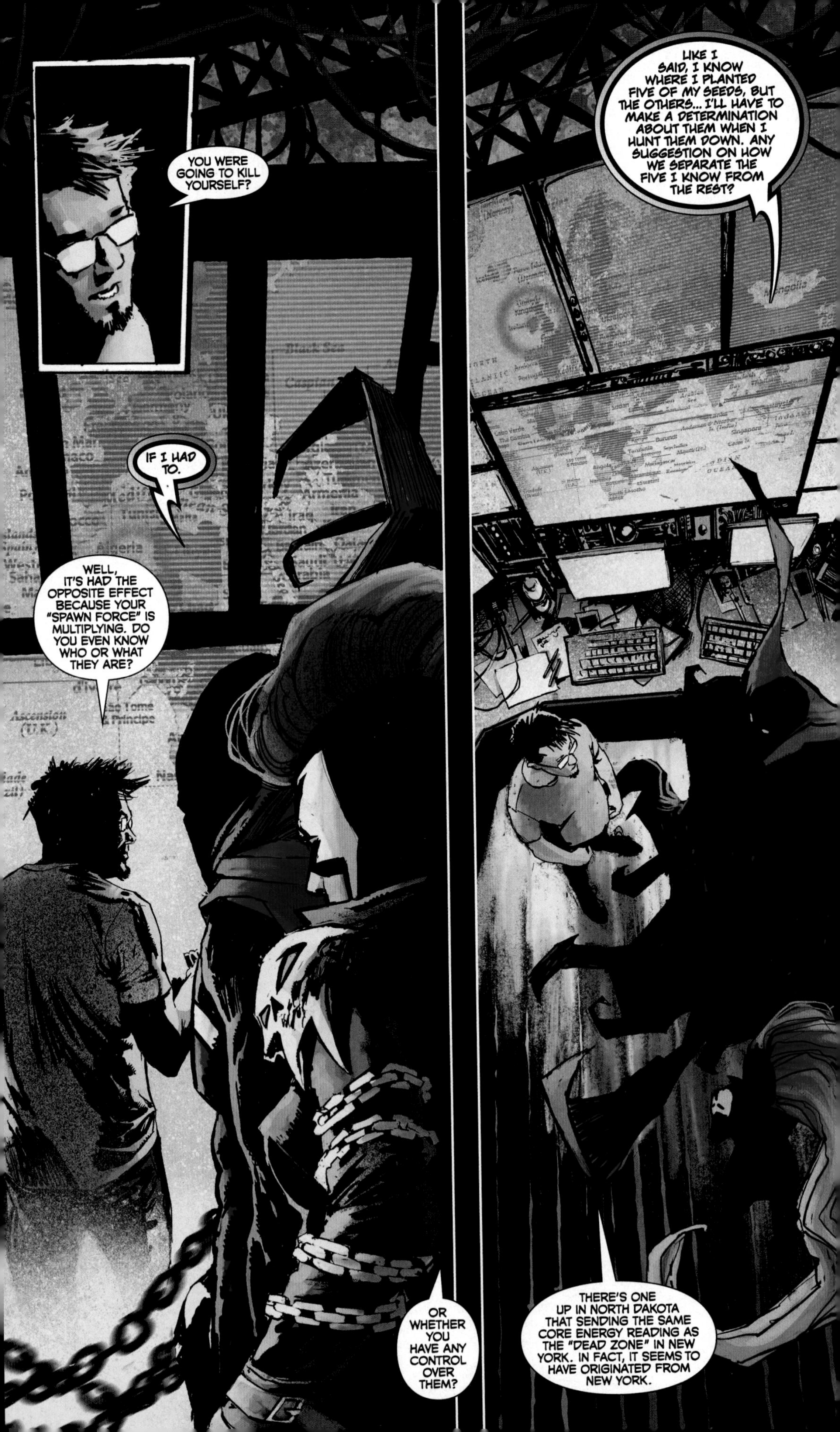

YOU WERE GOING TO KILL YOURSELF?
IF I HAD TO.
WELL, IT'S HAD THE OPPOSITE EFFECT BECAUSE YOUR "SPAWN FORCE" IS MULTIPLYING. DO YOU EVEN KNOW WHO OR WHAT THEY ARE?
OR WHETHER YOU HAVE ANY CONTROL OVER THEM?
LIKE I SAID, I KNOW WHERE I PLANTED FIVE OF MY SEEDS, BUT THE OTHERS... I'LL HAVE TO MAKE A DETERMINATION ABOUT THEM WHEN I HUNT THEM DOWN. ANY SUGGESTION ON HOW WE SEPARATE THE FIVE I KNOW FROM THE REST?
THERE'S ONE UP IN NORTH DAKOTA THAT SENDING THE SAME CORE ENERGY READING AS THE "DEAD ZONE" IN NEW YORK. IN FACT, IT SEEMS TO HAVE ORIGINATED FROM NEW YORK.

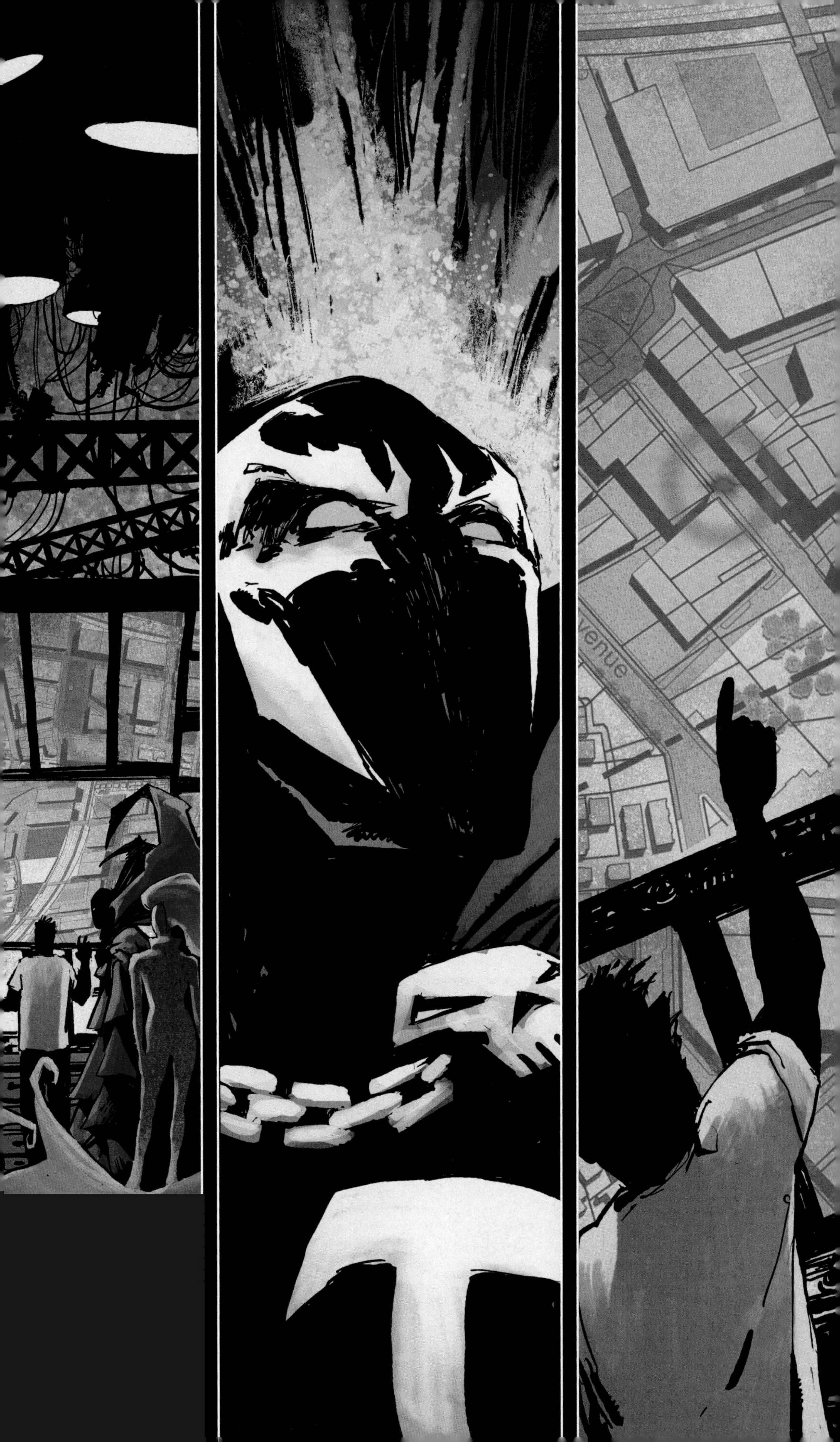

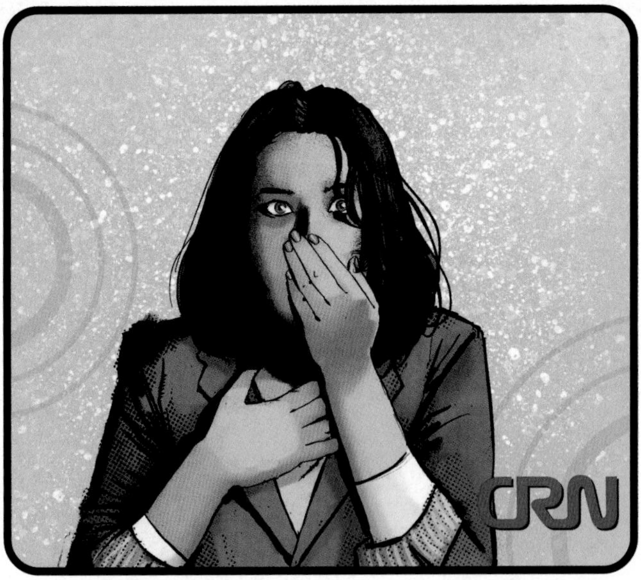
CRN

JUST COMING IN AT THIS EARLY HOUR ARE REPORTS OF WHAT MAY BE A MASS SHOOTING IN WESTHOPE, NORTH DAKOTA JUST A FEW MILES SOUTH OF THE CANADIAN BORDER.

ARMED MEN REPORTEDLY ENTERED THE TOWN SQUARE AND OPENED FIRE INTO TH CROWD GATHERED FOR A CHRISTMAS TR LIGHTING CEREMONY. DETAILS ARE FEW THIS TIME, DUE TO THE TINY POPULATION THIS REMOTE AREA.

SOCIAL MEDIA, MEANWHILE, IS BEING FLOODED WITH IMAGES OF PANIC AND BLOODSHEAD. AMONG THE GATHERED REVELERS THERE APPEAR TO BE MANY W ARE WOUNDED AND, POSSIBLY, DEAD.

LOCAL COVERAGE CAME TO AN ABRUPT HALT WHEN NEWS CREWS FLED FOR THEIR OWN SAFETY.

WE WILL BE LIVE WITH UPDATES ON THIS STORY AS MORE INFORMATION BECOME AVAILABLE.

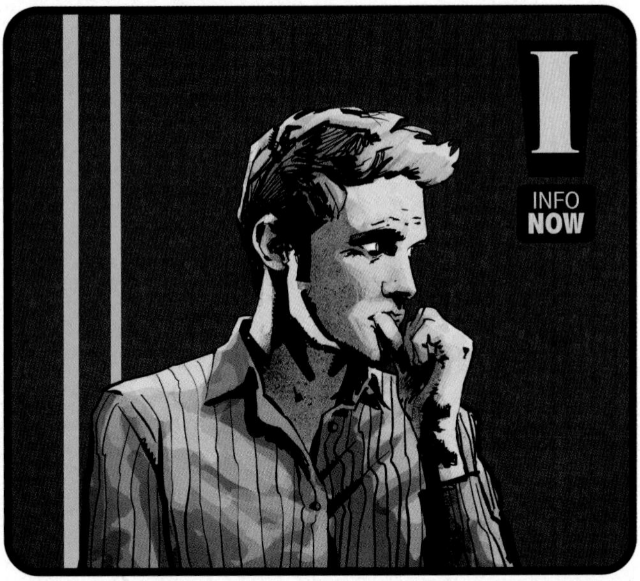
I
INFO
NOW

IT IS UNCLEAR IF STATE POLICE ARE ON T SCENE YET, LET ALONE WHETHER THEY HAVE ***ENGAGED*** THE GUNMEN.

INFORMATION IS COMING IN VIA ***SOCIAL MEDIA,*** FASTER THAN IT CAN BE ANALYZE AS WE SIFT THROUGH INCOMING PHOTOS AND TWEETS, THOUGH, AT LEAST ***TWO GUNMEN*** HAVE BEEN CONFIRMED. HOWEVE THEY ARE UNIDENTIFIED. AT THIS MOMEN NO ONE HAS ANY IDEA AS TO A ***MOTIVE***

THE CONSENSUS SEEMS TO BE THIS: ME WITH GUNS ***OPENED FIRE,*** FOLLOWED BY FLASH OF ***GREEN LIGHT.*** THERE'S NO WAY ALL TO DETERMINE WHETHER THESE EVEN ARE LINKED. NO ONE HAS OFFERED AN EXPLANATION, OR EVEN SPECULATION, RE GARDING THE ***NATURE*** OF THE GREEN LIG

YOU CAN DEPEND ON US FOR ***ONGOIN COVERAGE*** AS THIS STORY UNFOLDS.

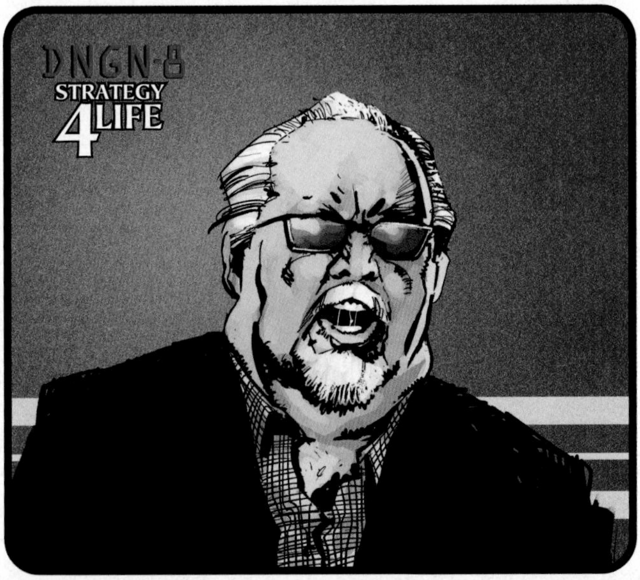
DNGN-8
STRATEGY
4LIFE

WHERE THE HECK ARE THE GOOD GUYS WITH THE GUNS
THIS IS ***NORTH DAKOTA*** WE'RE TALKIN ABOUT, FOR PETE'S SAKE!

STATE POLICE HAVE CONFIRMED THEY AR EN ROUTE AS WE SPEAK. "IT'S POSSIBLY EXPLOSION OF SOME KIND," IS THE BEST TH CAN COME UP WITH. ***TELL ME ANOTHE ONE, COPPER...*** THE SELFIES ARE SHOW HUNDREDS OF ***LITTLE*** EXPLOSIONS, AN JUST AS MANY ***BULLET*** CASINGS. ***AND FRONT OF A CHRISTMAS TREE*** THERE USED TO BE RESPECT FOR ***TRADITIC*** BACK IN BETTER TIMES!!

MOLES, TROLLS, GRASSY KNOLLS... GIVE A GOOD ***CONSPIRACY*** AT THIS TIME O THE MORNING. I DON'T WANT TO BE THINKI ABOUT BURYING MY RELATIVES IN THE MIDDLE OF ***WINTER.***

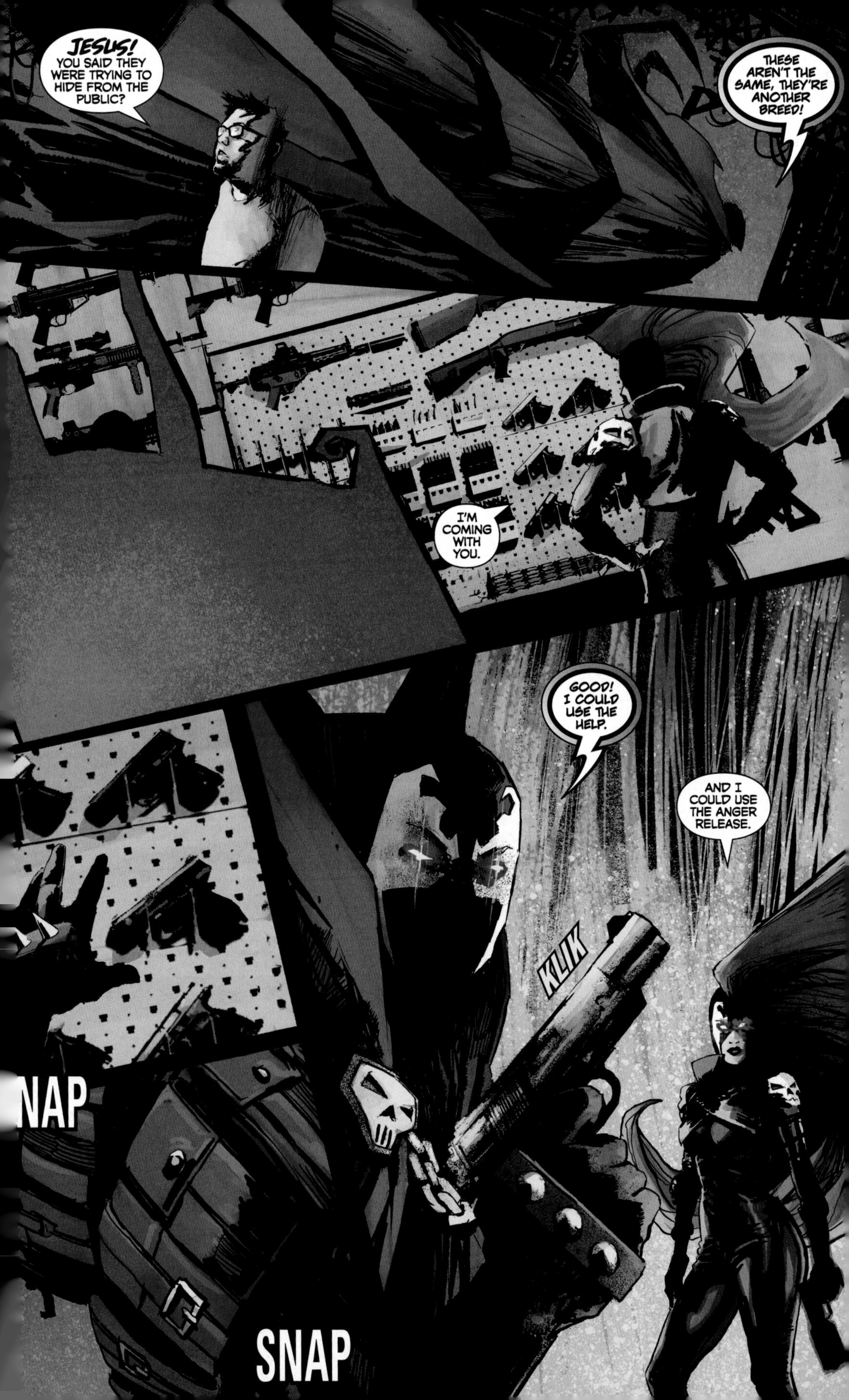
JESUS! YOU SAID THEY WERE TRYING TO HIDE FROM THE PUBLIC?
THESE AREN'T THE SAME, THEY'RE ANOTHER BREED!
I'M COMING WITH YOU.
GOOD! I COULD USE THE HELP.
AND I COULD USE THE ANGER RELEASE.
KLIK
SNAP
SNAP

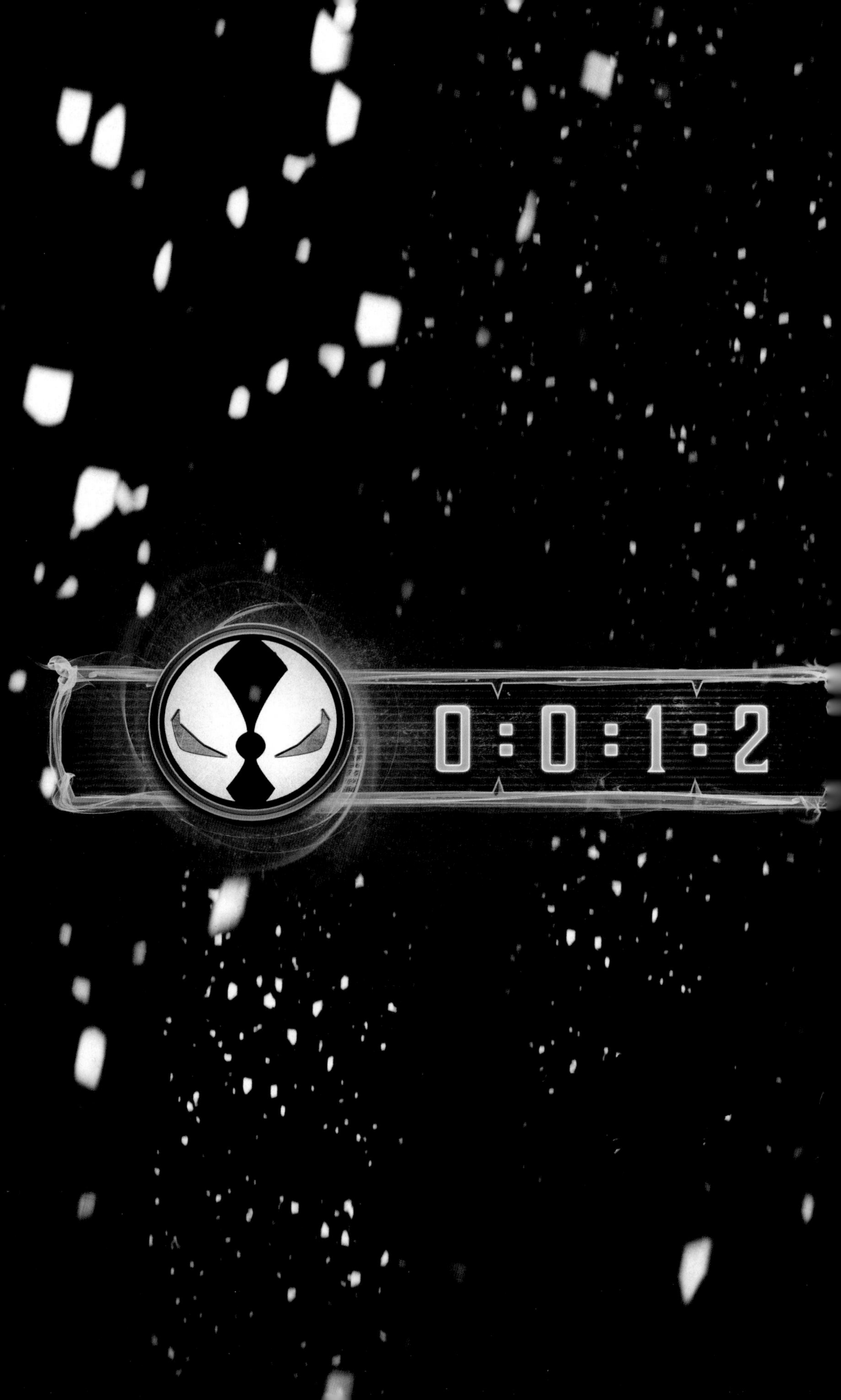
0:0:1:2

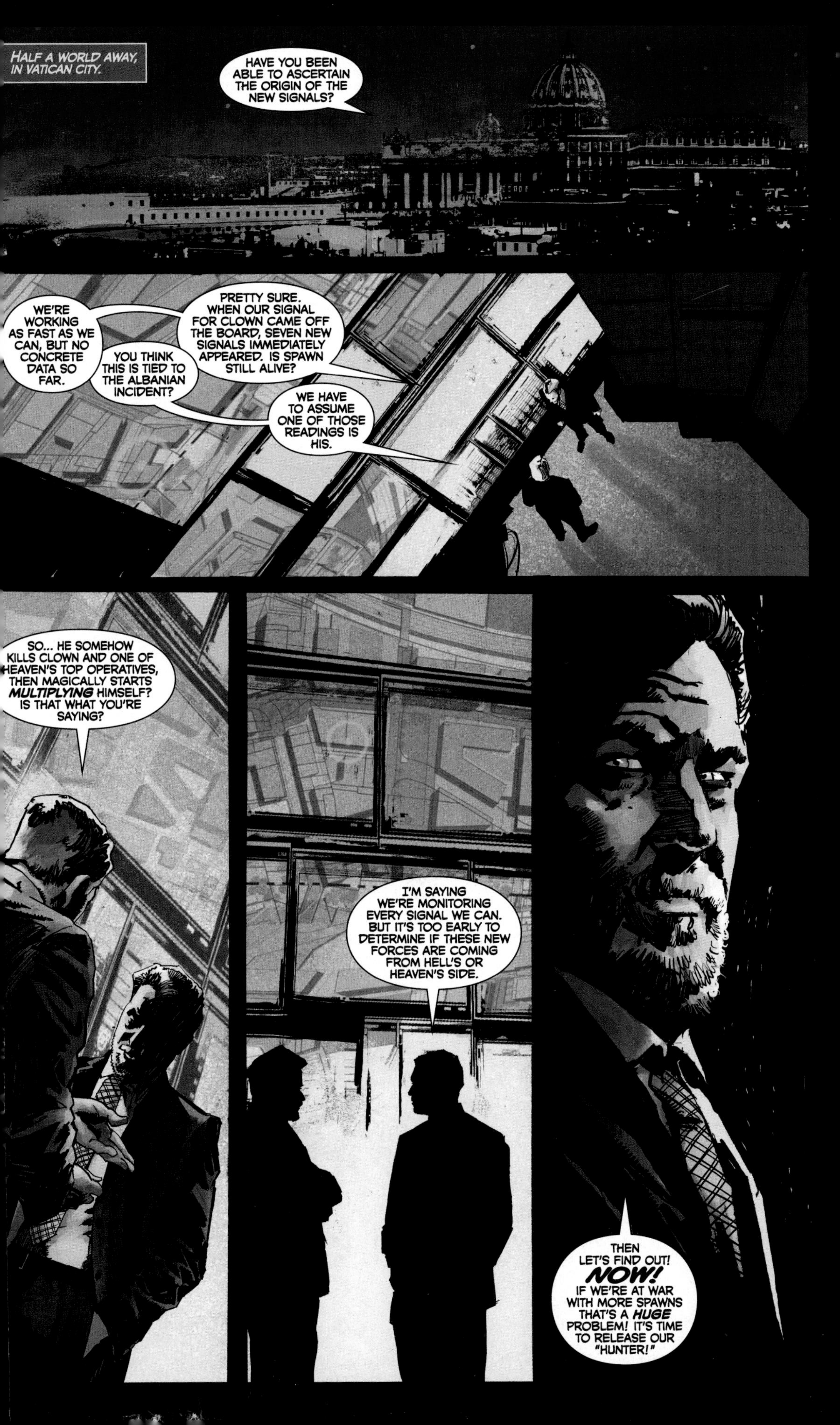
HALF A WORLD AWAY, IN VATICAN CITY.
HAVE YOU BEEN ABLE TO ASCERTAIN THE ORIGIN OF THE NEW SIGNALS?
WE'RE WORKING AS FAST AS WE CAN, BUT NO CONCRETE DATA SO FAR.
PRETTY SURE. WHEN OUR SIGNAL FOR CLOWN CAME OFF THE BOARD, SEVEN NEW SIGNALS IMMEDIATELY APPEARED. IS SPAWN STILL ALIVE?
YOU THINK THIS IS TIED TO THE ALBANIAN INCIDENT?
WE HAVE TO ASSUME ONE OF THOSE READINGS IS HIS.
SO... HE SOMEHOW KILLS CLOWN AND ONE OF HEAVEN'S TOP OPERATIVES, THEN MAGICALLY STARTS MULTIPLYING HIMSELF? IS THAT WHAT YOU'RE SAYING?
I'M SAYING WE'RE MONITORING EVERY SIGNAL WE CAN. BUT IT'S TOO EARLY TO DETERMINE IF THESE NEW FORCES ARE COMING FROM HELL'S OR HEAVEN'S SIDE.
THEN LET'S FIND OUT! NOW! IF WE'RE AT WAR WITH MORE SPAWNS THAT'S A HUGE PROBLEM! IT'S TIME TO RELEASE OUR "HUNTER!"

IN A SUBTERRANEAN BASEMENT BELOW THE VATICAN...
KILL THE LIGHTS.
WE KNOW YOU LIKE THE DARKNESS BETTER.
AND WE BOTH KNOW YOU'VE BEEN DOWN HERE A VERY LONG TIME. CONSTANTLY SCREAMING ABOUT YOUR RIGHTEOUSNESS, ABOUT YOUR DEVOTION. WELL, MY SON, THE LORD HAS SENT ME A MESSAGE.
HE WANTS YOU TO PERFORM A MISSION FOR HIM.
TO PROVE IF YOU'RE TRULY ONE OF US.

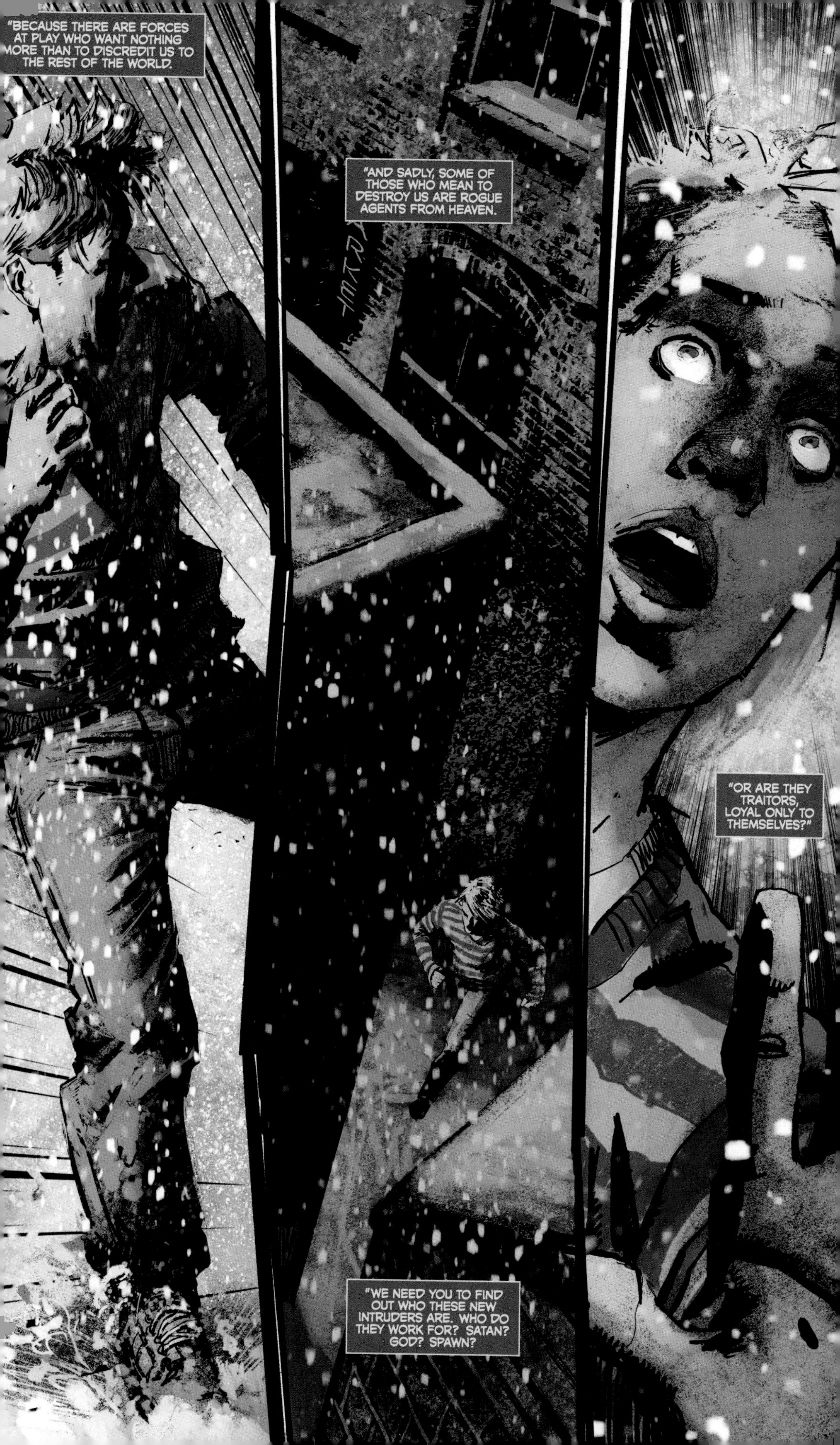
"BECAUSE THERE ARE FORCES AT PLAY WHO WANT NOTHING MORE THAN TO DISCREDIT US TO THE REST OF THE WORLD.
"AND SADLY, SOME OF THOSE WHO MEAN TO DESTROY US ARE ROGUE AGENTS FROM HEAVEN.
"WE NEED YOU TO FIND OUT WHO THESE NEW INTRUDERS ARE. WHO DO THEY WORK FOR? SATAN? GOD? SPAWN?
"OR ARE THEY TRAITORS, LOYAL ONLY TO THEMSELVES?"

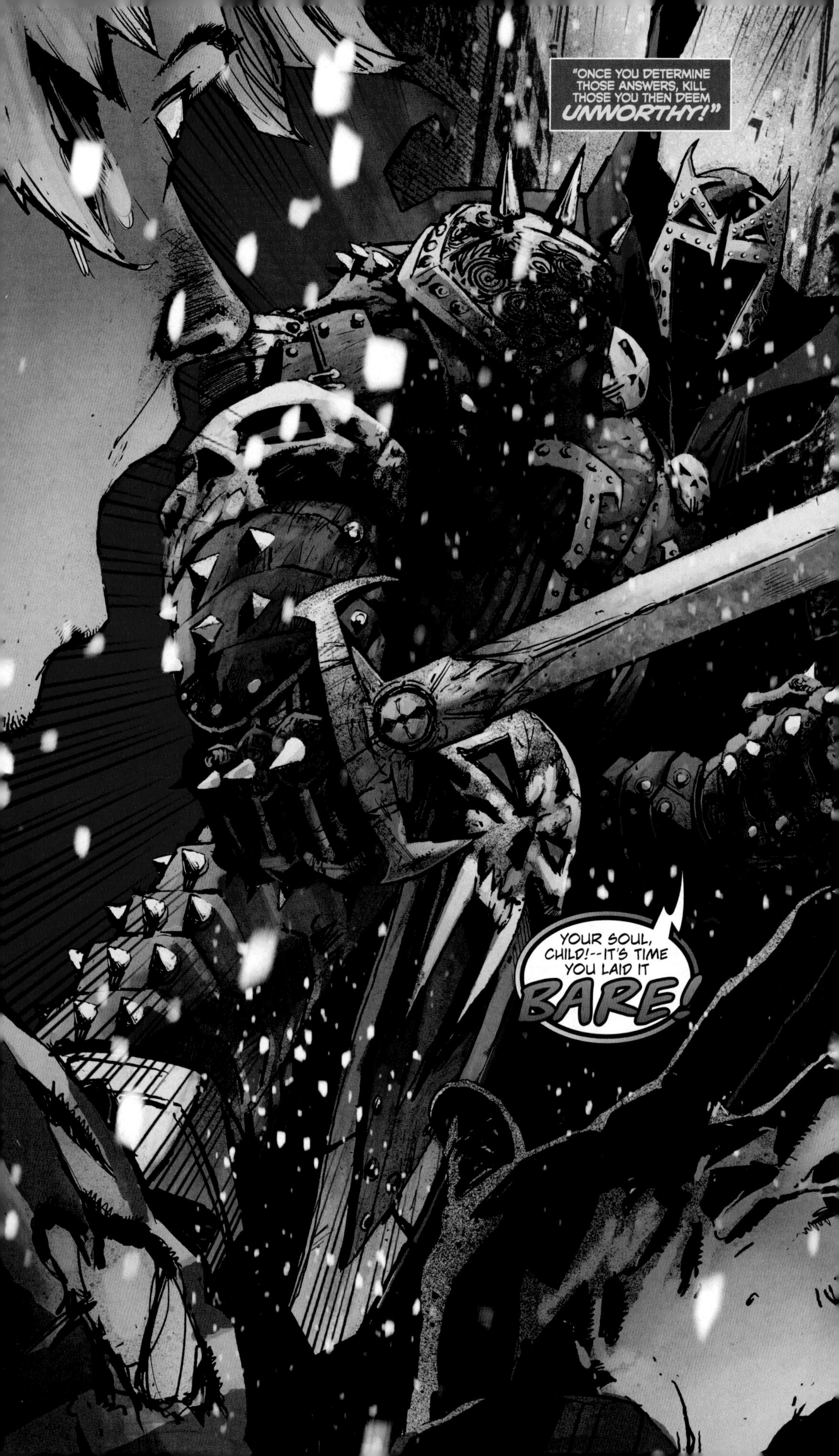
"ONCE YOU DETERMINE THOSE ANSWERS, KILL THOSE YOU THEN DEEM UNWORTHY!"
YOUR SOUL, CHILD!--IT'S TIME YOU LAID IT BARE!

CHAPTER TWO

"The Miracle"

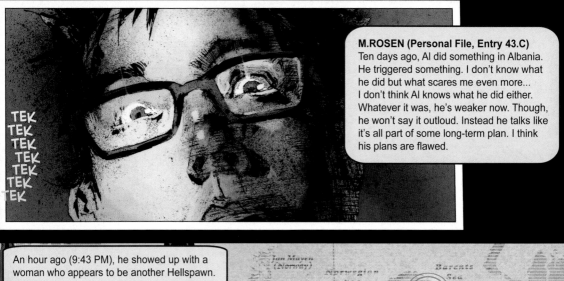

TEK TEK TEK TEK TEK TEK TEK
M.ROSEN (Personal File, Entry 43.C)
Ten days ago, Al did something in Albania. He triggered something. I don't know what he did but what scares me even more... I don't think Al knows what he did either. Whatever it was, he's weaker now. Though, he won't say it outloud. Instead he talks like it's all part of some long-term plan. I think his plans are flawed.
An hour ago (9:43 PM), he showed up with a woman who appears to be another Hellspawn.
He seems to trust her, but the Al Simmons I know (which hasn't been that long) doesn't trust very easily. Further, she brought a data-dump that Al wanted me to decrypt. The problem is that strangers bringing me strange data sets off all kinds of alarms.
Against my better judgment I cracked the files without running any virus detection—so far, the system hasn't crashed. The data mapped some energy signatures that have pinged across the globe since Al "detonated" his costume in Albania. But why do all the signals match the same readings given off by Al's powers?
Al doesn't know why, so I will investigate on my own. Right now, Al and his "sister" are on the trail of one of the markers. But one marker, in upstate New York, its activity seems different than the others. I'll run it through a separate series of algorithms.
IT CAN'T BE.
I also just pulled scrambled security footage from a private hospital. Something happened there at the exact same moment Al went "nuclear" in Albania.
This film is showing me... a miracle!.

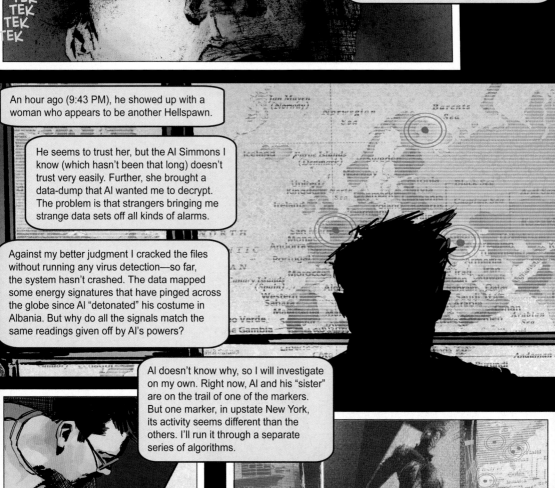

It's **Jim Downing!** How does he fit into all of Al's plans? And why didn't Al say anything about this? It's why I keep thinking Al doesn't know what he's triggered. He knew the relationship I had with Jim. How close we were before Jim lapsed into another coma. Jim had to be one of the five people Al placed his "power seeds" into. Possibly even the first one.

My other files are filled with notes, theories and firsthand accounts of my time with Jim. On top of which, Jim may have been the very first piece Al placed on the board. I say "may have been" because Al has plans embedded in other plans. So, I can't be sure. Then, there's the big questions... What side is Jim even one?!? Hell, what side am I on??????

I'm getting worried about Al. He's spreading himself way too thin. The number of enemies he's trying to fight at once... The scale of the war he's battling... It's too much for one man to do alone. Maybe that's why he picked Jim. I know Al said he thought he was going to die in Albania but if he didn't, he'd have the upper-hand... He'd build an army, starting with the first five "seeds" he planted. And, of course, Jim would be one of those five.

Al wants to be the good guy--the hero--but his sins, his anger, they give Simmons a dark side. A side I can't fully trust. Maybe that's why he chose Jim, because he knows Jim's personality's nearly the opposite of his own. A smart leader always finds those who can fill the leader's weaknesses.

I need to find Jim, because he's a target now, too. Al said he rigged the outcome of his fight with Heaven and Hell by placing slivers of his powers in people he believes would take up his cause if (when) he falls. What he didn't do, I'm betting, is give any of those five the option to say no. Or tell them they would become targets. Apparently, one of his "chosen" is already dead--a girl named, Nyx. Did research on her but found nothing. Obviously, that wasn't her real name.

I'll keep investigating because her life could help lead to answers about her death. But, more importantly... Jim's back. And, I don't know what the other's Al "cursed" with his powers are all about, but Jim Downing is a unique beast--his soul has lived in both Heaven and Hell. According to Spawn lore that's a rare combo. He's been **damned** and **saved**. That just might make him a bigger target than Al himself. I wonder... Is Al channeling some of Jim's personality already?

It would be easy to see Al's recent actions as being inspired by Jim's own--going public, seeking the spotlight, letting the world know that Lt. Col. Al Simmons was alive and "well". Would Al have made those moves without Jim's example? Hard to say. Harder to say... How will Al react as his public persona continues to gain attention? Could be a timebomb.

But Al has touched one person he isn't thinking about... **ME!** I'm caught in the middle of events I can barely keep track of much less comprehend. At times I feel like a soldier in an impossible war then I flip to feeling like a prisoner. I'm just human. Al seems to forget that. Everything around us isn't normal except me. I can die! He didn't give me any of his damn powers. Maybe he thinks he can just replace me. Maybe he really doesn't give a shit.

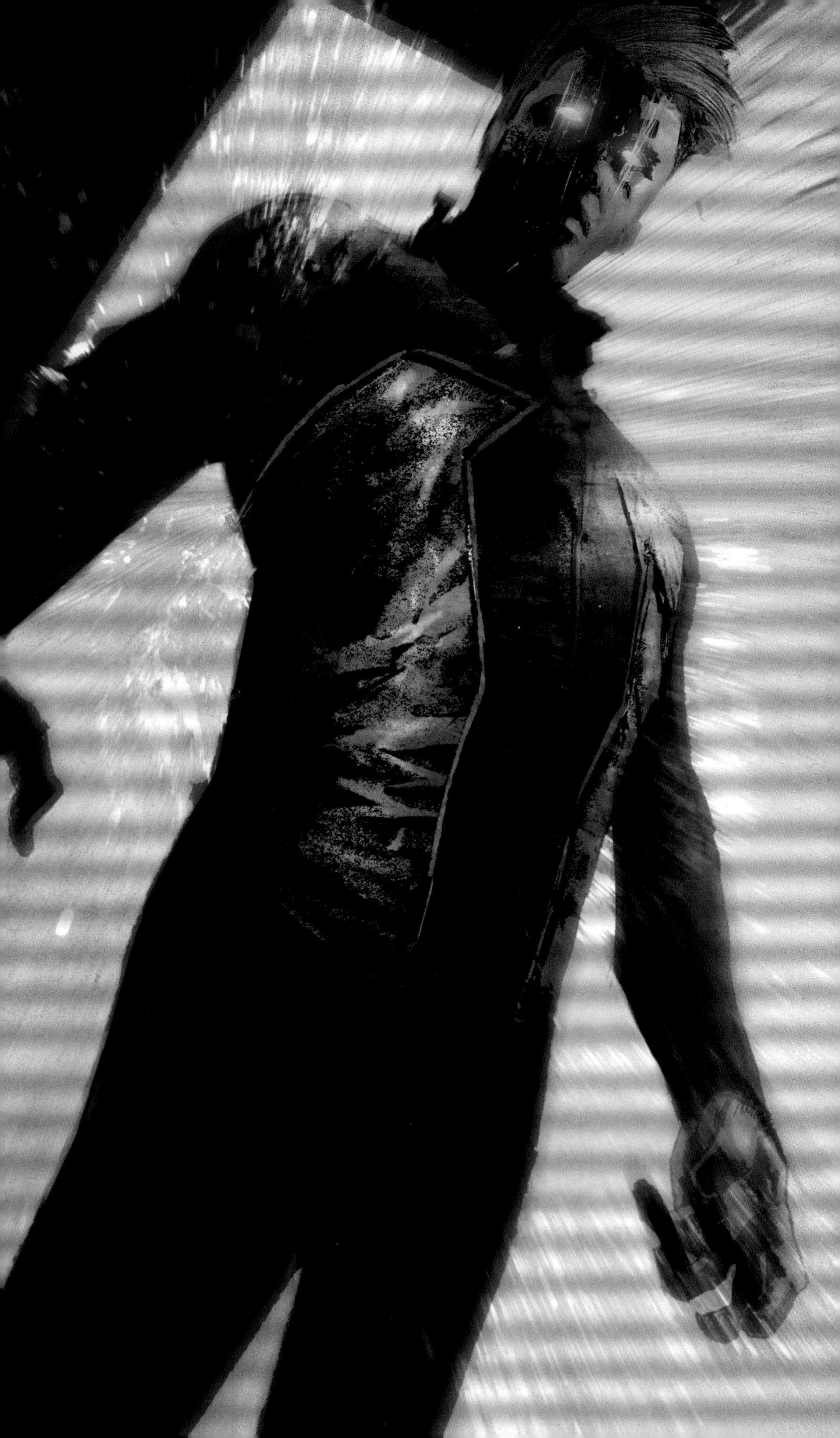

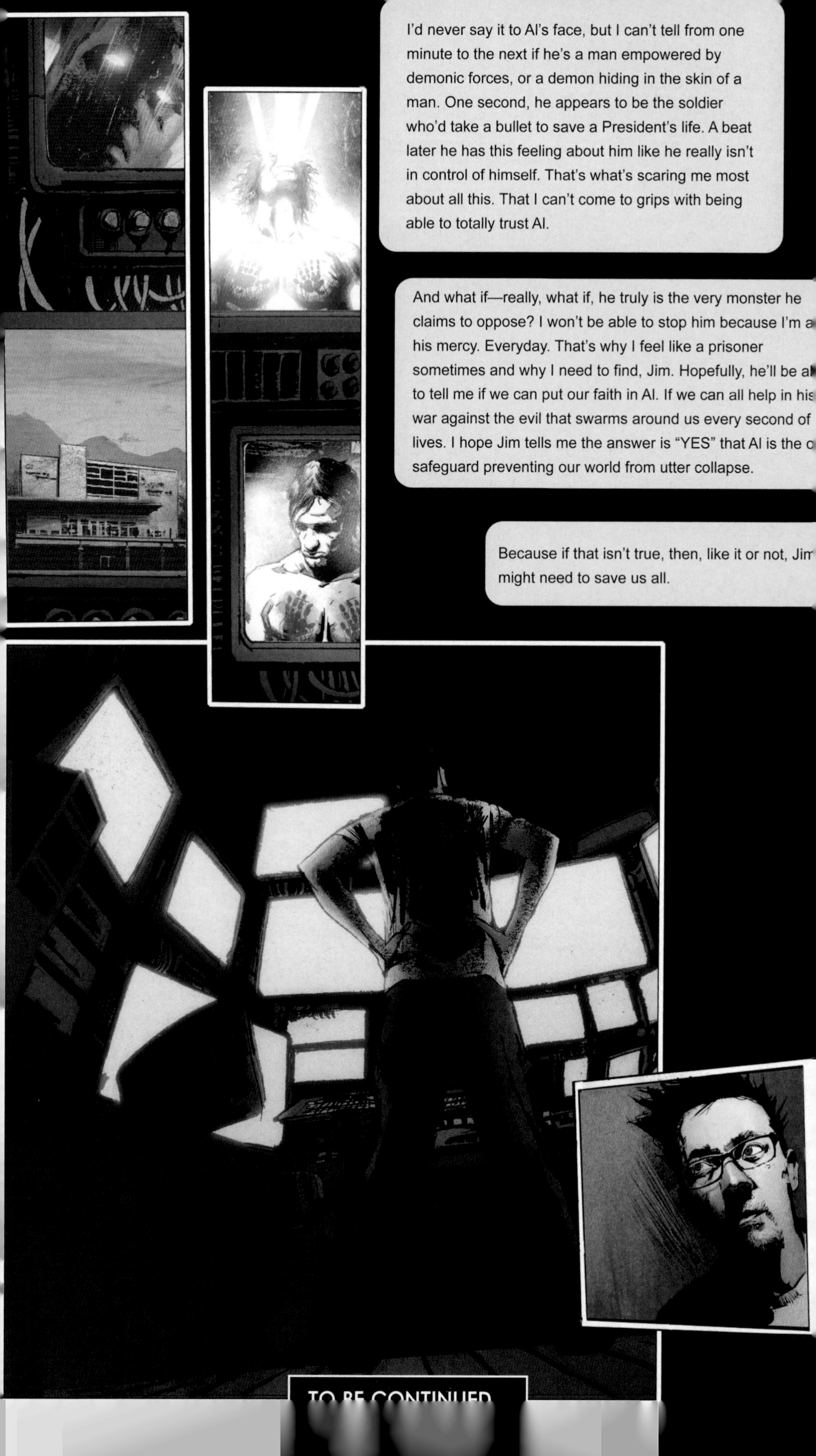

I'd never say it to Al's face, but I can't tell from one minute to the next if he's a man empowered by demonic forces, or a demon hiding in the skin of a man. One second, he appears to be the soldier who'd take a bullet to save a President's life. A beat later he has this feeling about him like he really isn't in control of himself. That's what's scaring me most about all this. That I can't come to grips with being able to totally trust Al.
And what if—really, what if, he truly is the very monster he claims to oppose? I won't be able to stop him because I'm a his mercy. Everyday. That's why I feel like a prisoner sometimes and why I need to find, Jim. Hopefully, he'll be a to tell me if we can put our faith in Al. If we can all help in his war against the evil that swarms around us every second of lives. I hope Jim tells me the answer is "YES" that Al is the safeguard preventing our world from utter collapse.
Because if that isn't true, then, like it or not, Jim might need to save us all.
TO BE CONTINUED

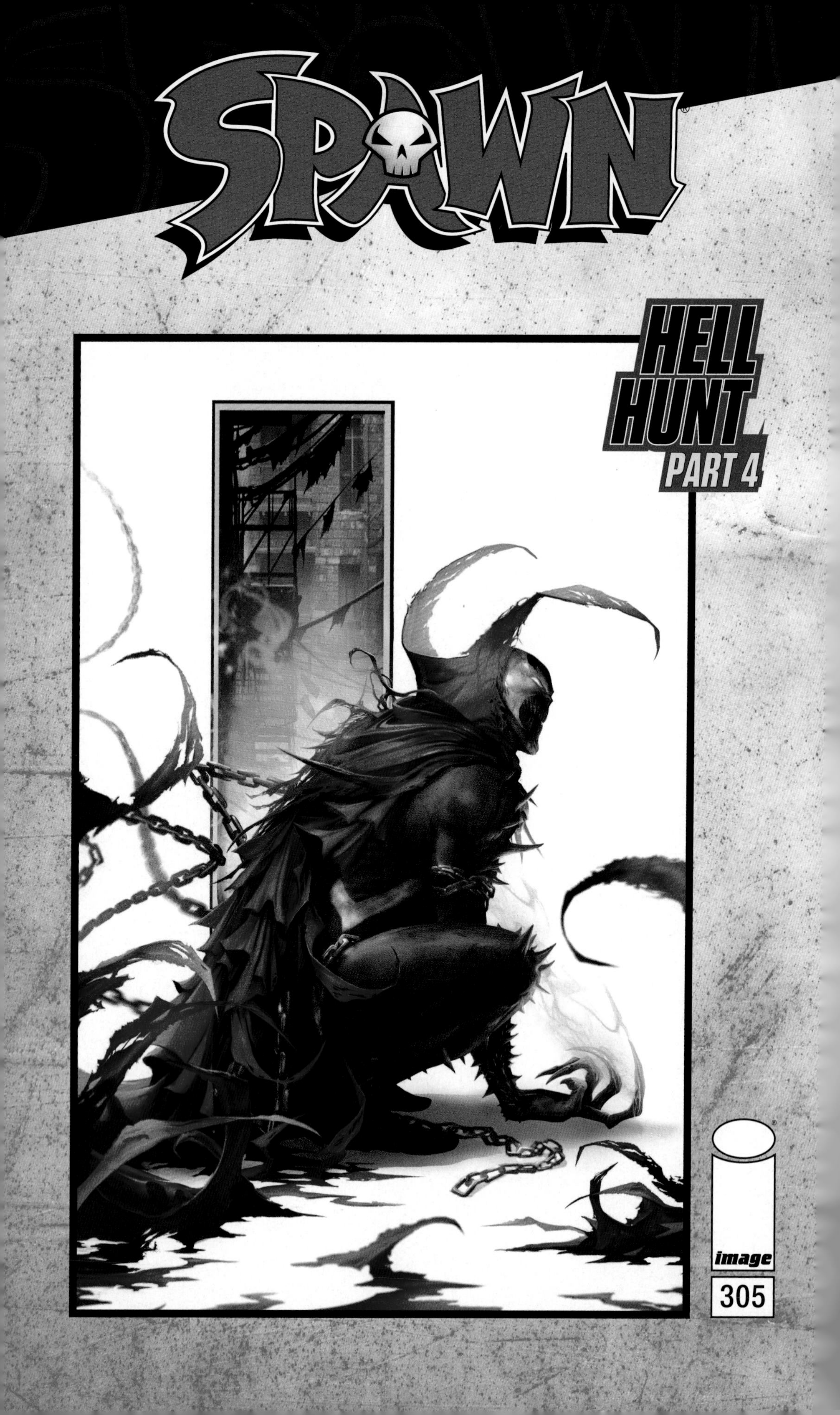
SPAWN
HELL HUNT
PART 4
image
305

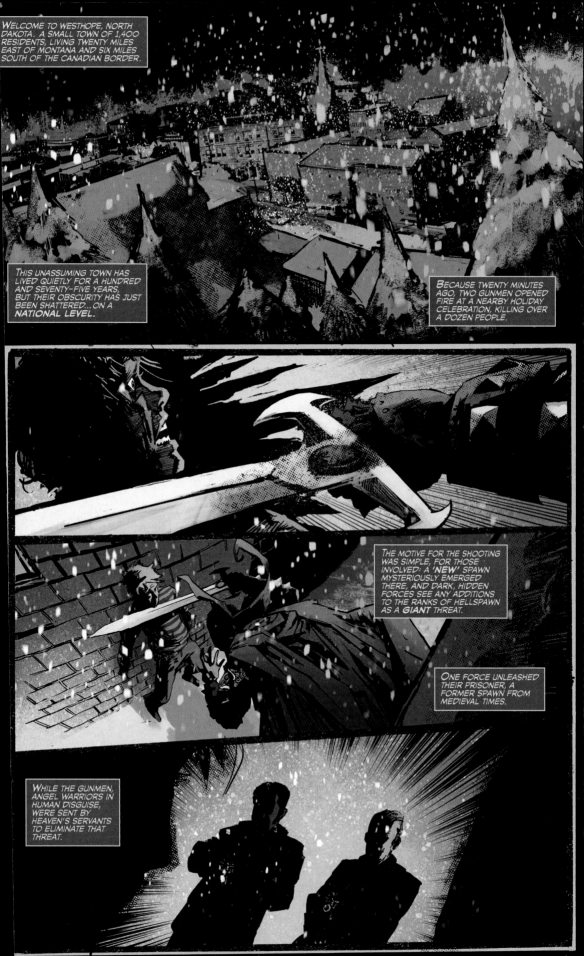

WELCOME TO WESTHOPE, NORTH DAKOTA. A SMALL TOWN OF 1,400 RESIDENTS, LIVING TWENTY MILES EAST OF MONTANA AND SIX MILES SOUTH OF THE CANADIAN BORDER.

THIS UNASSUMING TOWN HAS LIVED QUIETLY FOR A HUNDRED AND SEVENTY-FIVE YEARS, BUT THEIR OBSCURITY HAS JUST BEEN SHATTERED...ON A *NATIONAL LEVEL.*

BECAUSE TWENTY MINUTES AGO, TWO GUNMEN OPENED FIRE AT A NEARBY HOLIDAY CELEBRATION, KILLING OVER A DOZEN PEOPLE.

THE MOTIVE FOR THE SHOOTING WAS SIMPLE, FOR THOSE INVOLVED: A *'NEW'* SPAWN MYSTERIOUSLY EMERGED THERE, AND DARK, HIDDEN FORCES SEE ANY ADDITIONS TO THE RANKS OF HELLSPAWN AS A *GIANT* THREAT.

ONE FORCE UNLEASHED THEIR PRISONER, A FORMER SPAWN FROM MEDIEVAL TIMES.

WHILE THE GUNMEN, ANGEL WARRIORS IN HUMAN DISGUISE, WERE SENT BY HEAVEN'S SERVANTS TO ELIMINATE THAT THREAT.

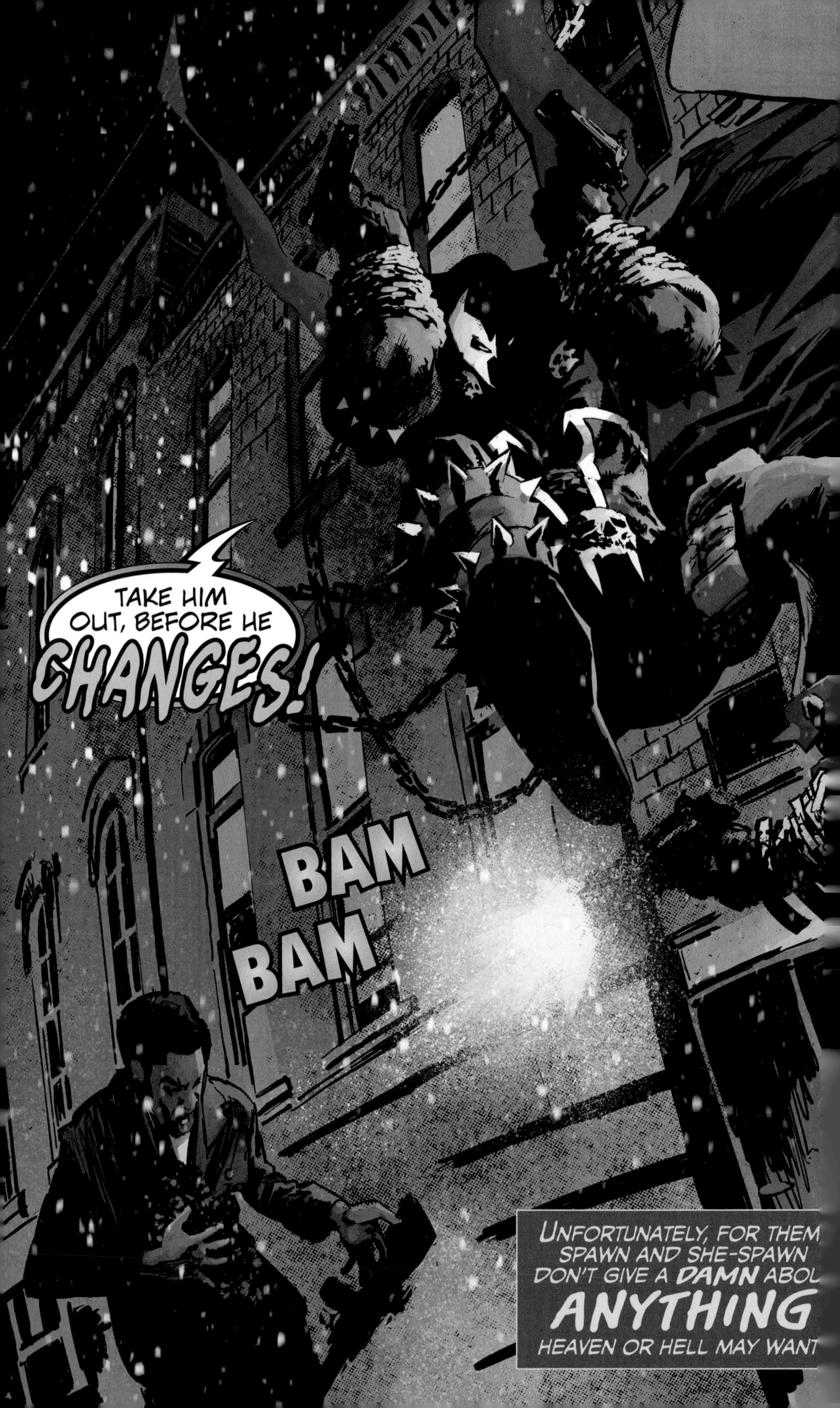

TAKE HIM OUT, BEFORE HE CHANGES!
BAM
BAM
UNFORTUNATELY, FOR THEM SPAWN AND SHE-SPAWN DON'T GIVE A DAMN ABOU ANYTHING HEAVEN OR HELL MAY WANT

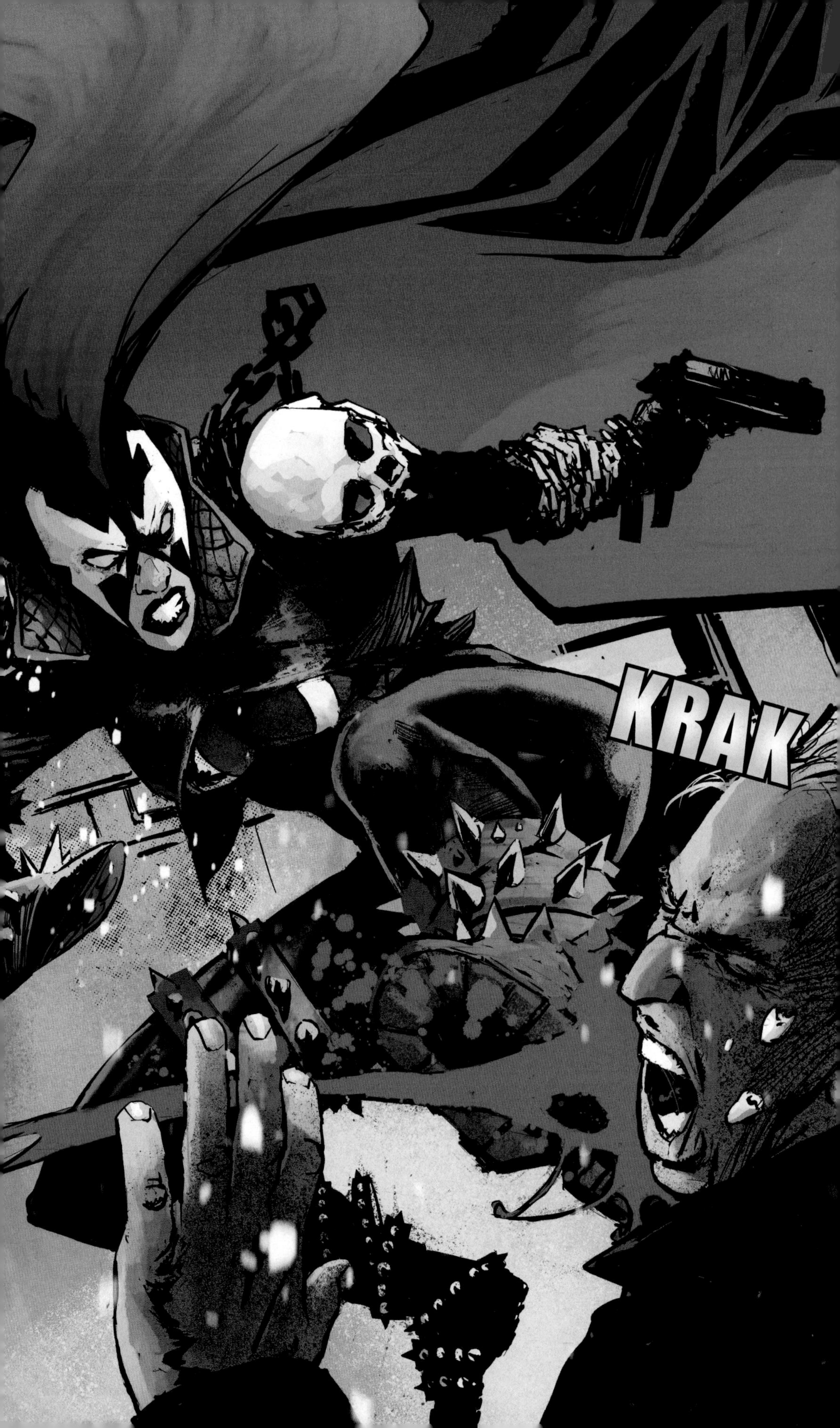
KRAK

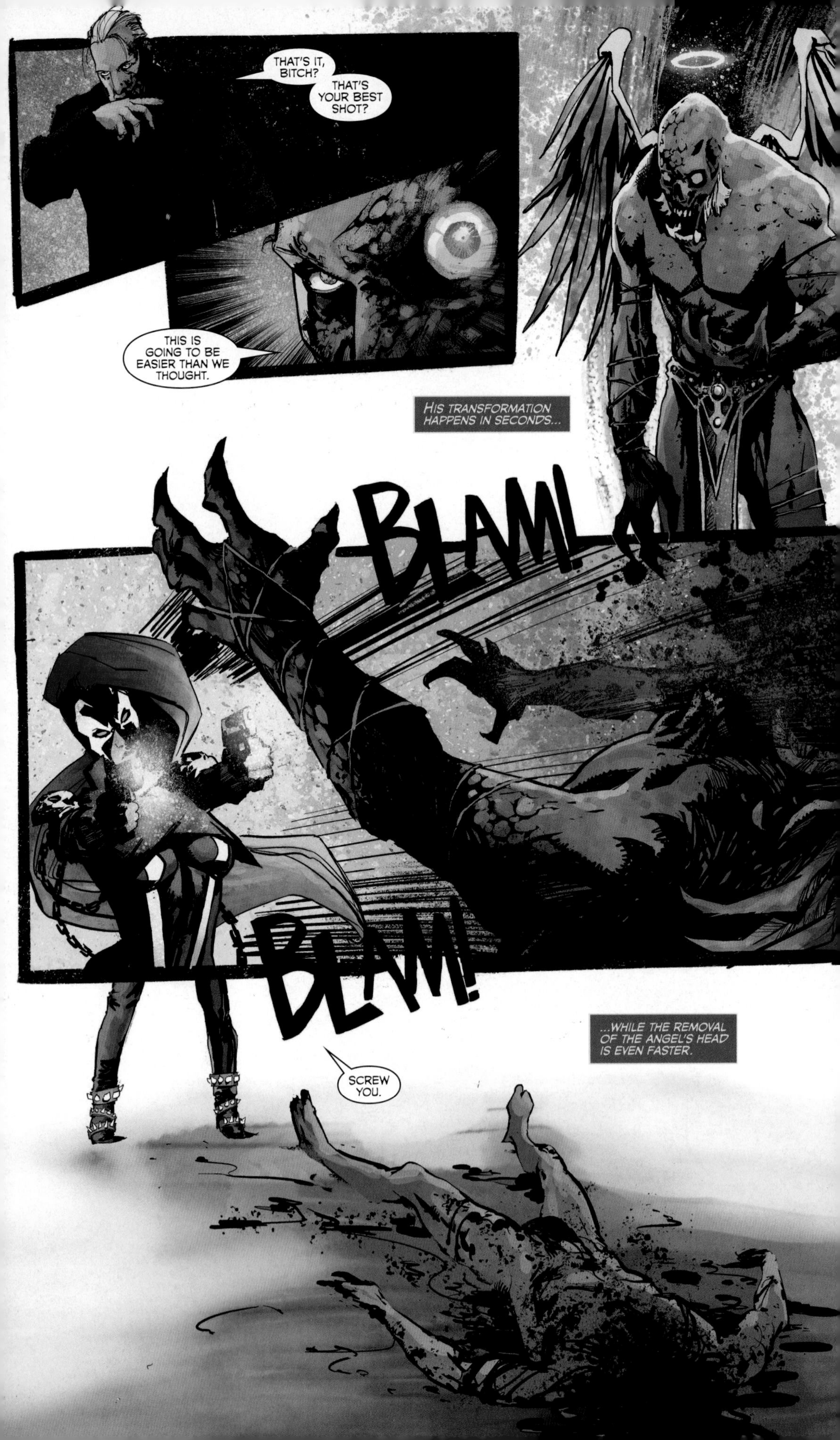

THAT'S IT, BITCH?
THAT'S YOUR BEST SHOT?
THIS IS GOING TO BE EASIER THAN WE THOUGHT.
HIS TRANSFORMATION HAPPENS IN SECONDS...
BLAM!
BLAM!
...WHILE THE REMOVAL OF THE ANGEL'S HEAD IS EVEN FASTER.
SCREW YOU.

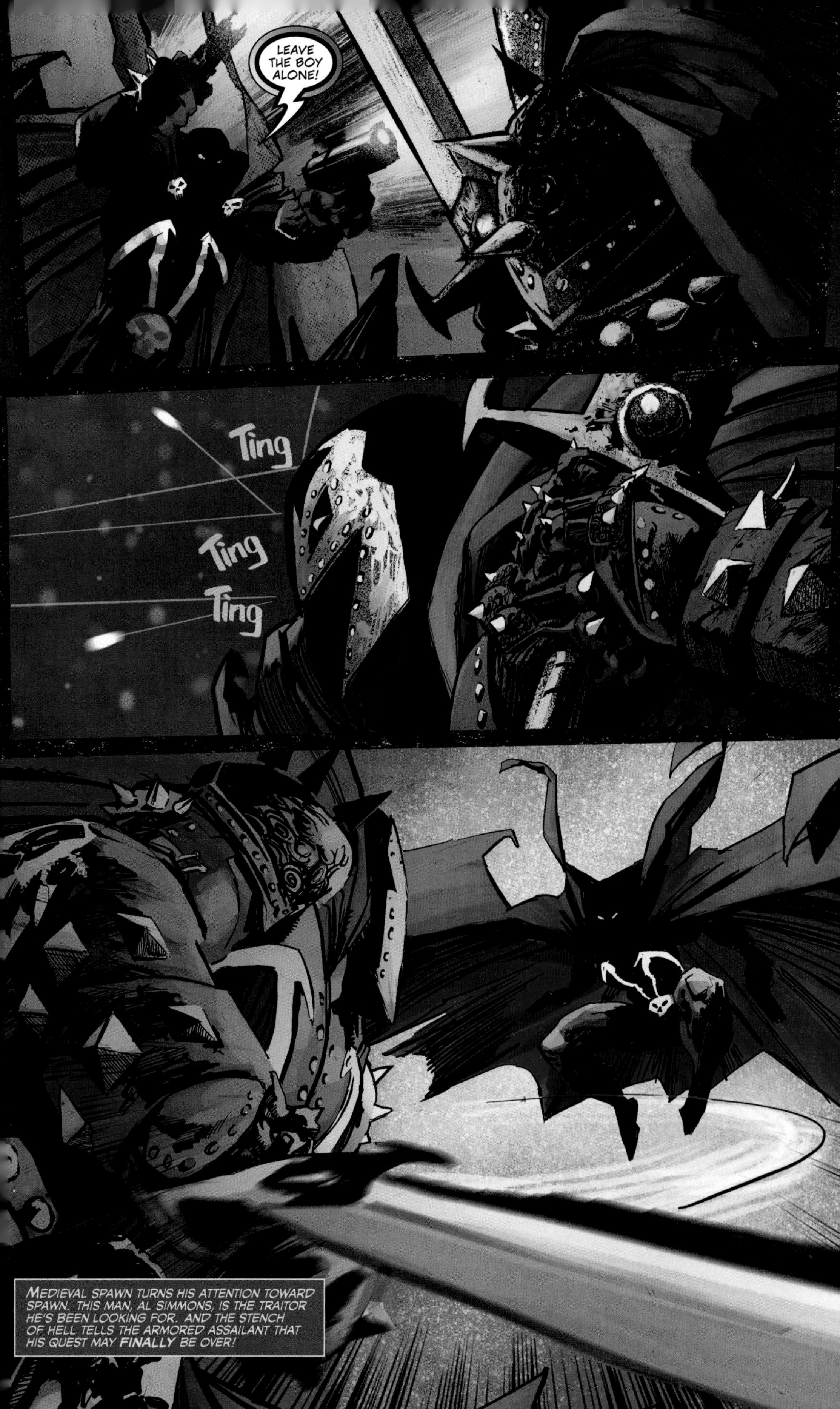
LEAVE THE BOY ALONE!
Ting
Ting
Ting
MEDIEVAL SPAWN TURNS HIS ATTENTION TOWARD SPAWN. THIS MAN, AL SIMMONS, IS THE TRAITOR HE'S BEEN LOOKING FOR. AND THE STENCH OF HELL TELLS THE ARMORED ASSAILANT THAT HIS QUEST MAY **FINALLY** BE OVER!

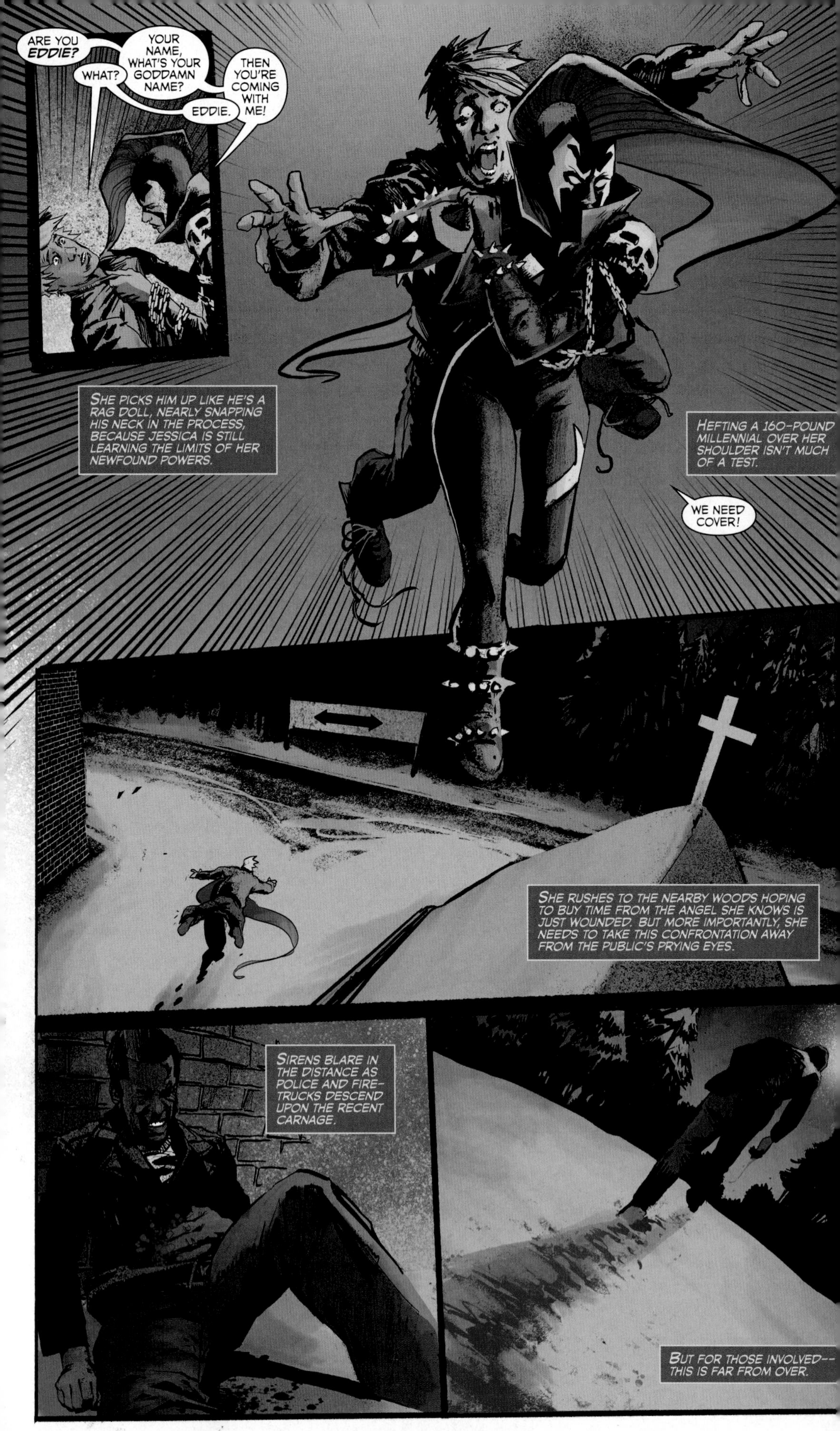
ARE YOU EDDIE?
WHAT?
YOUR NAME, WHAT'S YOUR GODDAMN NAME?
EDDIE.
THEN YOU'RE COMING WITH ME!
SHE PICKS HIM UP LIKE HE'S A RAG DOLL, NEARLY SNAPPING HIS NECK IN THE PROCESS, BECAUSE JESSICA IS STILL LEARNING THE LIMITS OF HER NEWFOUND POWERS.
HEFTING A 160-POUND MILLENNIAL OVER HER SHOULDER ISN'T MUCH OF A TEST.
WE NEED COVER!
SHE RUSHES TO THE NEARBY WOODS HOPING TO BUY TIME FROM THE ANGEL SHE KNOWS IS JUST WOUNDED. BUT MORE IMPORTANTLY, SHE NEEDS TO TAKE THIS CONFRONTATION AWAY FROM THE PUBLIC'S PRYING EYES.
SIRENS BLARE IN THE DISTANCE AS POLICE AND FIRE-TRUCKS DESCEND UPON THE RECENT CARNAGE.
BUT FOR THOSE INVOLVED-- THIS IS FAR FROM OVER.

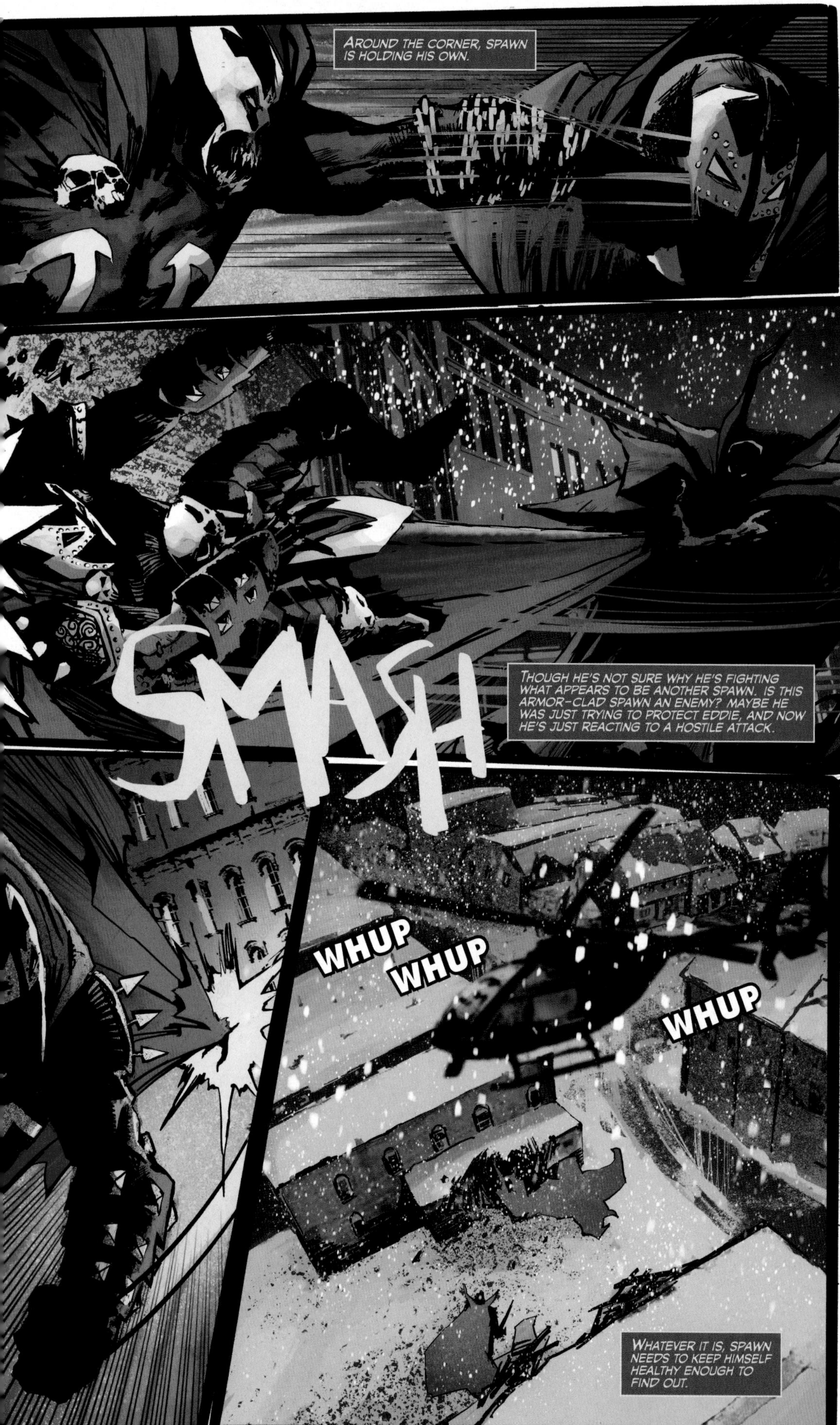
AROUND THE CORNER, SPAWN IS HOLDING HIS OWN.
SMASH
THOUGH HE'S NOT SURE WHY HE'S FIGHTING WHAT APPEARS TO BE ANOTHER SPAWN. IS THIS ARMOR-CLAD SPAWN AN ENEMY? MAYBE HE WAS JUST TRYING TO PROTECT EDDIE, AND NOW HE'S JUST REACTING TO A HOSTILE ATTACK.
WHUP
WHUP
WHUP
WHATEVER IT IS, SPAWN NEEDS TO KEEP HIMSELF HEALTHY ENOUGH TO FIND OUT.

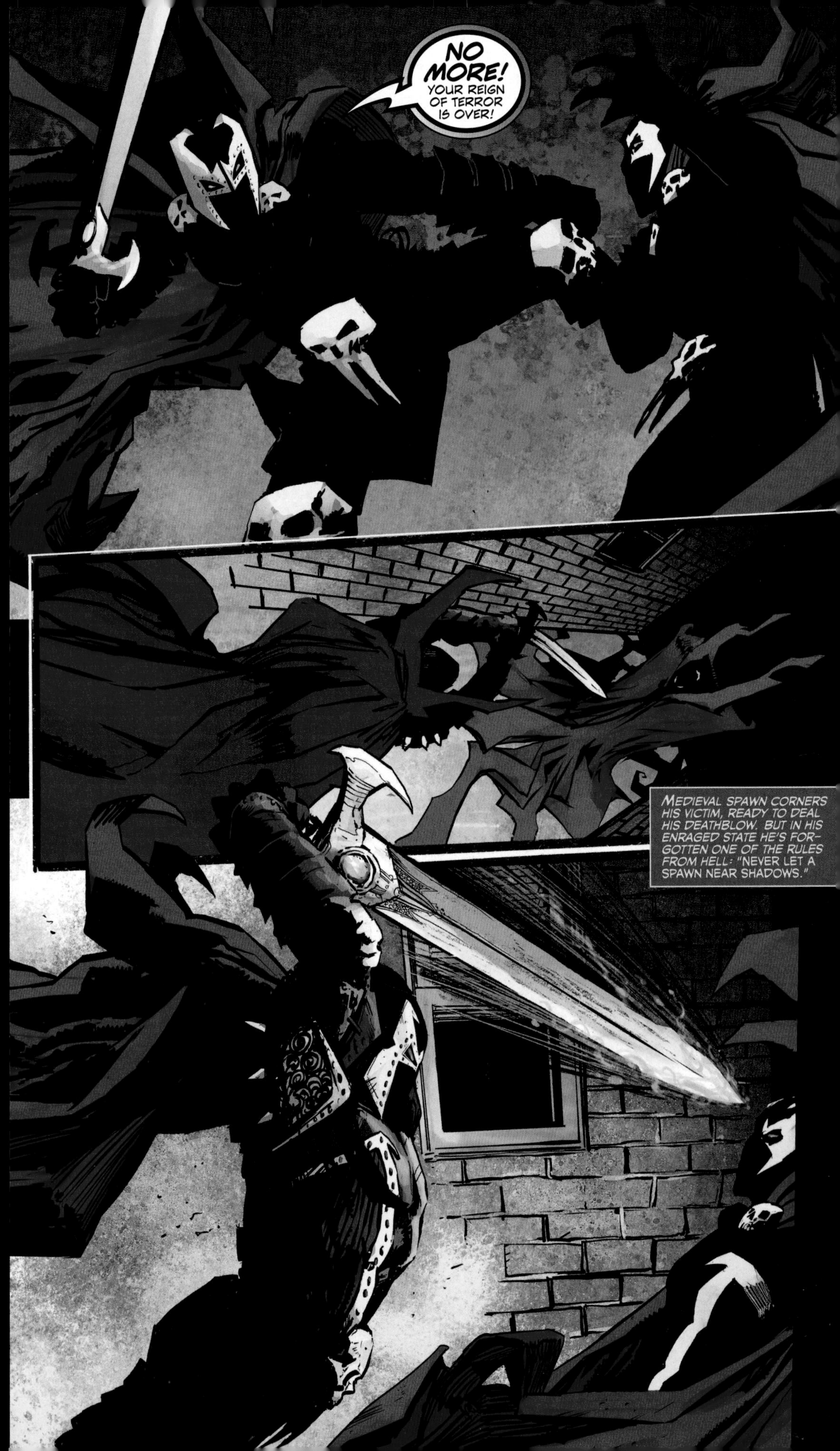
NO MORE! YOUR REIGN OF TERROR IS OVER!
MEDIEVAL SPAWN CORNERS HIS VICTIM, READY TO DEAL HIS DEATHBLOW. BUT IN HIS ENRAGED STATE HE'S FORGOTTEN ONE OF THE RULES FROM HELL: "NEVER LET A SPAWN NEAR SHADOWS."

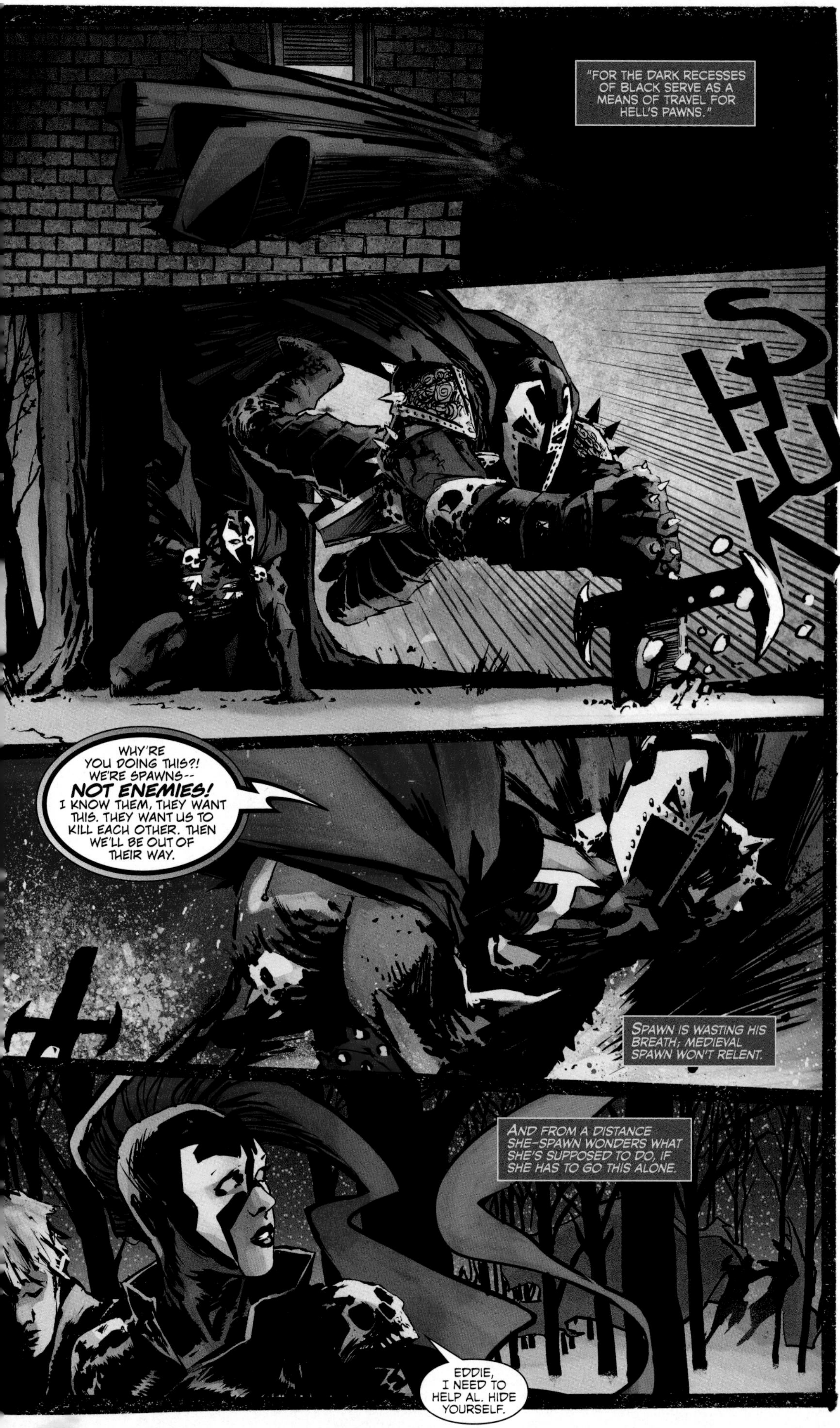
"FOR THE DARK RECESSES OF BLACK SERVE AS A MEANS OF TRAVEL FOR HELL'S PAWNS."
SHUK
WHY'RE YOU DOING THIS?! WE'RE SPAWNS-- NOT ENEMIES! I KNOW THEM, THEY WANT THIS. THEY WANT US TO KILL EACH OTHER. THEN WE'LL BE OUT OF THEIR WAY.
SPAWN IS WASTING HIS BREATH; MEDIEVAL SPAWN WON'T RELENT.
AND FROM A DISTANCE SHE-SPAWN WONDERS WHAT SHE'S SUPPOSED TO DO, IF SHE HAS TO GO THIS ALONE.
EDDIE, I NEED TO HELP AL. HIDE YOURSELF.

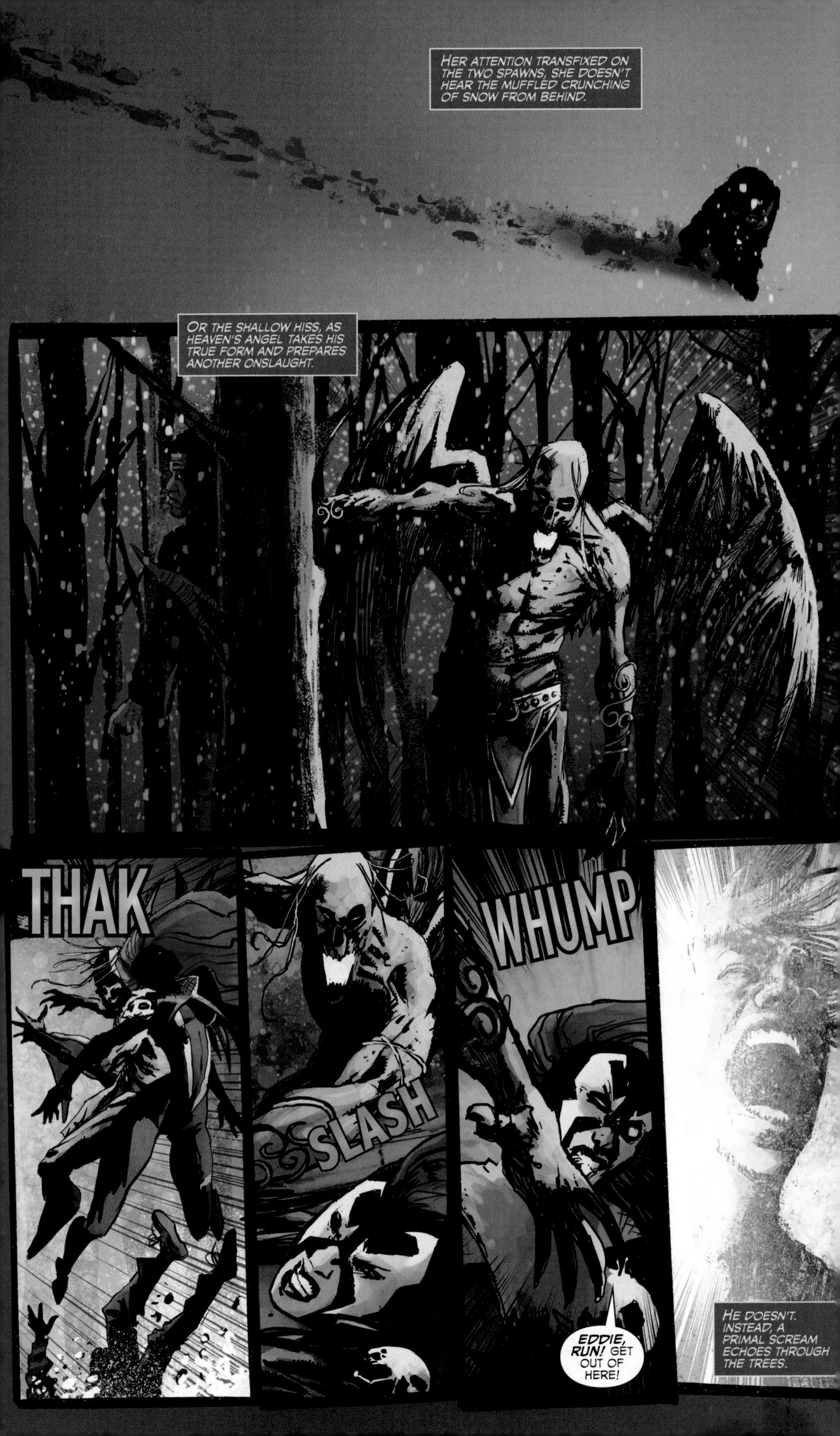
HER ATTENTION TRANSFIXED ON THE TWO SPAWNS, SHE DOESN'T HEAR THE MUFFLED CRUNCHING OF SNOW FROM BEHIND.
OR THE SHALLOW HISS, AS HEAVEN'S ANGEL TAKES HIS TRUE FORM AND PREPARES ANOTHER ONSLAUGHT.
THAK
SLASH
WHUMP
EDDIE, RUN! GET OUT OF HERE!
HE DOESN'T. INSTEAD, A PRIMAL SCREAM ECHOES THROUGH THE TREES.

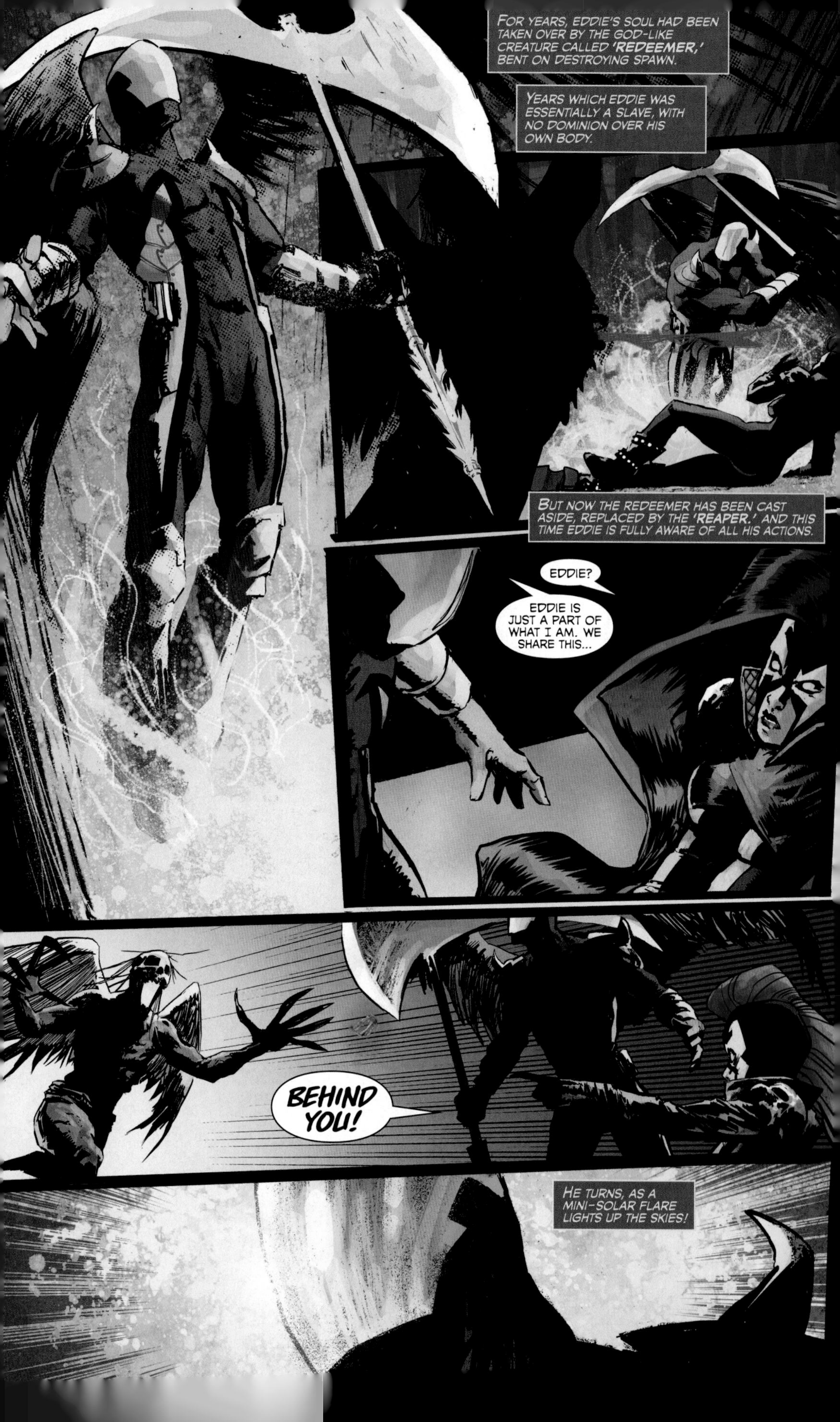

FOR YEARS, EDDIE'S SOUL HAD BEEN TAKEN OVER BY THE GOD-LIKE CREATURE CALLED 'REDEEMER,' BENT ON DESTROYING SPAWN.
YEARS WHICH EDDIE WAS ESSENTIALLY A SLAVE, WITH NO DOMINION OVER HIS OWN BODY.
BUT NOW THE REDEEMER HAS BEEN CAST ASIDE, REPLACED BY THE 'REAPER.' AND THIS TIME EDDIE IS FULLY AWARE OF ALL HIS ACTIONS.
EDDIE?
EDDIE IS JUST A PART OF WHAT I AM. WE SHARE THIS...
BEHIND YOU!
HE TURNS, AS A MINI-SOLAR FLARE LIGHTS UP THE SKIES!

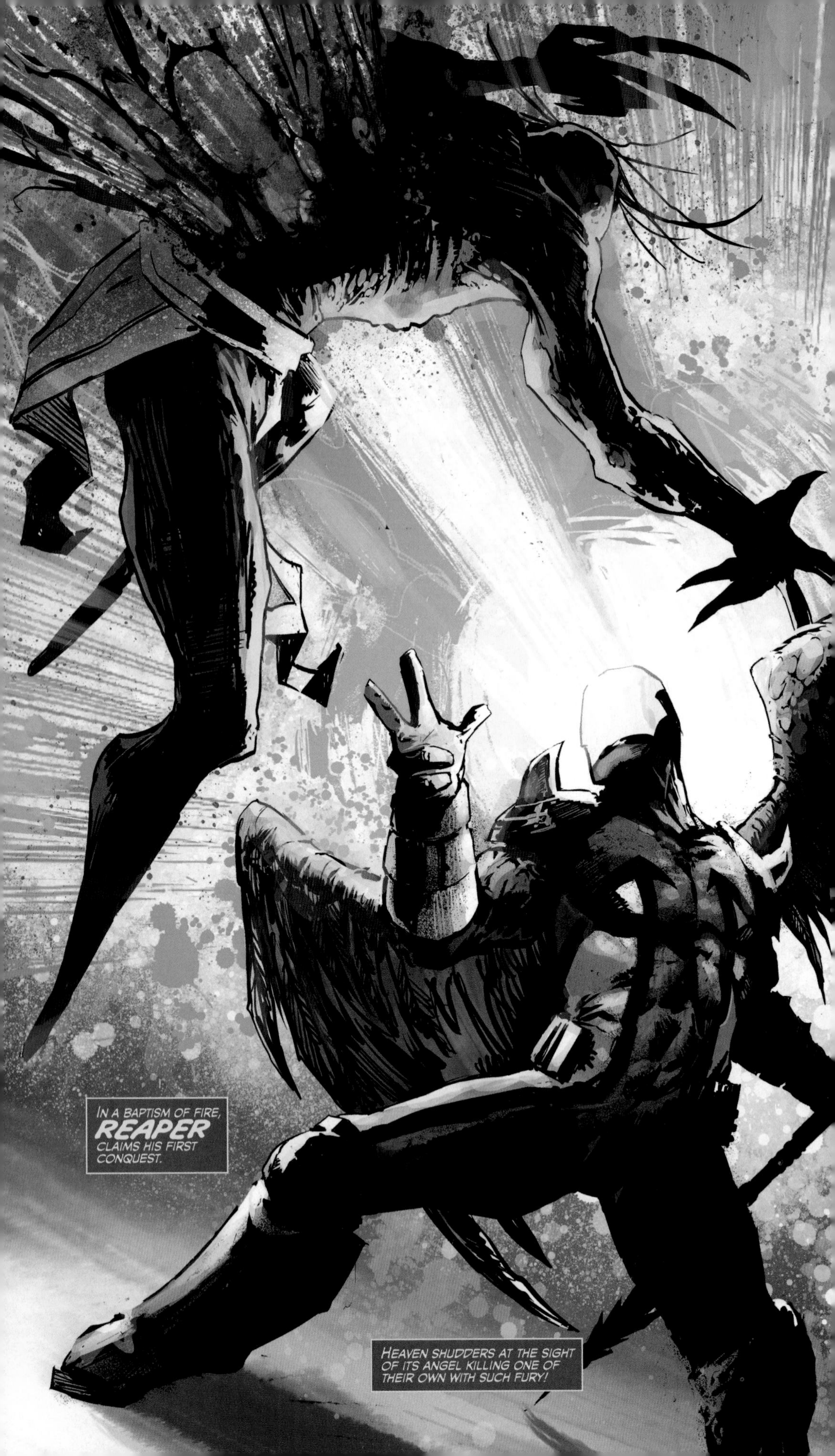
IN A BAPTISM OF FIRE, REAPER CLAIMS HIS FIRST CONQUEST.
HEAVEN SHUDDERS AT THE SIGHT OF ITS ANGEL KILLING ONE OF THEIR OWN WITH SUCH FURY!

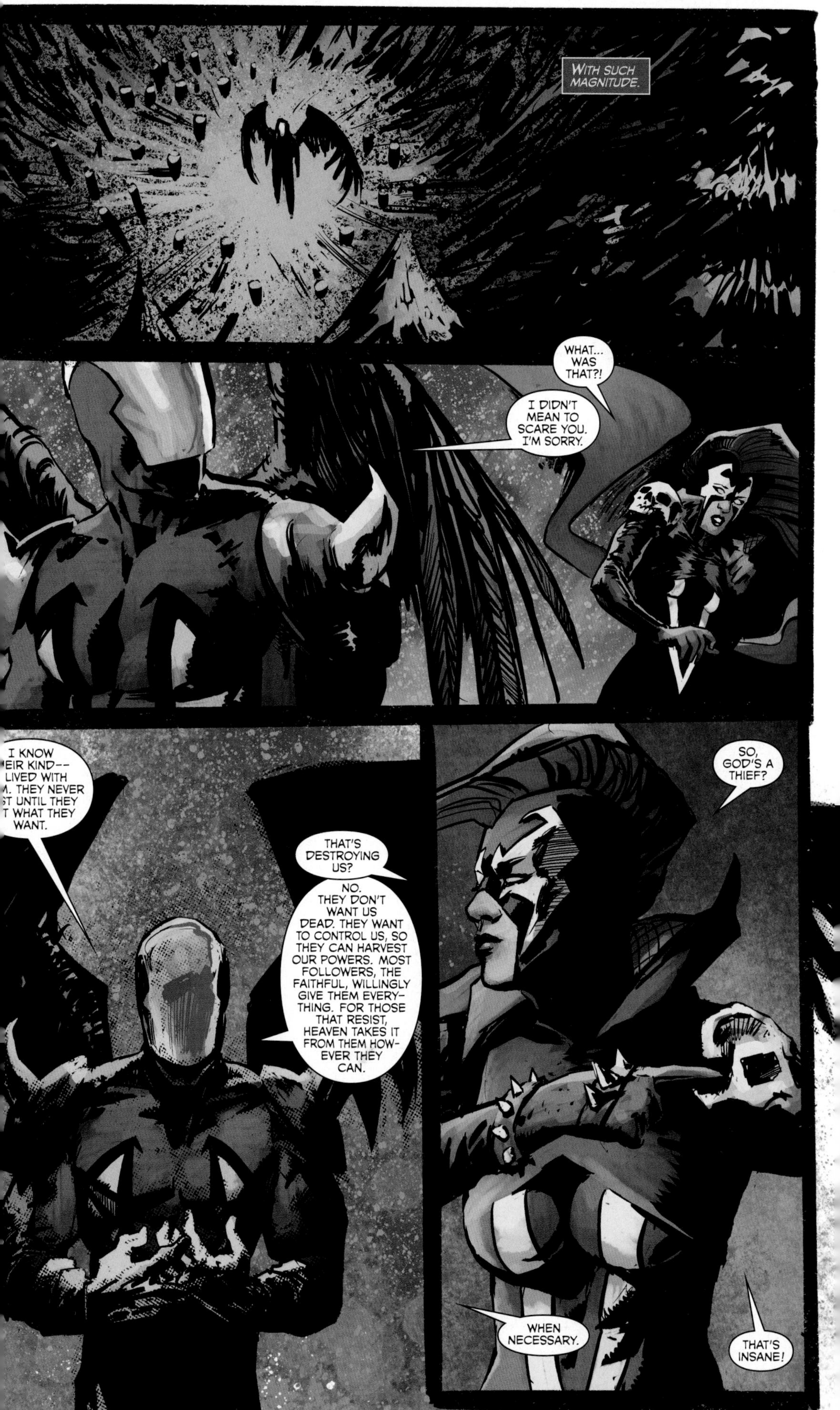

WITH SUCH MAGNITUDE.
WHAT... WAS THAT?!
I DIDN'T MEAN TO SCARE YOU. I'M SORRY.
I KNOW EIR KIND-- LIVED WITH M. THEY NEVER ST UNTIL THEY T WHAT THEY WANT.
THAT'S DESTROYING US?
NO. THEY DON'T WANT US DEAD. THEY WANT TO CONTROL US, SO THEY CAN HARVEST OUR POWERS. MOST FOLLOWERS, THE FAITHFUL, WILLINGLY GIVE THEM EVERY-THING. FOR THOSE THAT RESIST, HEAVEN TAKES IT FROM THEM HOW-EVER THEY CAN.
SO, GOD'S A THIEF?
WHEN NECESSARY.
THAT'S INSANE!

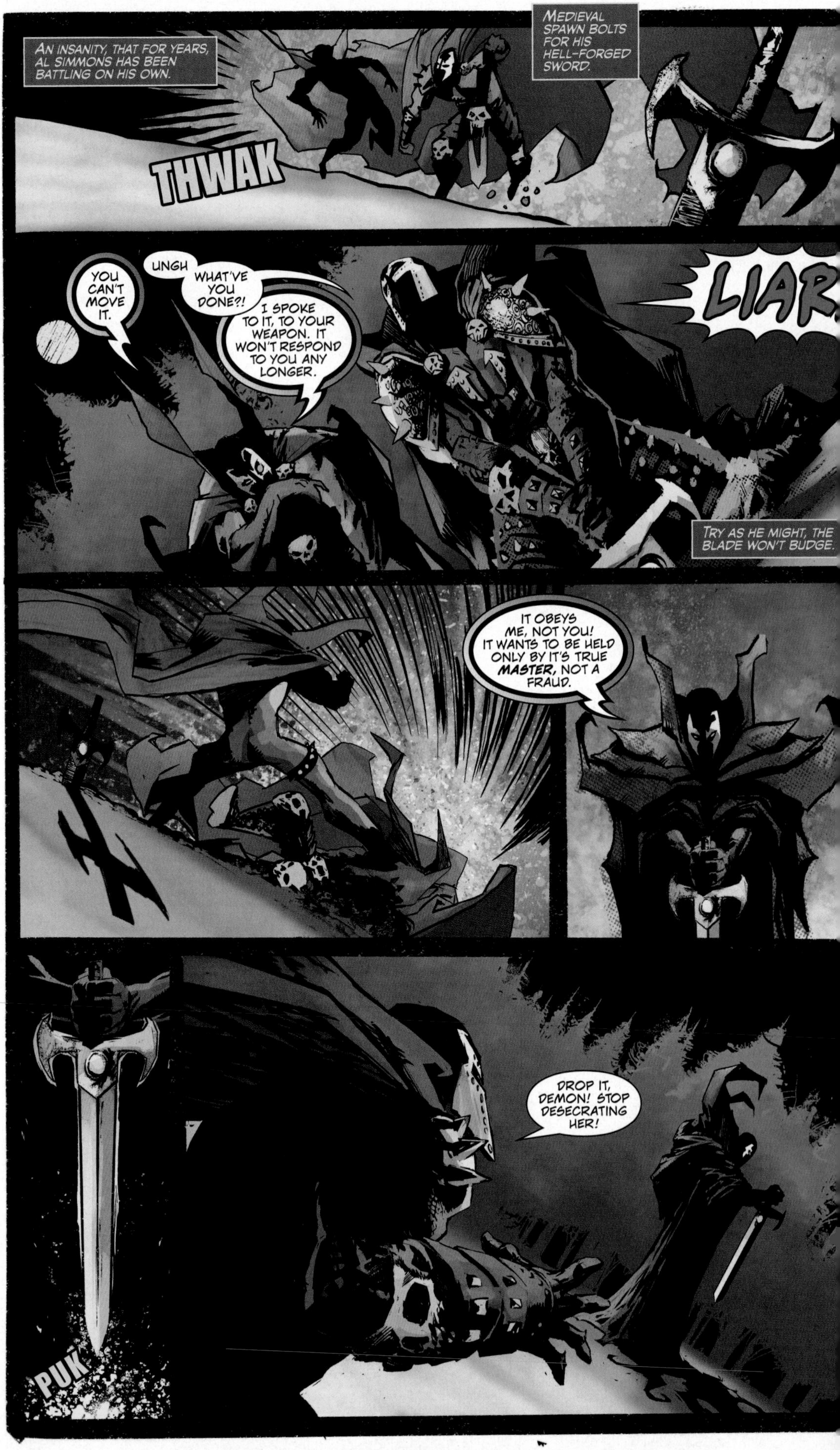

AN INSANITY, THAT FOR YEARS, AL SIMMONS HAS BEEN BATTLING ON HIS OWN.
MEDIEVAL SPAWN BOLTS FOR HIS HELL-FORGED SWORD.
THWAK
YOU CAN'T MOVE IT.
UNGH
WHAT'VE YOU DONE?!
I SPOKE TO IT, TO YOUR WEAPON. IT WON'T RESPOND TO YOU ANY LONGER.
LIAR
TRY AS HE MIGHT, THE BLADE WON'T BUDGE.
IT OBEYS ME, NOT YOU! IT WANTS TO BE HELD ONLY BY IT'S TRUE MASTER, NOT A FRAUD.
DROP IT, DEMON! STOP DESECRATING HER!
PUK

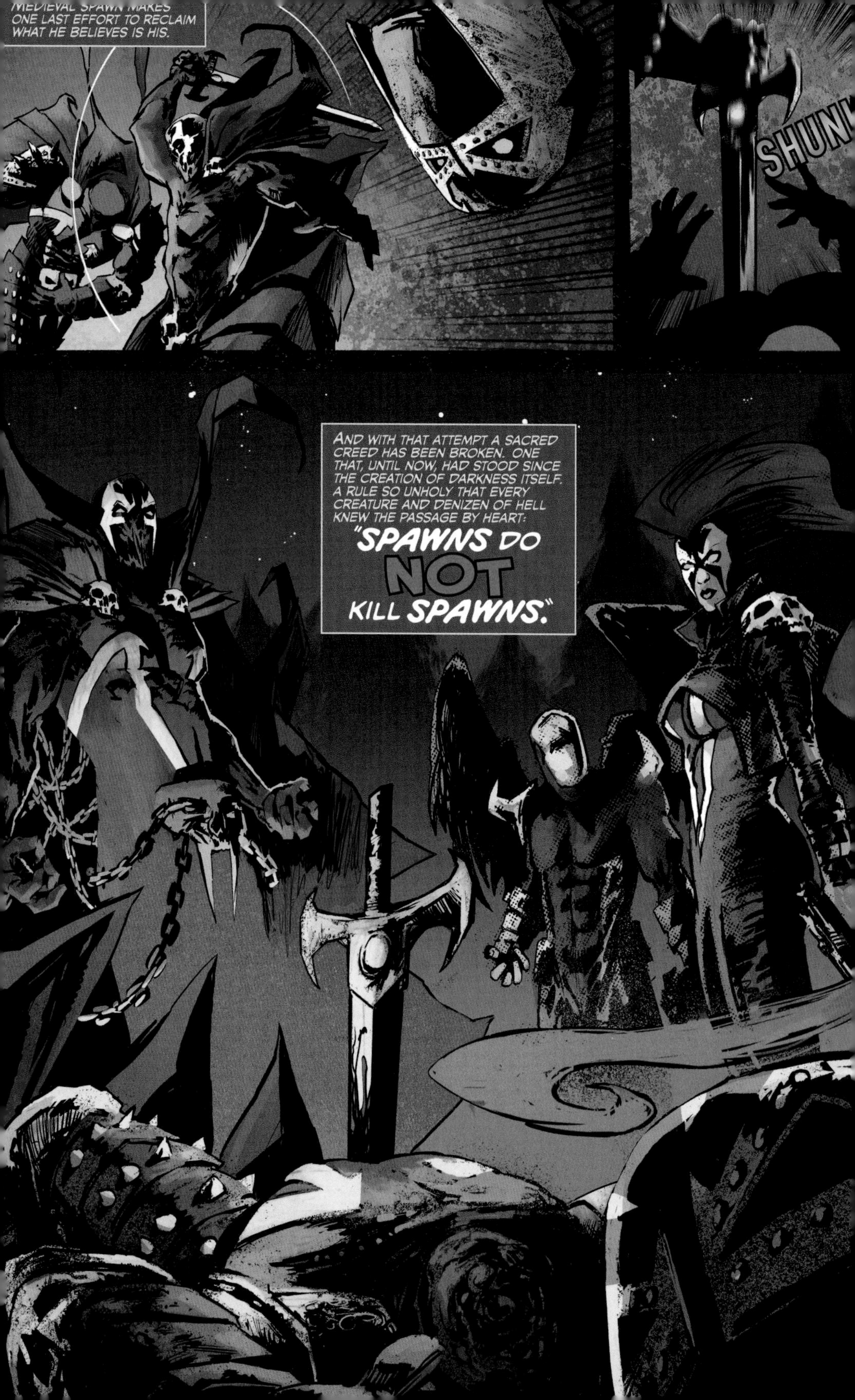
MEDIEVAL SPAWN MAKES ONE LAST EFFORT TO RECLAIM WHAT HE BELIEVES IS HIS.
SHUN
AND WITH THAT ATTEMPT A SACRED CREED HAS BEEN BROKEN. ONE THAT, UNTIL NOW, HAD STOOD SINCE THE CREATION OF DARKNESS ITSELF. A RULE SO UNHOLY THAT EVERY CREATURE AND DENIZEN OF HELL KNEW THE PASSAGE BY HEART: "SPAWNS DO NOT KILL SPAWNS."

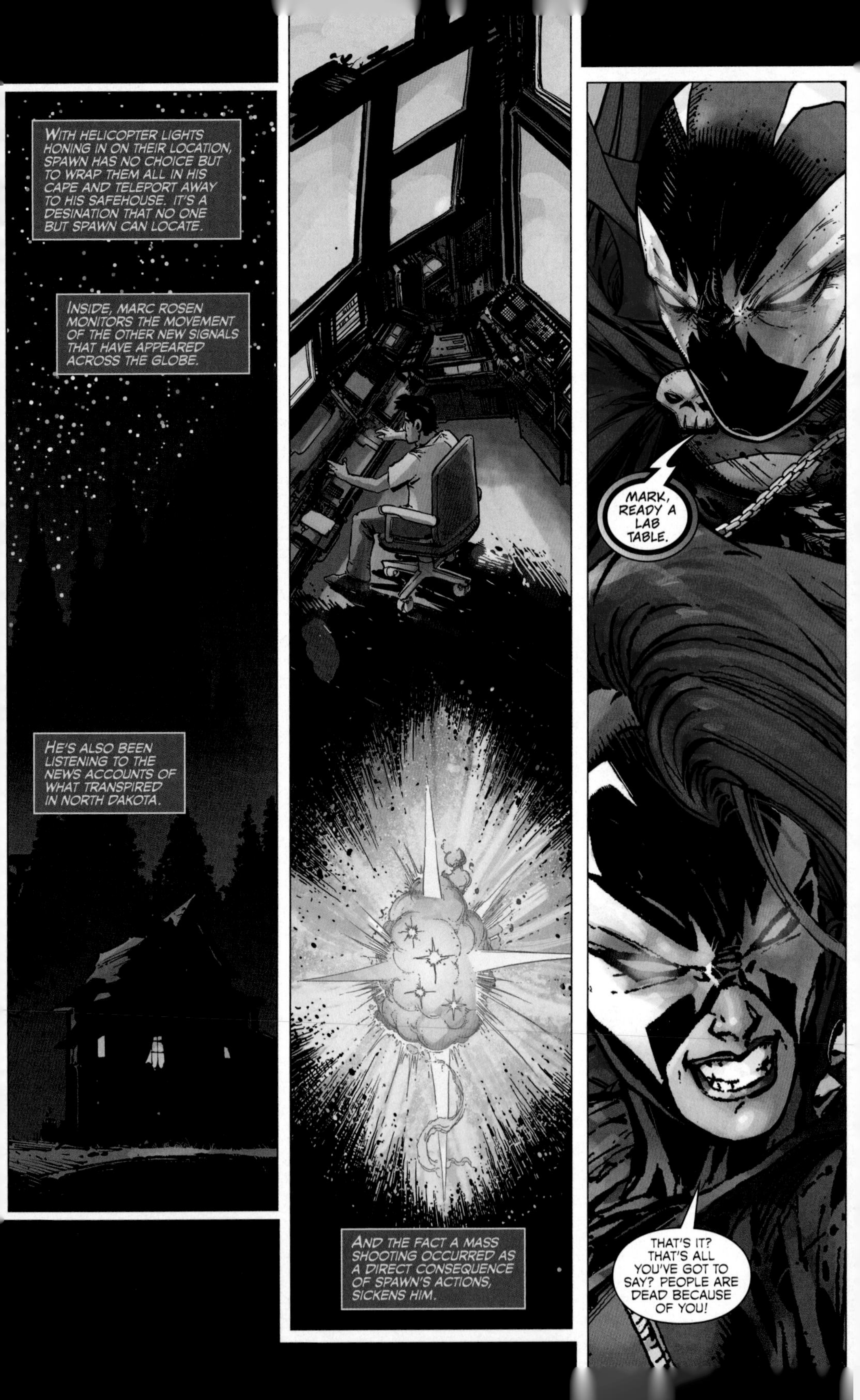
WITH HELICOPTER LIGHTS HONING IN ON THEIR LOCATION, SPAWN HAS NO CHOICE BUT TO WRAP THEM ALL IN HIS CAPE AND TELEPORT AWAY TO HIS SAFEHOUSE. IT'S A DESINATION THAT NO ONE BUT SPAWN CAN LOCATE.
INSIDE, MARC ROSEN MONITORS THE MOVEMENT OF THE OTHER NEW SIGNALS THAT HAVE APPEARED ACROSS THE GLOBE.
HE'S ALSO BEEN LISTENING TO THE NEWS ACCOUNTS OF WHAT TRANSPIRED IN NORTH DAKOTA.
AND THE FACT A MASS SHOOTING OCCURRED AS A DIRECT CONSEQUENCE OF SPAWN'S ACTIONS, SICKENS HIM.
MARK, READY A LAB TABLE.
THAT'S IT? THAT'S ALL YOU'VE GOT TO SAY? PEOPLE ARE DEAD BECAUSE OF YOU!

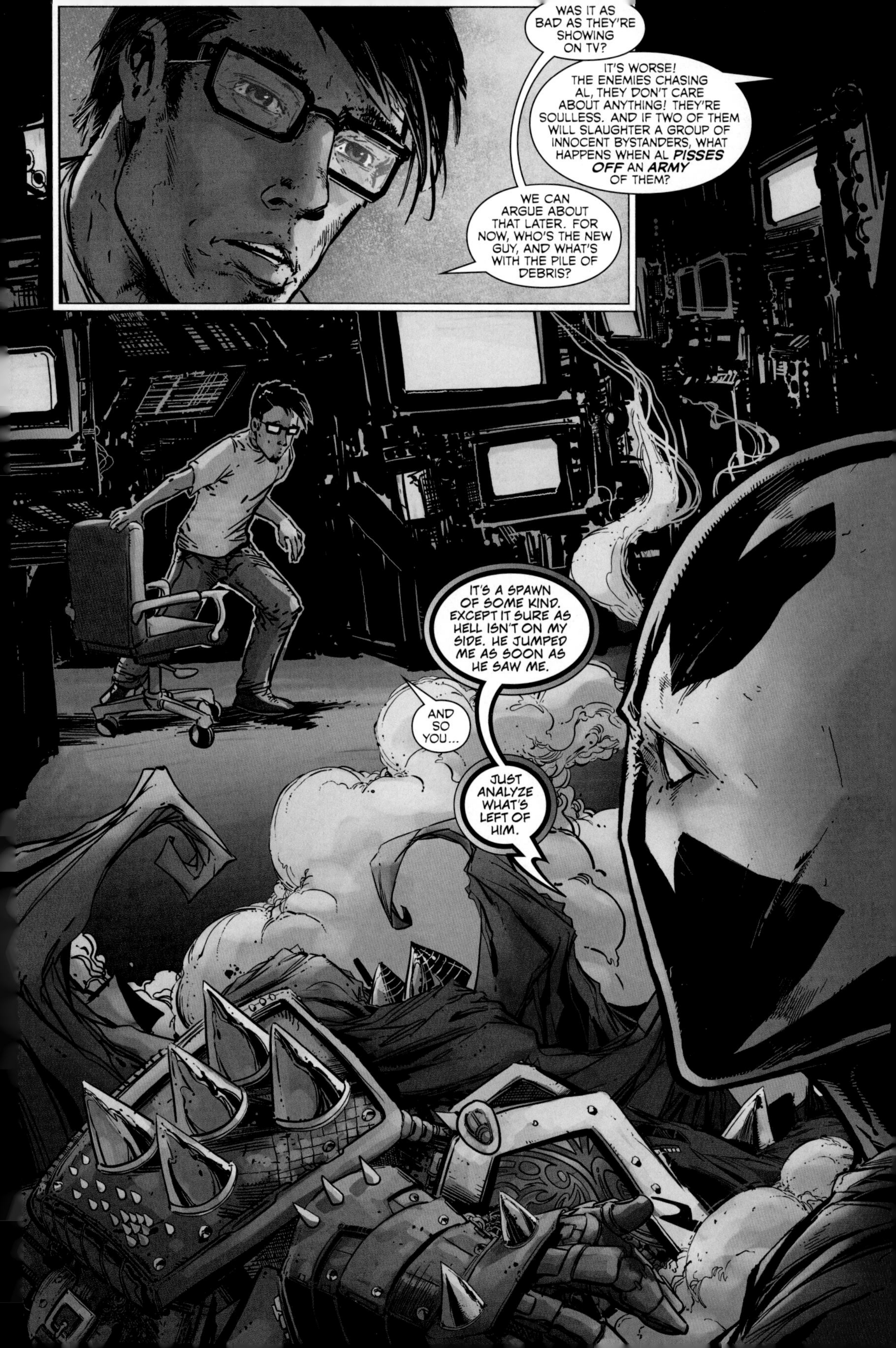
WAS IT AS BAD AS THEY'RE SHOWING ON TV?
IT'S WORSE! THE ENEMIES CHASING AL, THEY DON'T CARE ABOUT ANYTHING! THEY'RE SOULLESS. AND IF TWO OF THEM WILL SLAUGHTER A GROUP OF INNOCENT BYSTANDERS, WHAT HAPPENS WHEN AL ***PISSES OFF*** AN ***ARMY*** OF THEM?
WE CAN ARGUE ABOUT THAT LATER. FOR NOW, WHO'S THE NEW GUY, AND WHAT'S WITH THE PILE OF DEBRIS?
IT'S A SPAWN OF SOME KIND. EXCEPT IT SURE AS HELL ISN'T ON MY SIDE. HE JUMPED ME AS SOON AS HE SAW ME.
AND SO YOU...
JUST ANALYZE WHAT'S LEFT OF HIM.

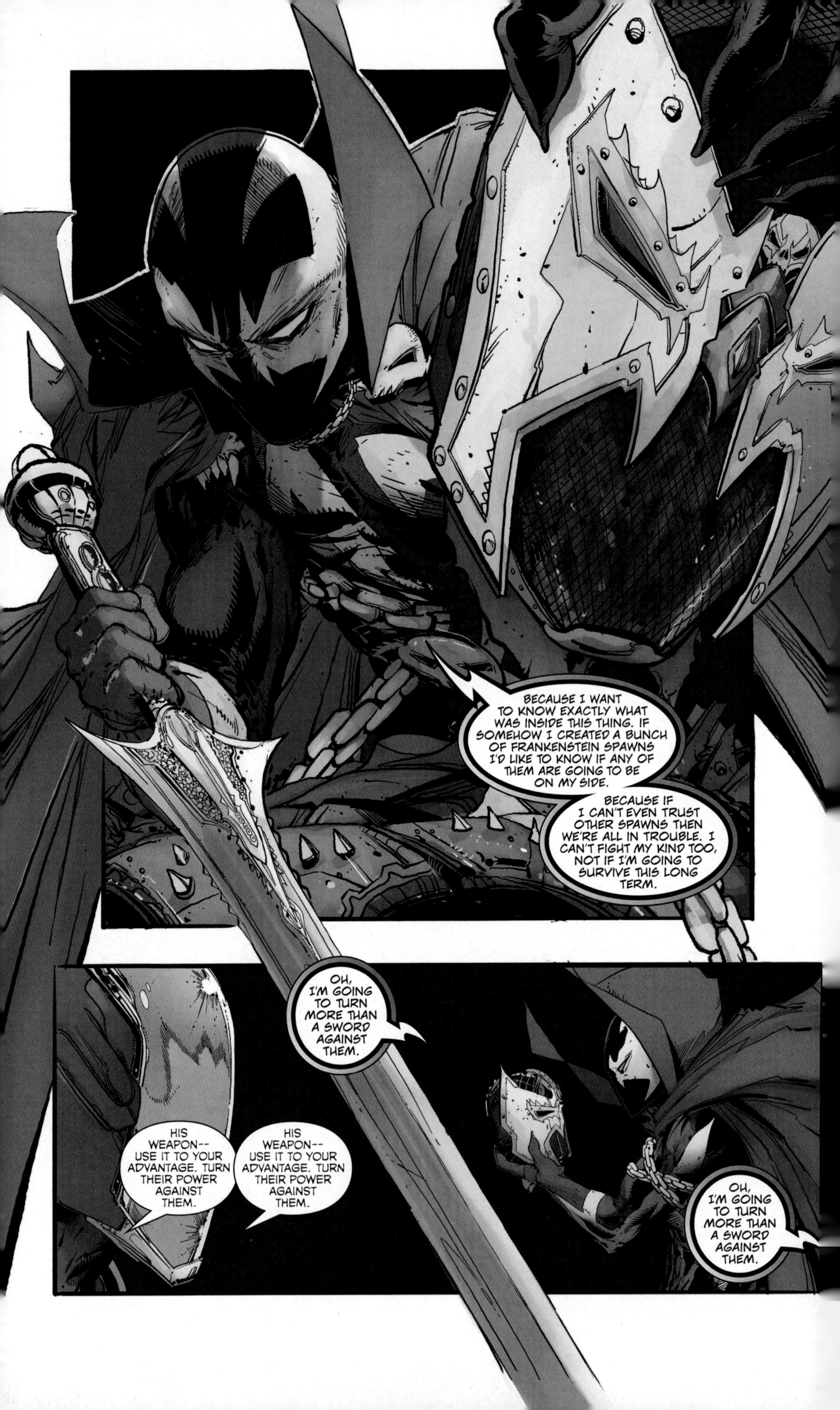

BECAUSE I WANT TO KNOW EXACTLY WHAT WAS INSIDE THIS THING. IF SOMEHOW I CREATED A BUNCH OF FRANKENSTEIN SPAWNS I'D LIKE TO KNOW IF ANY OF THEM ARE GOING TO BE ON MY SIDE.
BECAUSE IF I CAN'T EVEN TRUST OTHER SPAWNS THEN WE'RE ALL IN TROUBLE. I CAN'T FIGHT MY KIND TOO, NOT IF I'M GOING TO SURVIVE THIS LONG TERM.
OH, I'M GOING TO TURN MORE THAN A SWORD AGAINST THEM.
HIS WEAPON-- USE IT TO YOUR ADVANTAGE. TURN THEIR POWER AGAINST THEM.
HIS WEAPON-- USE IT TO YOUR ADVANTAGE. TURN THEIR POWER AGAINST THEM.
OH, I'M GOING TO TURN MORE THAN A SWORD AGAINST THEM.

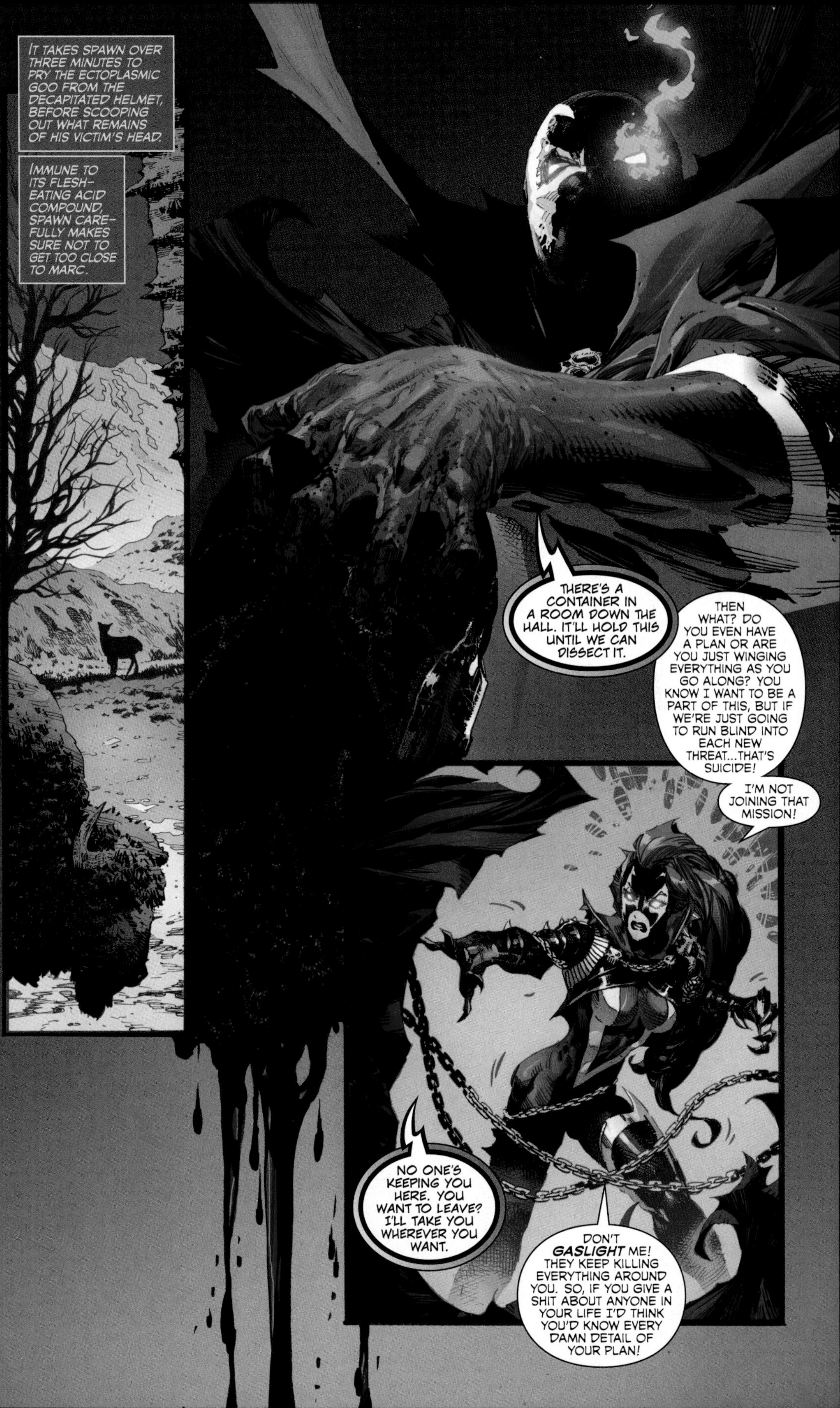
IT TAKES SPAWN OVER THREE MINUTES TO PRY THE ECTOPLASMIC GOO FROM THE DECAPITATED HELMET, BEFORE SCOOPING OUT WHAT REMAINS OF HIS VICTIM'S HEAD.
IMMUNE TO ITS FLESH-EATING ACID COMPOUND, SPAWN CAREFULLY MAKES SURE NOT TO GET TOO CLOSE TO MARC.
THERE'S A CONTAINER IN A ROOM DOWN THE HALL. IT'LL HOLD THIS UNTIL WE CAN DISSECT IT.
THEN WHAT? DO YOU EVEN HAVE A PLAN OR ARE YOU JUST WINGING EVERYTHING AS YOU GO ALONG? YOU KNOW I WANT TO BE A PART OF THIS, BUT IF WE'RE JUST GOING TO RUN BLIND INTO EACH NEW THREAT...THAT'S SUICIDE!
I'M NOT JOINING THAT MISSION!
NO ONE'S KEEPING YOU HERE. YOU WANT TO LEAVE? I'LL TAKE YOU WHEREVER YOU WANT.
DON'T **GASLIGHT** ME! THEY KEEP KILLING EVERYTHING AROUND YOU. SO, IF YOU GIVE A SHIT ABOUT ANYONE IN YOUR LIFE I'D THINK YOU'D KNOW EVERY DAMN DETAIL OF YOUR PLAN!

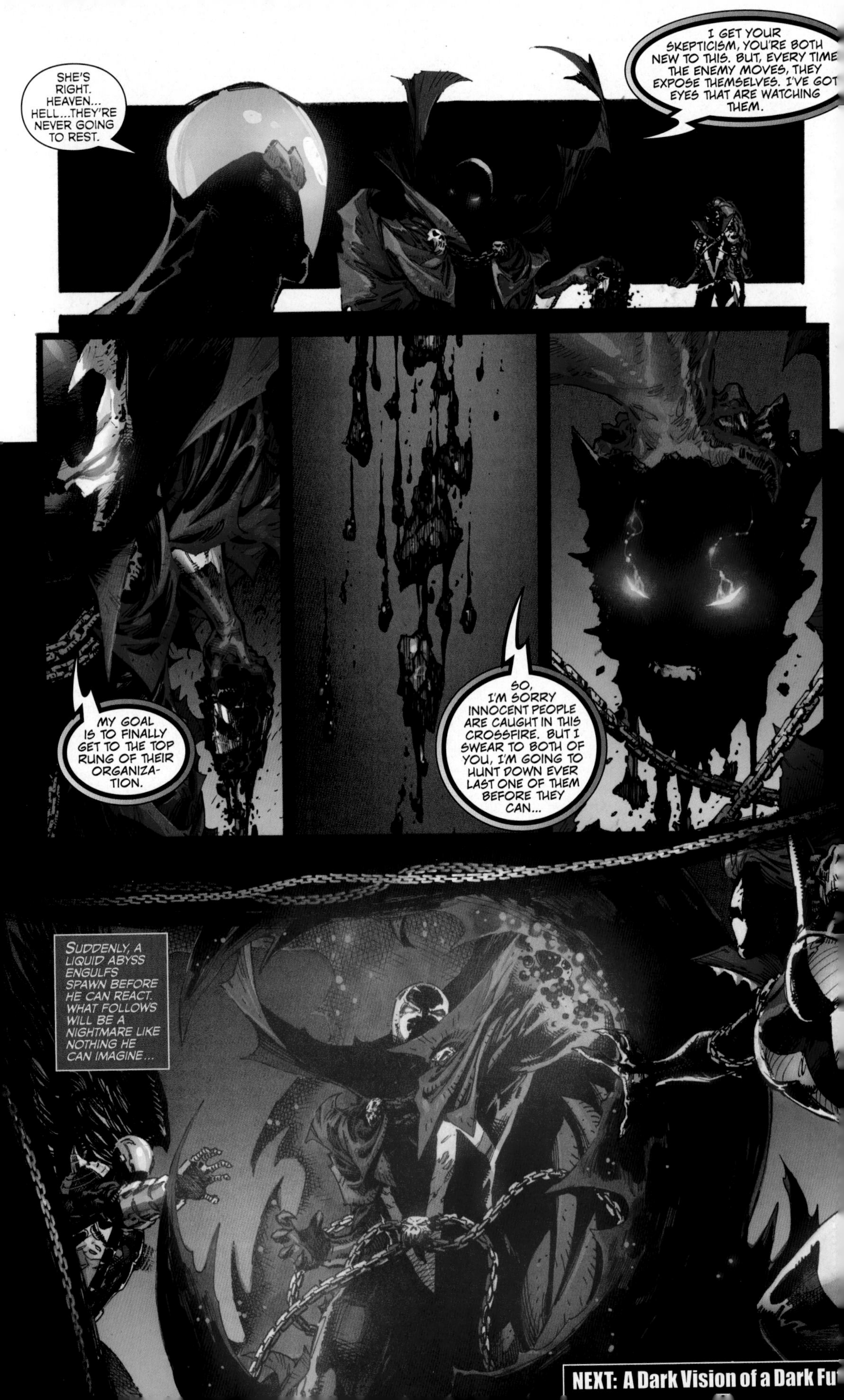
SHE'S RIGHT. HEAVEN... HELL...THEY'RE NEVER GOING TO REST.
I GET YOUR SKEPTICISM, YOU'RE BOTH NEW TO THIS. BUT, EVERY TIME THE ENEMY MOVES, THEY EXPOSE THEMSELVES. I'VE GOT EYES THAT ARE WATCHING THEM.
MY GOAL IS TO FINALLY GET TO THE TOP RUNG OF THEIR ORGANIZA-TION.
SO, I'M SORRY INNOCENT PEOPLE ARE CAUGHT IN THIS CROSSFIRE. BUT I SWEAR TO BOTH OF YOU, I'M GOING TO HUNT DOWN EVER LAST ONE OF THEM BEFORE THEY CAN...
SUDDENLY, A LIQUID ABYSS ENGULFS SPAWN BEFORE HE CAN REACT. WHAT FOLLOWS WILL BE A NIGHTMARE LIKE NOTHING HE CAN IMAGINE...
NEXT: A Dark Vision of a Dark Fu

SPAWN

PROPHECY OF DEATH
PART 1

image

306

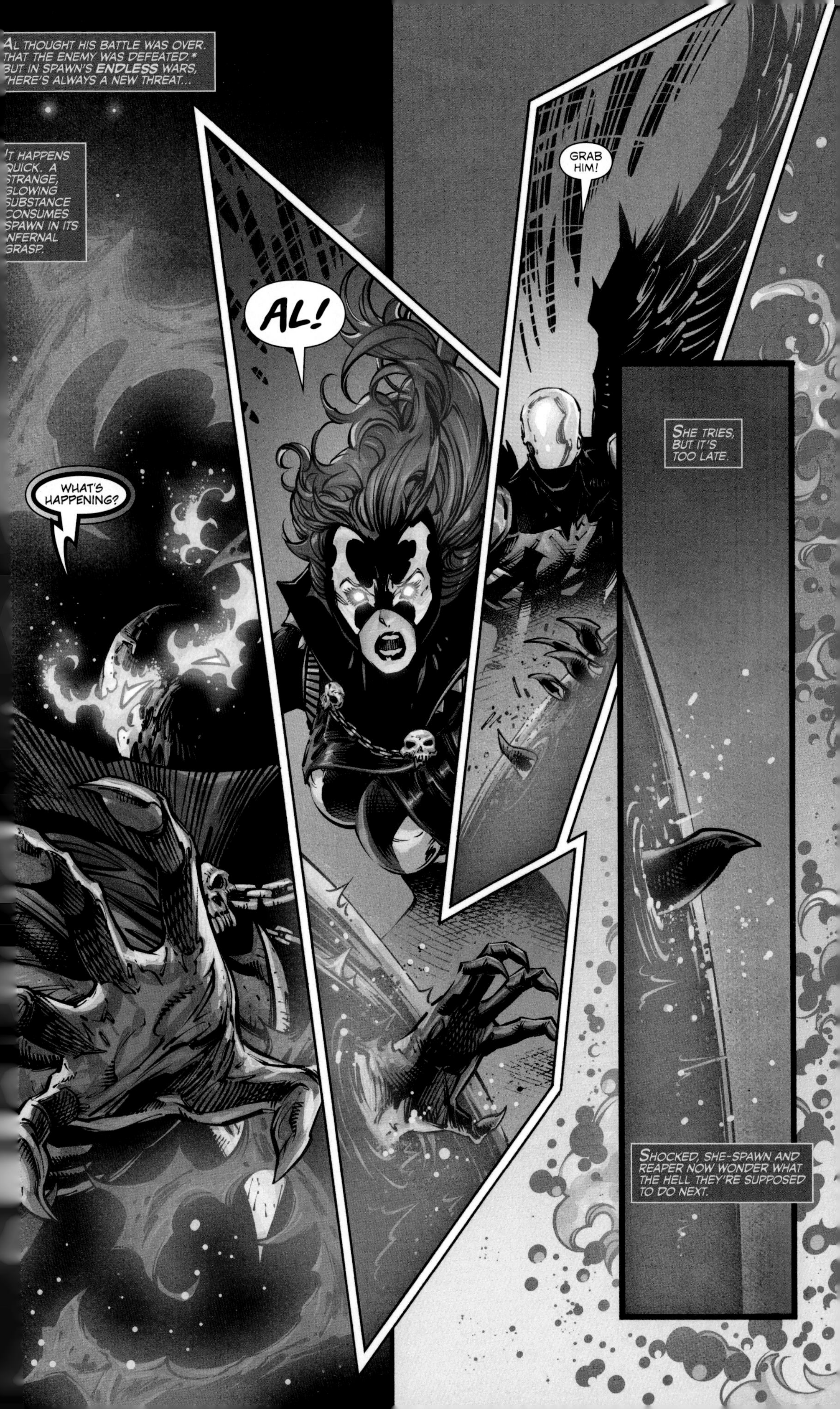
AL THOUGHT HIS BATTLE WAS OVER. THAT THE ENEMY WAS DEFEATED.* BUT IN SPAWN'S ENDLESS WARS, THERE'S ALWAYS A NEW THREAT...
IT HAPPENS QUICK. A STRANGE, GLOWING SUBSTANCE CONSUMES SPAWN IN ITS INFERNAL GRASP.
WHAT'S HAPPENING?
AL!
GRAB HIM!
SHE TRIES, BUT IT'S TOO LATE.
SHOCKED, SHE-SPAWN AND REAPER NOW WONDER WHAT THE HELL THEY'RE SUPPOSED TO DO NEXT.

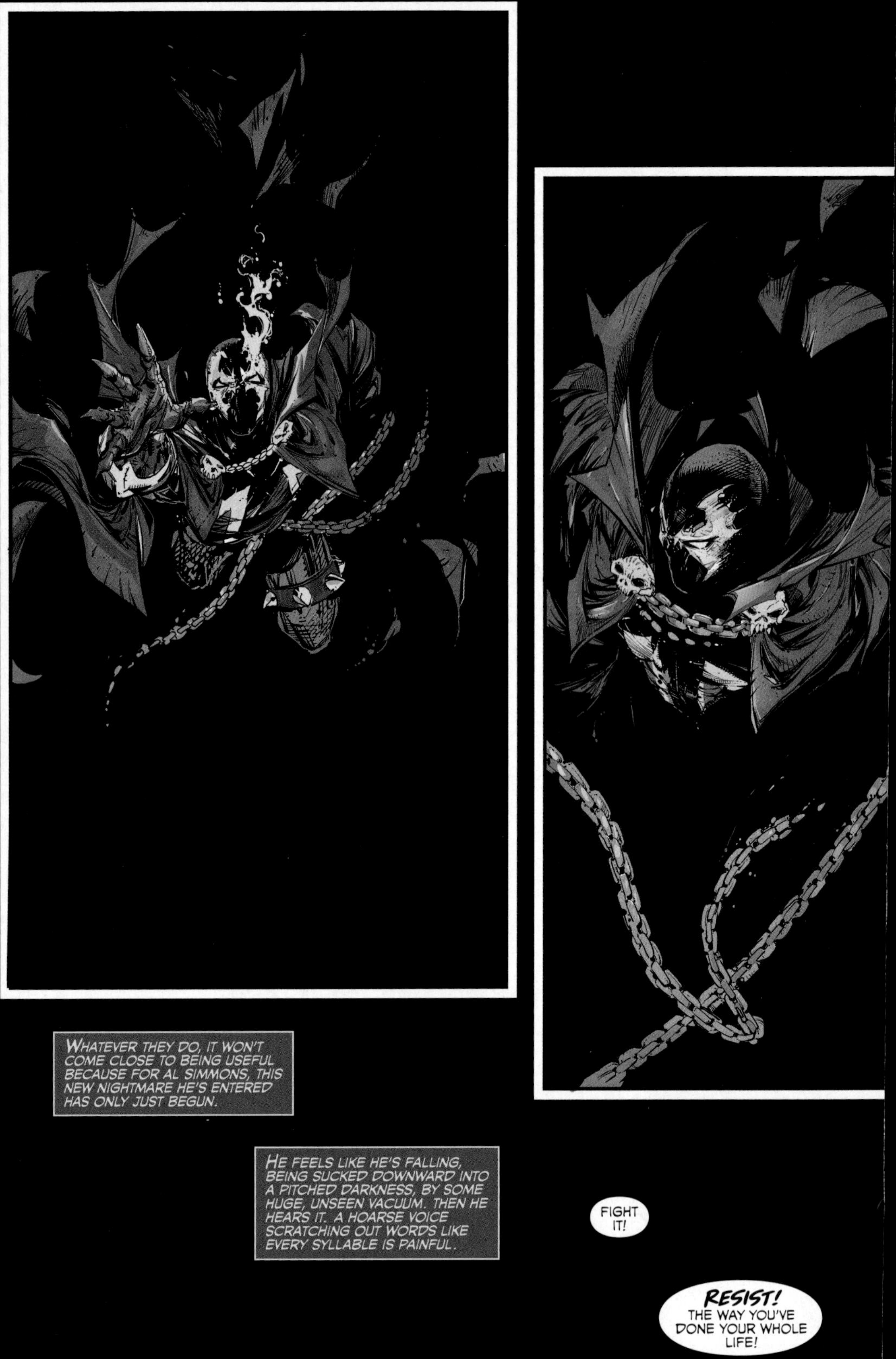
WHATEVER THEY DO, IT WON'T COME CLOSE TO BEING USEFUL BECAUSE FOR AL SIMMONS, THIS NEW NIGHTMARE HE'S ENTERED HAS ONLY JUST BEGUN.
HE FEELS LIKE HE'S FALLING, BEING SUCKED DOWNWARD INTO A PITCHED DARKNESS, BY SOME HUGE, UNSEEN VACUUM. THEN HE HEARS IT. A HOARSE VOICE SCRATCHING OUT WORDS LIKE EVERY SYLLABLE IS PAINFUL.
FIGHT IT!
RESIST! THE WAY YOU'VE DONE YOUR WHOLE LIFE!

AND JUST AS HE'S ABOUT TO BLACK OUT, THE VOICE WHISPERS ONE LAST WORD...

PLEASE.

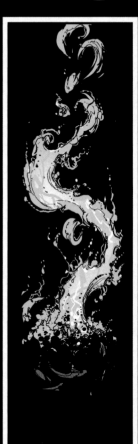

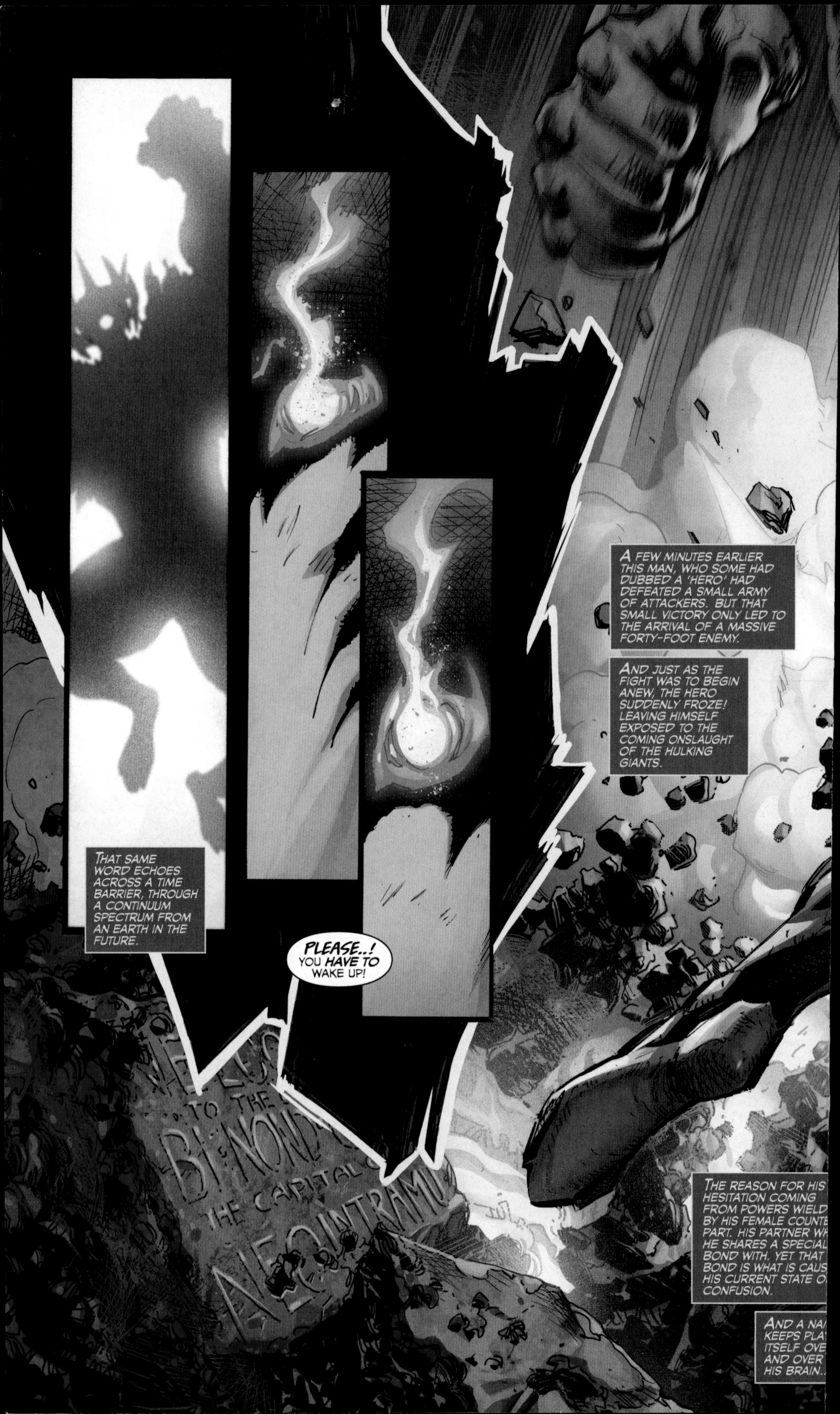
A FEW MINUTES EARLIER THIS MAN, WHO SOME HAD DUBBED A 'HERO' HAD DEFEATED A SMALL ARMY OF ATTACKERS. BUT THAT SMALL VICTORY ONLY LED TO THE ARRIVAL OF A MASSIVE FORTY-FOOT ENEMY.
AND JUST AS THE FIGHT WAS TO BEGIN ANEW, THE HERO SUDDENLY FROZE! LEAVING HIMSELF EXPOSED TO THE COMING ONSLAUGHT OF THE HULKING GIANTS.
THE REASON FOR HIS HESITATION COMING FROM POWERS WIELD BY HIS FEMALE COUNTE PART. HIS PARTNER WH HE SHARES A SPECIAL BOND WITH. YET THAT BOND IS WHAT IS CAUS HIS CURRENT STATE O CONFUSION.
AND A NA KEEPS PLA ITSELF OVE AND OVER HIS BRAIN..
THAT SAME WORD ECHOES ACROSS A TIME BARRIER, THROUGH A CONTINUUM SPECTRUM FROM AN EARTH IN THE FUTURE.
PLEASE..! YOU HAVE TO WAKE UP!

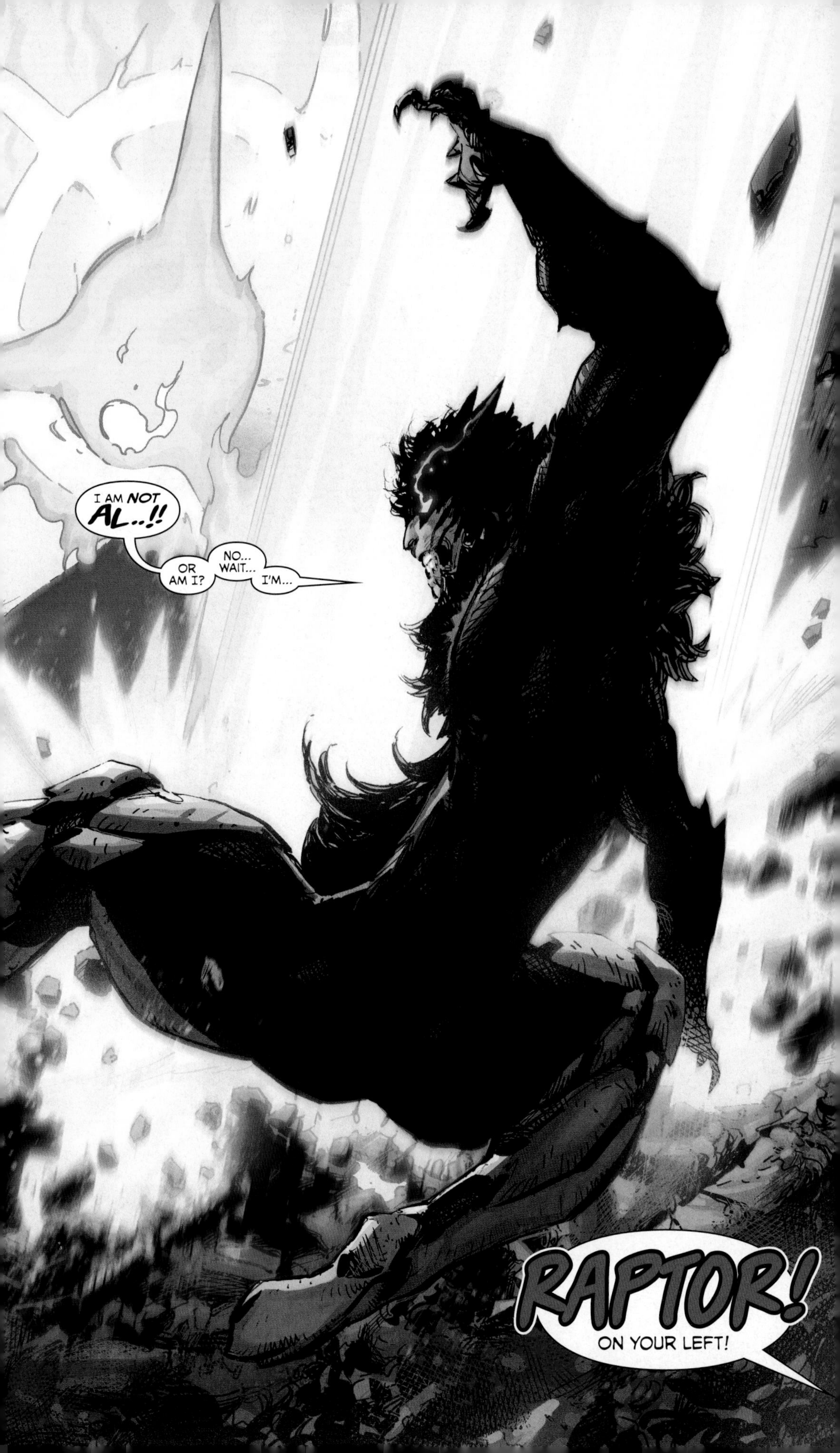
I AM NOT AL..!!
OR AM I?
NO... WAIT... I'M...
RAPTOR! ON YOUR LEFT!

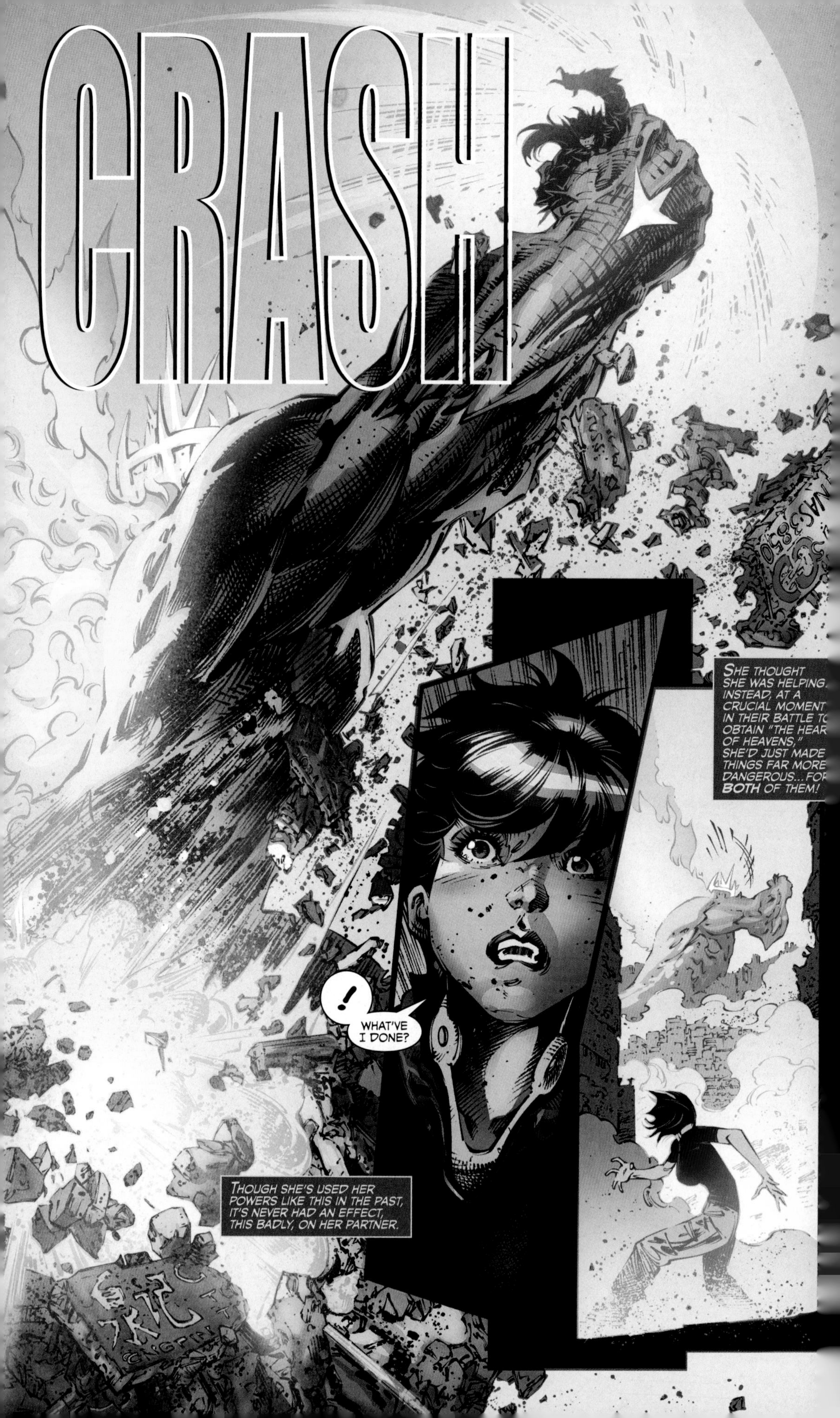
CRASH
SHE THOUGHT SHE WAS HELPING. INSTEAD, AT A CRUCIAL MOMENT IN THEIR BATTLE TC OBTAIN "THE HEAR OF HEAVENS," SHE'D JUST MADE THINGS FAR MORE DANGEROUS... FOR BOTH OF THEM!
!
WHAT'VE I DONE?
THOUGH SHE'S USED HER POWERS LIKE THIS IN THE PAST, IT'S NEVER HAD AN EFFECT, THIS BADLY, ON HER PARTNER.

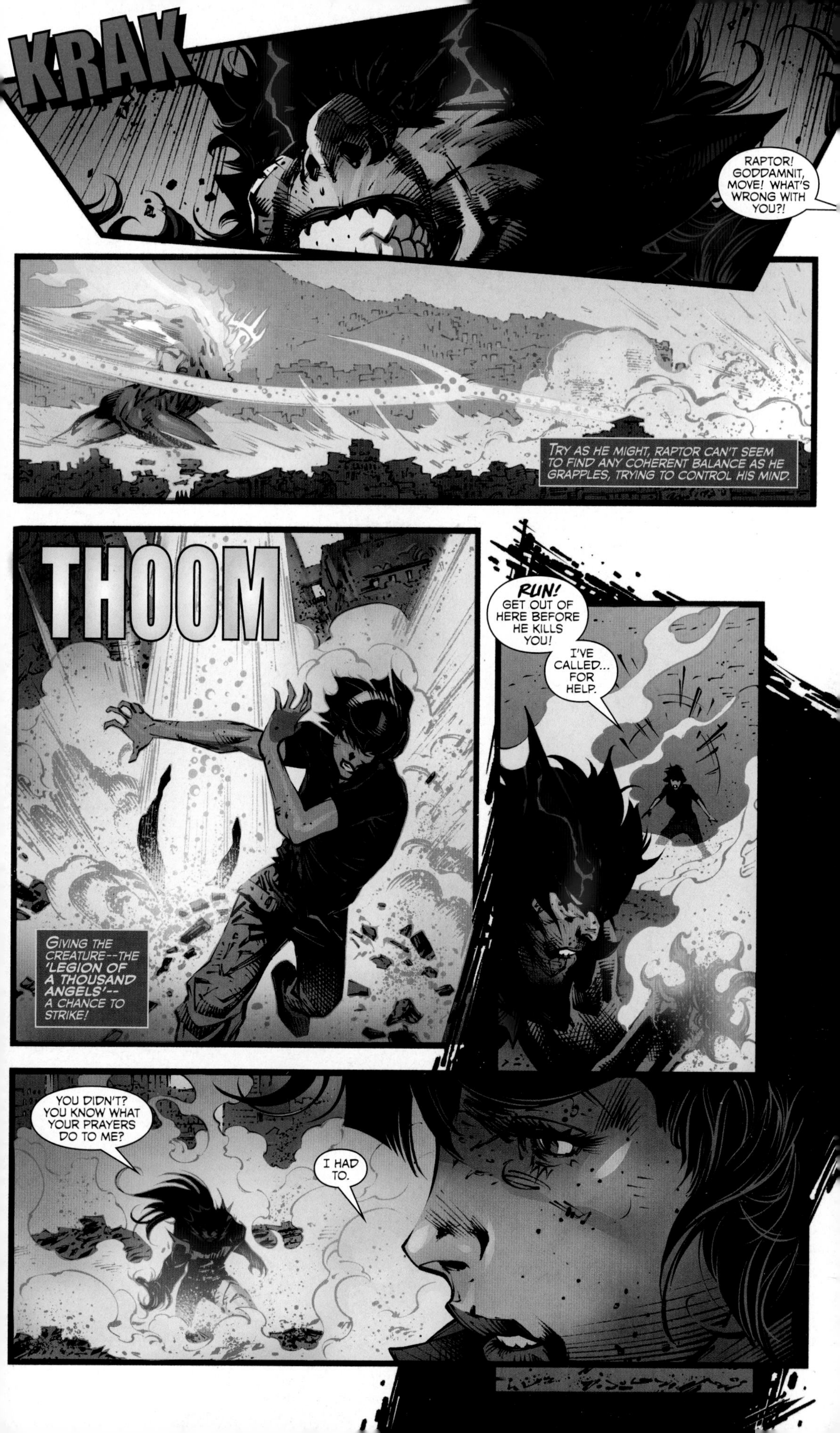
KRAK
RAPTOR! GODDAMNIT, MOVE! WHAT'S WRONG WITH YOU?!
TRY AS HE MIGHT, RAPTOR CAN'T SEEM TO FIND ANY COHERENT BALANCE AS HE GRAPPLES, TRYING TO CONTROL HIS MIND.
THOOM
GIVING THE CREATURE--THE 'LEGION OF A THOUSAND ANGELS'-- A CHANCE TO STRIKE!
RUN! GET OUT OF HERE BEFORE HE KILLS YOU!
I'VE CALLED... FOR HELP.
YOU DIDN'T? YOU KNOW WHAT YOUR PRAYERS DO TO ME?
I HAD TO.

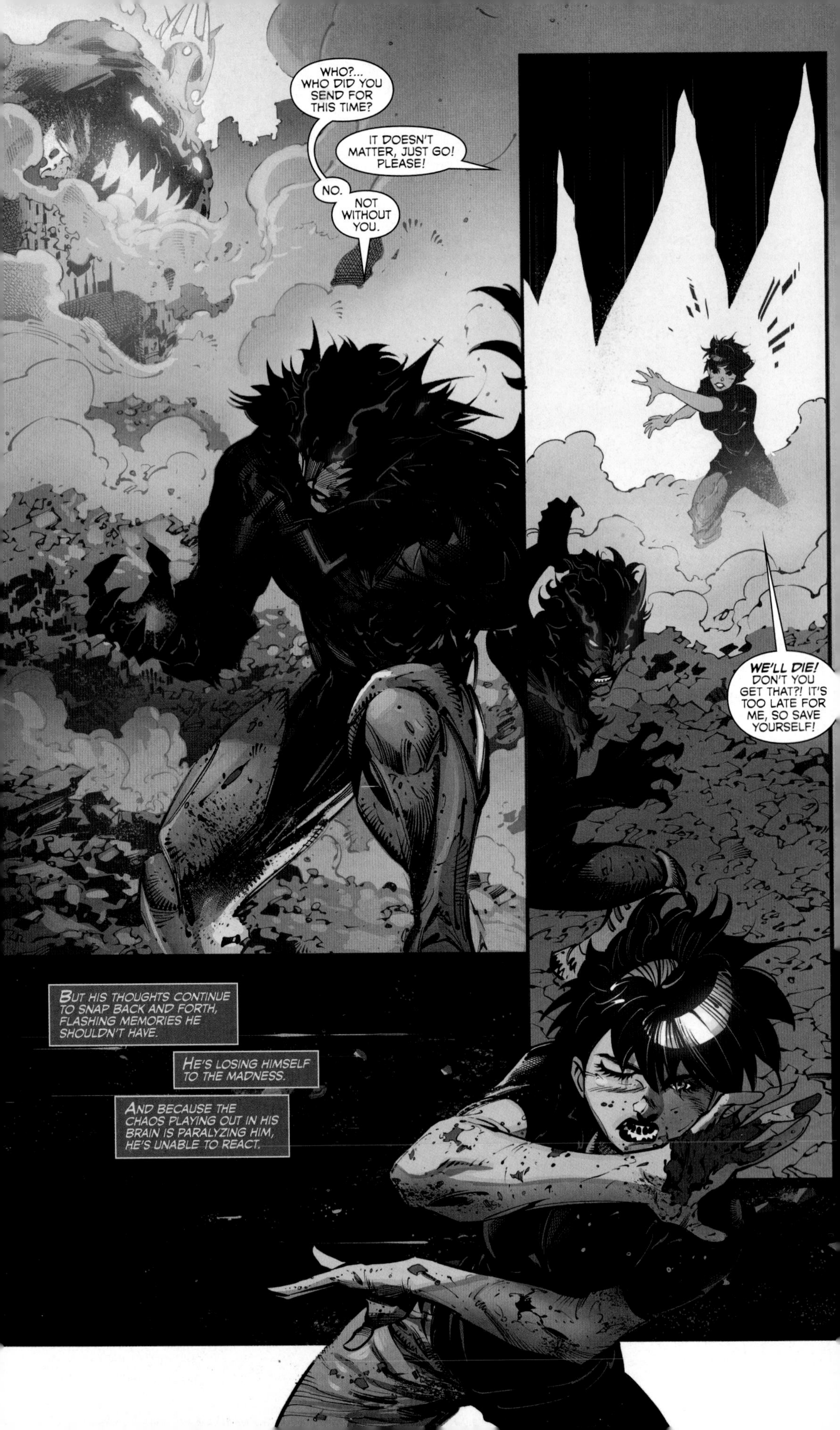
WHO?... WHO DID YOU SEND FOR THIS TIME?
IT DOESN'T MATTER, JUST GO! PLEASE!
NO.
NOT WITHOUT YOU.
WE'LL DIE! DON'T YOU GET THAT?! IT'S TOO LATE FOR ME, SO SAVE YOURSELF!
BUT HIS THOUGHTS CONTINUE TO SNAP BACK AND FORTH, FLASHING MEMORIES HE SHOULDN'T HAVE.
HE'S LOSING HIMSELF TO THE MADNESS.
AND BECAUSE THE CHAOS PLAYING OUT IN HIS BRAIN IS PARALYZING HIM, HE'S UNABLE TO REACT.

THOOM
THOOM
THOOM

RAPTOR...?

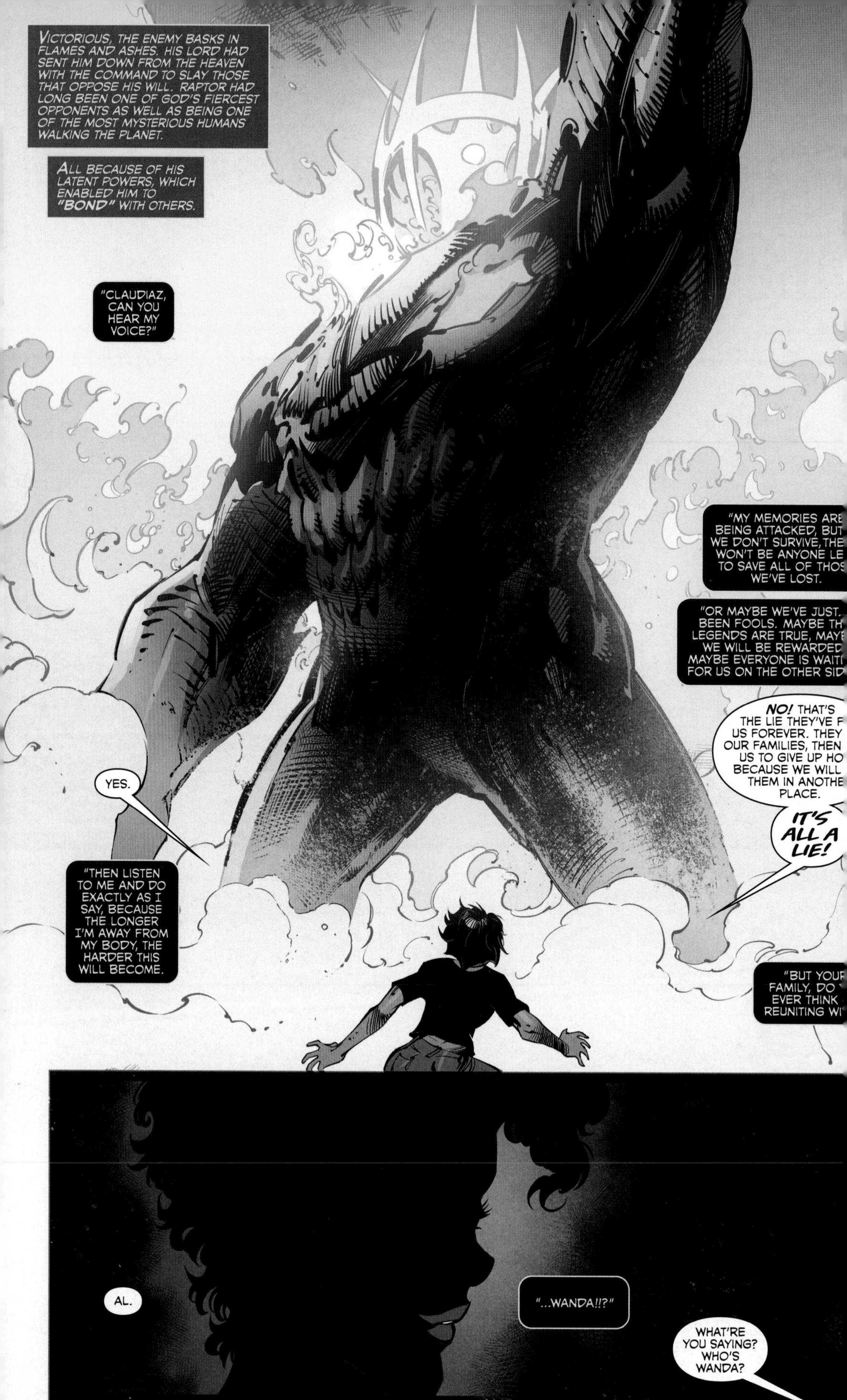
VICTORIOUS, THE ENEMY BASKS IN FLAMES AND ASHES. HIS LORD HAD SENT HIM DOWN FROM THE HEAVEN WITH THE COMMAND TO SLAY THOSE THAT OPPOSE HIS WILL. RAPTOR HAD LONG BEEN ONE OF GOD'S FIERCEST OPPONENTS AS WELL AS BEING ONE OF THE MOST MYSTERIOUS HUMANS WALKING THE PLANET.
ALL BECAUSE OF HIS LATENT POWERS, WHICH ENABLED HIM TO "BOND" WITH OTHERS.
"CLAUDIAZ, CAN YOU HEAR MY VOICE?"
YES.
"THEN LISTEN TO ME AND DO EXACTLY AS I SAY, BECAUSE THE LONGER I'M AWAY FROM MY BODY, THE HARDER THIS WILL BECOME.
"MY MEMORIES ARE BEING ATTACKED, BUT WE DON'T SURVIVE, THE WON'T BE ANYONE LE TO SAVE ALL OF THOS WE'VE LOST.
"OR MAYBE WE'VE JUST... BEEN FOOLS. MAYBE TH LEGENDS ARE TRUE, MAYE WE WILL BE REWARDED MAYBE EVERYONE IS WAITI FOR US ON THE OTHER SID
NO! THAT'S THE LIE THEY'VE F US FOREVER. THEY OUR FAMILIES, THEN US TO GIVE UP HO BECAUSE WE WILL THEM IN ANOTHE PLACE.
IT'S ALL A LIE!
"BUT YOUR FAMILY, DO EVER THINK REUNITING WI
AL.
"...WANDA!!?"
WHAT'RE YOU SAYING? WHO'S WANDA?

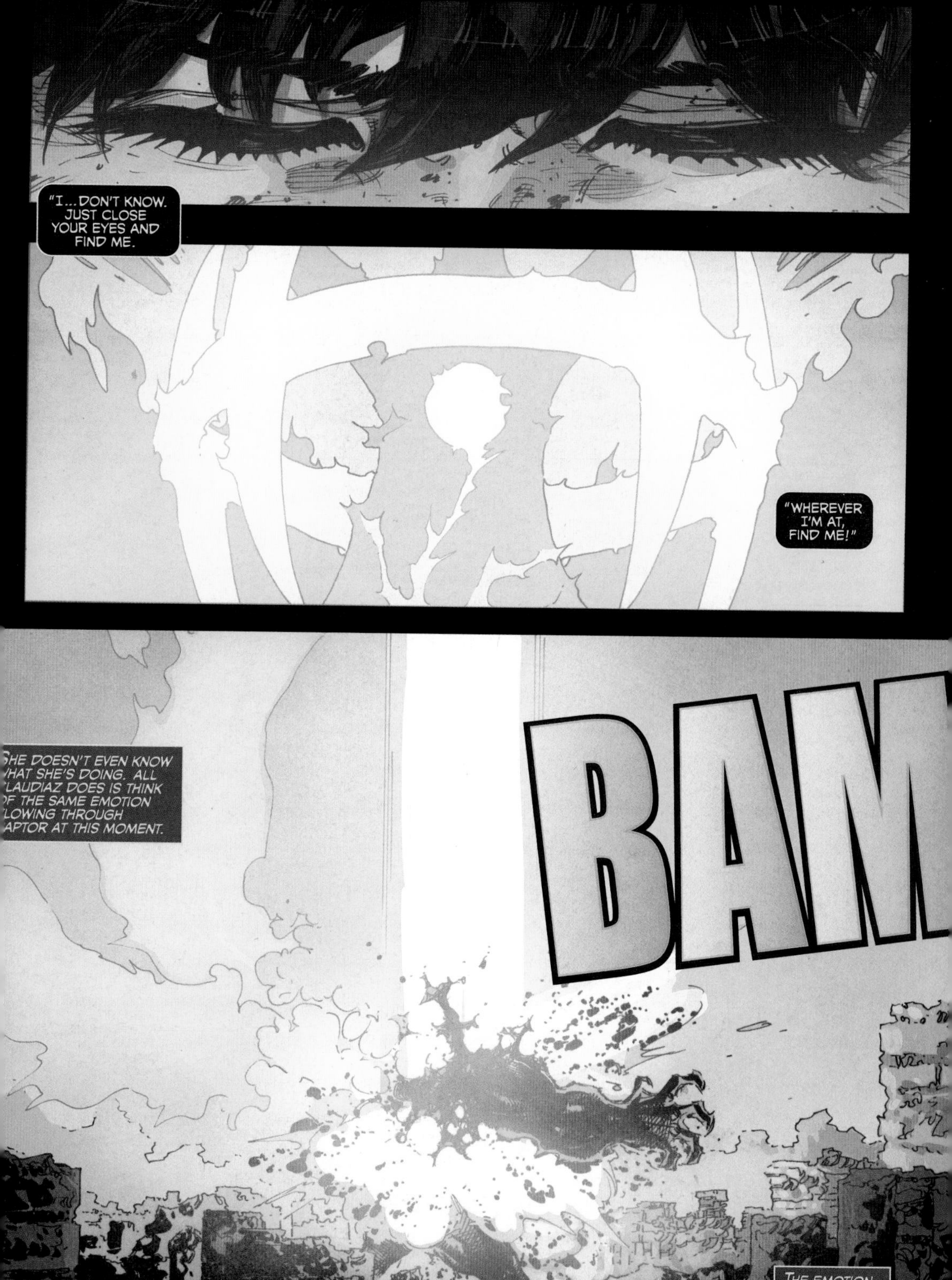
"I...DON'T KNOW. JUST CLOSE YOUR EYES AND FIND ME.
"WHEREVER I'M AT, FIND ME!"
SHE DOESN'T EVEN KNOW WHAT SHE'S DOING. ALL CLAUDIAZ DOES IS THINK OF THE SAME EMOTION FLOWING THROUGH RAPTOR AT THIS MOMENT.
BAM
THE EMOTION CALLED 'LOVE.'

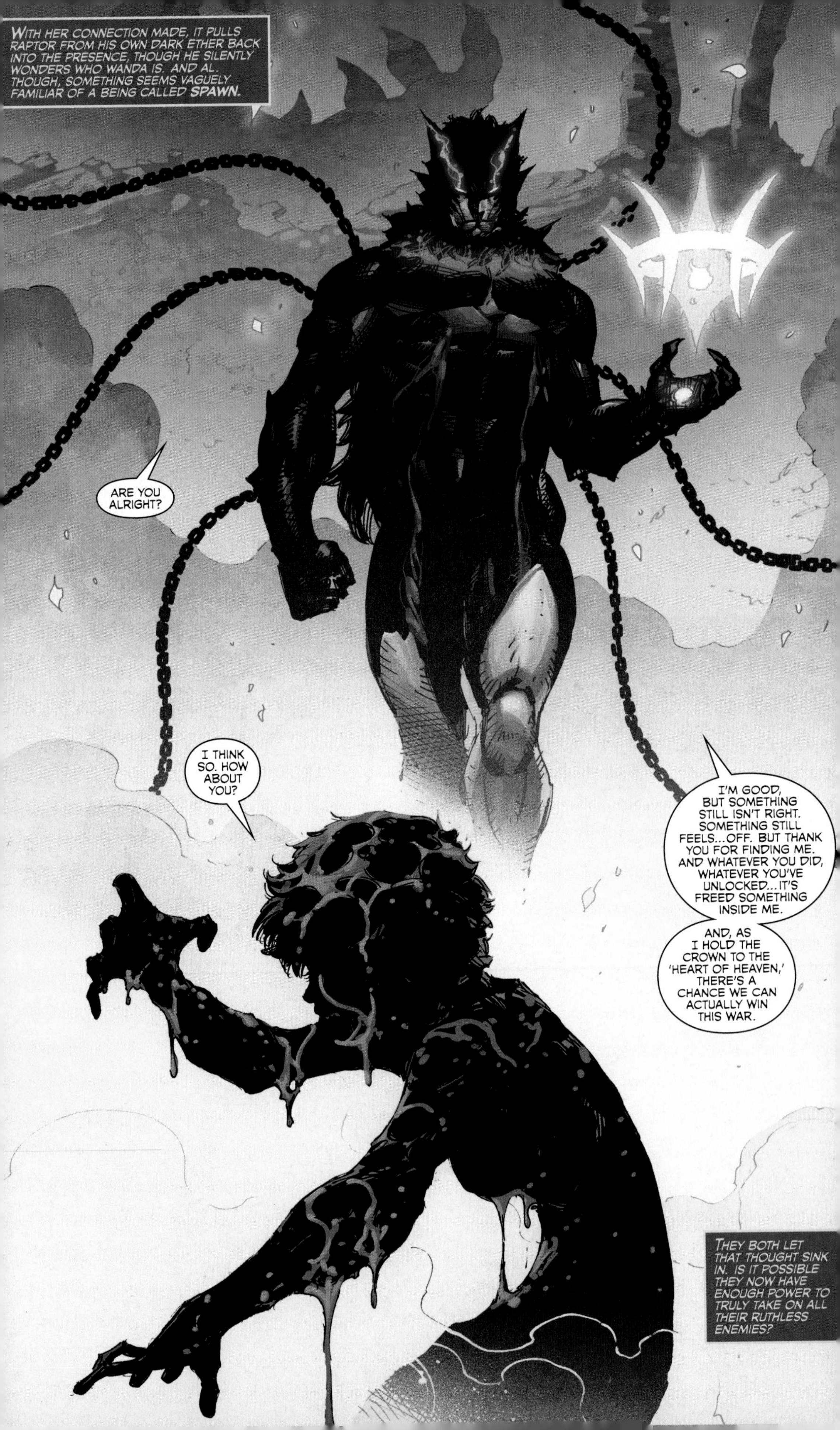
WITH HER CONNECTION MADE, IT PULLS RAPTOR FROM HIS OWN DARK ETHER BACK INTO THE PRESENCE, THOUGH HE SILENTLY WONDERS WHO WANDA IS. AND AL. THOUGH, SOMETHING SEEMS VAGUELY FAMILIAR OF A BEING CALLED SPAWN.
ARE YOU ALRIGHT?
I THINK SO. HOW ABOUT YOU?
I'M GOOD, BUT SOMETHING STILL ISN'T RIGHT. SOMETHING STILL FEELS...OFF. BUT THANK YOU FOR FINDING ME. AND WHATEVER YOU DID, WHATEVER YOU'VE UNLOCKED...IT'S FREED SOMETHING INSIDE ME.
AND, AS I HOLD THE CROWN TO THE 'HEART OF HEAVEN,' THERE'S A CHANCE WE CAN ACTUALLY WIN THIS WAR.
THEY BOTH LET THAT THOUGHT SINK IN. IS IT POSSIBLE THEY NOW HAVE ENOUGH POWER TO TRULY TAKE ON ALL THEIR RUTHLESS ENEMIES?

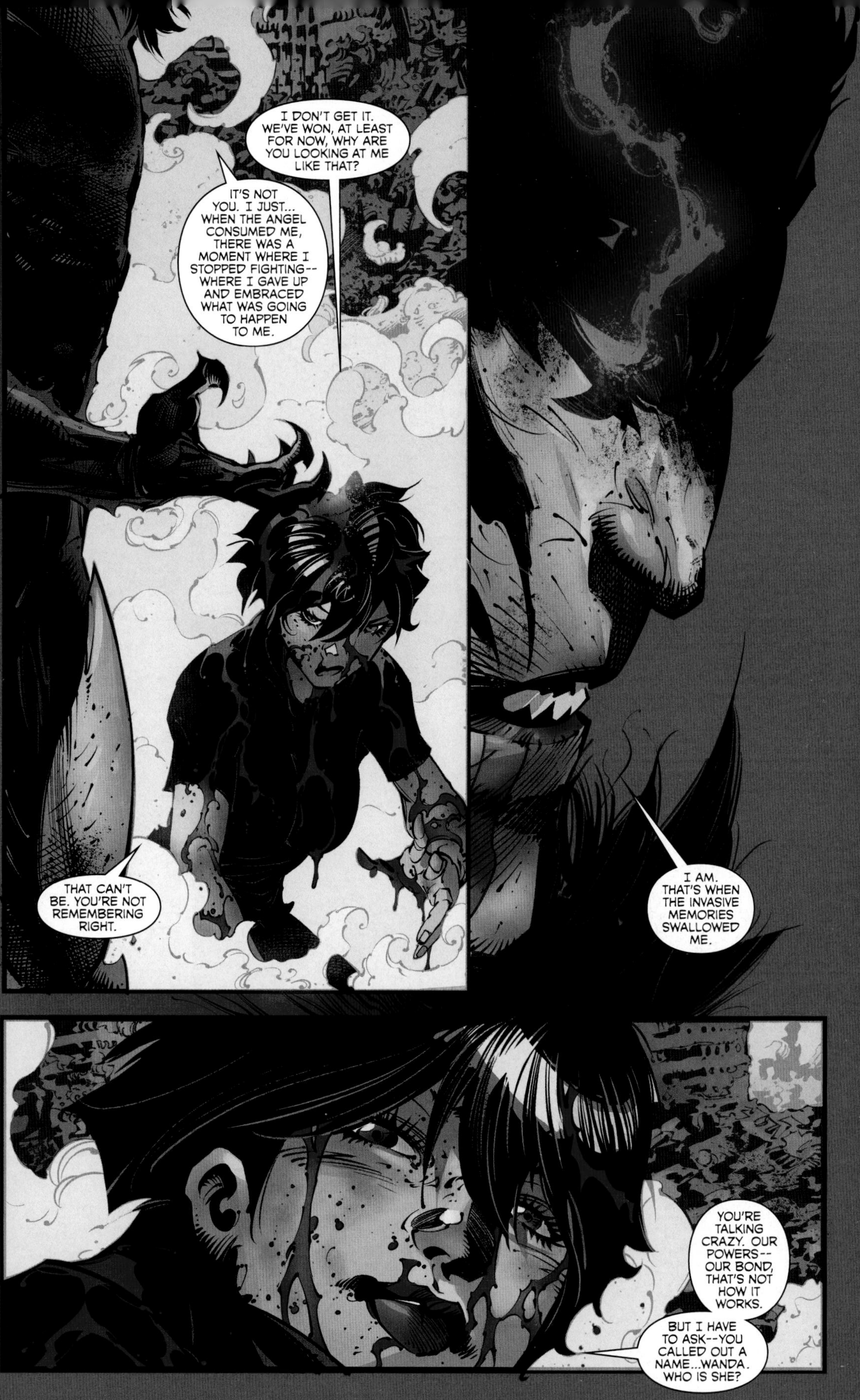
I DON'T GET IT. WE'VE WON, AT LEAST FOR NOW, WHY ARE YOU LOOKING AT ME LIKE THAT?
IT'S NOT YOU. I JUST... WHEN THE ANGEL CONSUMED ME, THERE WAS A MOMENT WHERE I STOPPED FIGHTING-- WHERE I GAVE UP AND EMBRACED WHAT WAS GOING TO HAPPEN TO ME.
THAT CAN'T BE. YOU'RE NOT REMEMBERING RIGHT.
I AM. THAT'S WHEN THE INVASIVE MEMORIES SWALLOWED ME.
YOU'RE TALKING CRAZY. OUR POWERS-- OUR BOND, THAT'S NOT HOW IT WORKS.
BUT I HAVE TO ASK--YOU CALLED OUT A NAME...WANDA. WHO IS SHE?

ELSEWHERE. INSIDE AN UNKNOWN PRISON COMPLEX.

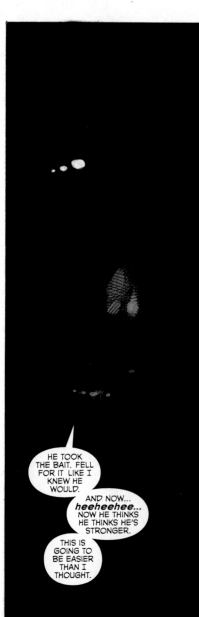

HE TOOK THE BAIT. FELL FOR IT LIKE I KNEW HE WOULD.

AND NOW... *heeheehee...* NOW HE THINKS HE THINKS HE'S STRONGER.

THIS IS GOING TO BE EASIER THAN I THOUGHT.

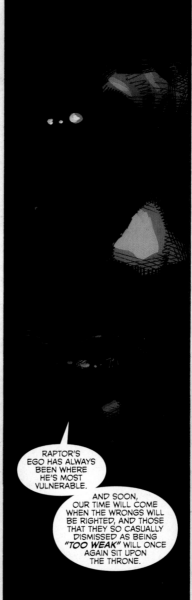

RAPTOR'S EGO HAS ALWAYS BEEN WHERE HE'S MOST VULNERABLE.

AND SOON, OUR TIME WILL COME WHEN THE WRONGS WILL BE RIGHTED, AND THOSE THAT THEY SO CASUALLY DISMISSED AS BEING *"TOO WEAK"* WILL ONCE AGAIN SIT UPON THE THRONE.

AND IT'LL BE THE SELF-RIGHTEOUS "HEROES" THAT WILL BE PUNISHED FOR THEIR CRIMES.

AND ALL WILL BE BACK AS IT SHOULD BE. EVERYTHING IN ITS RIGHT PLACE. ISN'T THAT RIGHT, BILLY?

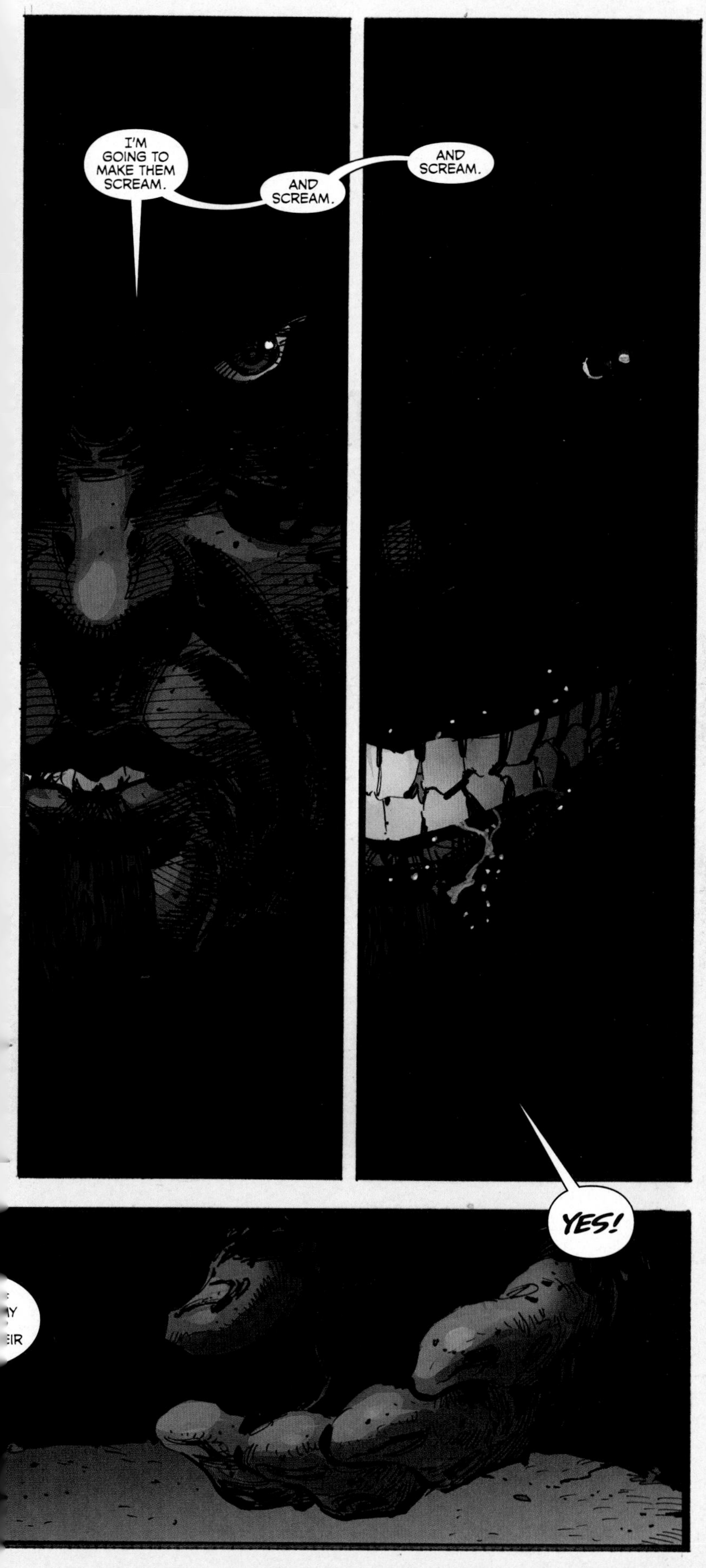
I'M GOING TO MAKE THEM SCREAM.
AND SCREAM.
AND SCREAM.
YES!

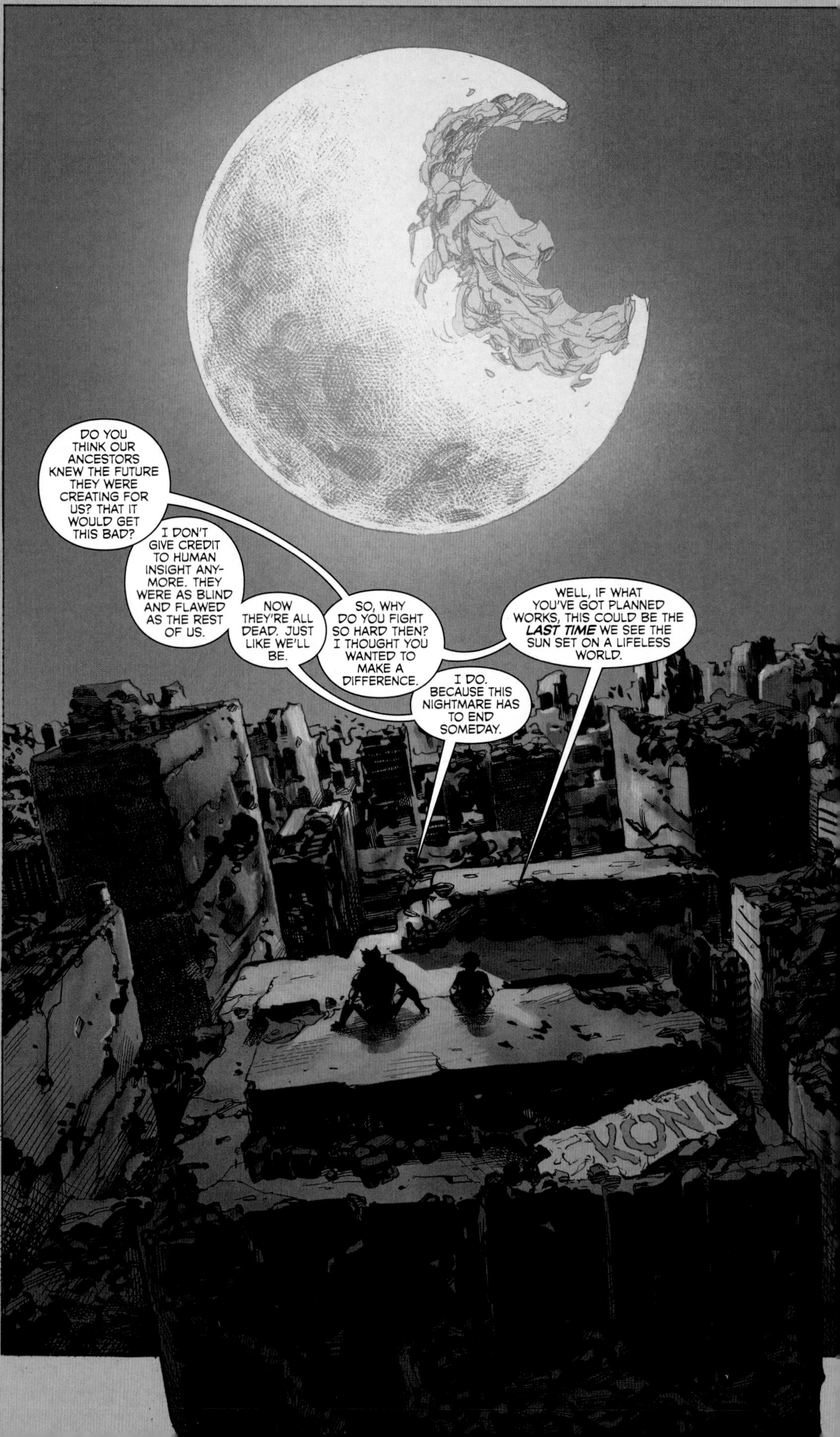

DO YOU THINK OUR ANCESTORS KNEW THE FUTURE THEY WERE CREATING FOR US? THAT IT WOULD GET THIS BAD?
I DON'T GIVE CREDIT TO HUMAN INSIGHT ANY-MORE. THEY WERE AS BLIND AND FLAWED AS THE REST OF US.
NOW THEY'RE ALL DEAD. JUST LIKE WE'LL BE.
SO, WHY DO YOU FIGHT SO HARD THEN? I THOUGHT YOU WANTED TO MAKE A DIFFERENCE.
I DO. BECAUSE THIS NIGHTMARE HAS TO END SOMEDAY.
WELL, IF WHAT YOU'VE GOT PLANNED WORKS, THIS COULD BE THE LAST TIME WE SEE THE SUN SET ON A LIFELESS WORLD.
KONI

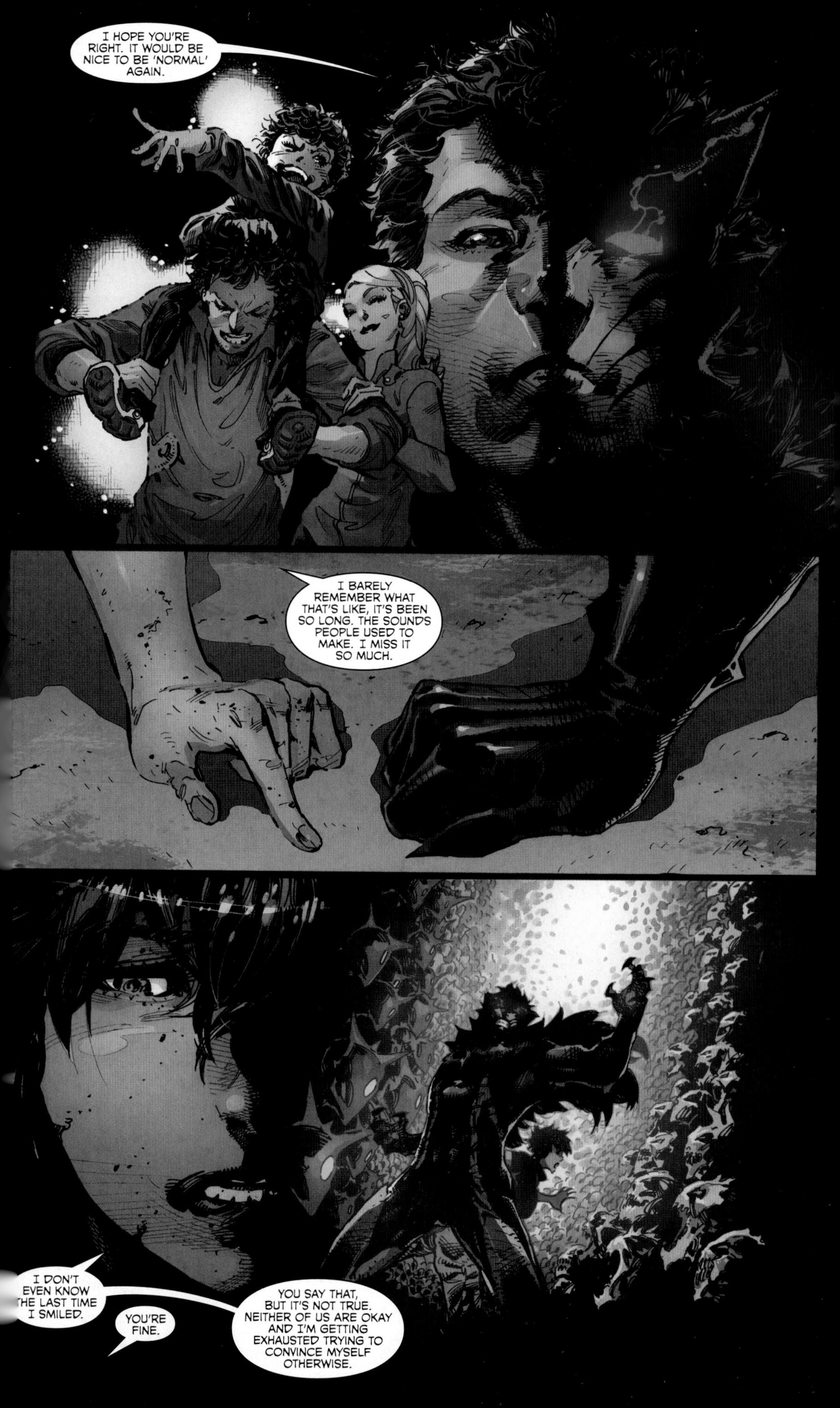
I HOPE YOU'RE RIGHT. IT WOULD BE NICE TO BE 'NORMAL' AGAIN.
I BARELY REMEMBER WHAT THAT'S LIKE, IT'S BEEN SO LONG. THE SOUNDS PEOPLE USED TO MAKE. I MISS IT SO MUCH.
I DON'T EVEN KNOW THE LAST TIME I SMILED.
YOU'RE FINE.
YOU SAY THAT, BUT IT'S NOT TRUE. NEITHER OF US ARE OKAY AND I'M GETTING EXHAUSTED TRYING TO CONVINCE MYSELF OTHERWISE.

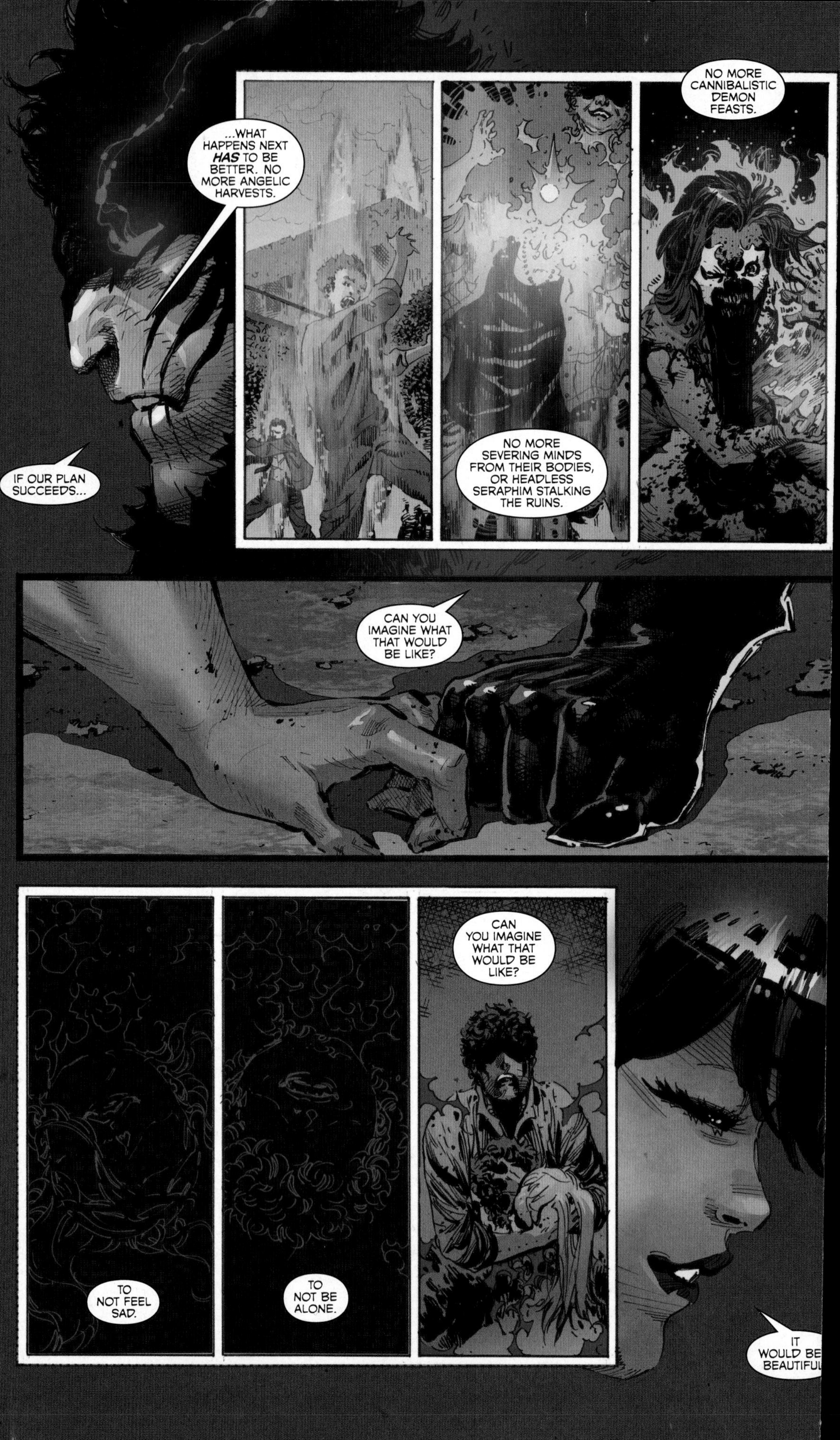
IF OUR PLAN SUCCEEDS...
...WHAT HAPPENS NEXT **HAS** TO BE BETTER. NO MORE ANGELIC HARVESTS.
NO MORE SEVERING MINDS FROM THEIR BODIES, OR HEADLESS SERAPHIM STALKING THE RUINS.
NO MORE CANNIBALISTIC DEMON FEASTS.
CAN YOU IMAGINE WHAT THAT WOULD BE LIKE?
TO NOT FEEL SAD.
TO NOT BE ALONE.
CAN YOU IMAGINE WHAT THAT WOULD BE LIKE?
IT WOULD BE BEAUTIFUL

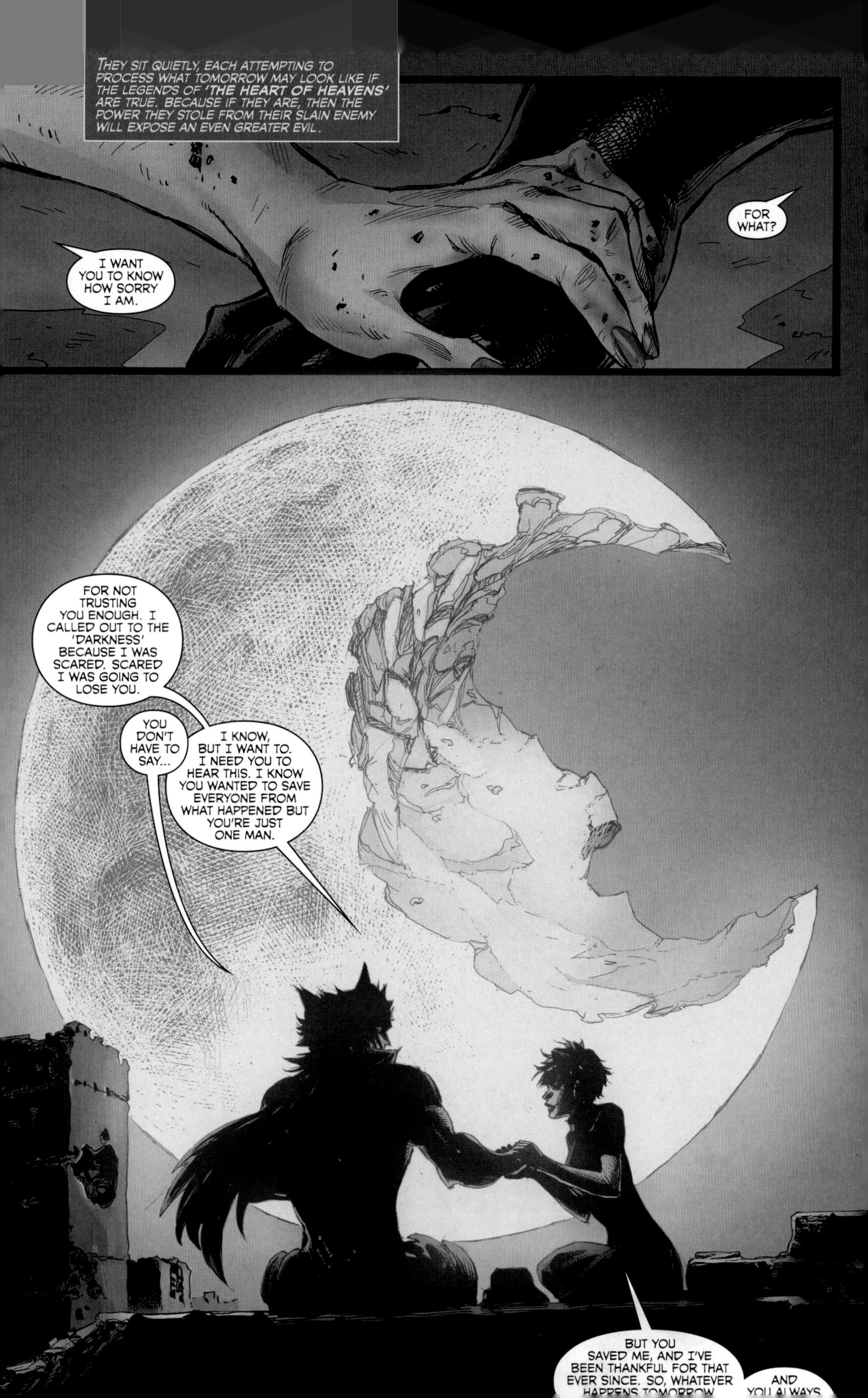
THEY SIT QUIETLY, EACH ATTEMPTING TO PROCESS WHAT TOMORROW MAY LOOK LIKE IF THE LEGENDS OF 'THE HEART OF HEAVENS' ARE TRUE. BECAUSE IF THEY ARE, THEN THE POWER THEY STOLE FROM THEIR SLAIN ENEMY WILL EXPOSE AN EVEN GREATER EVIL.
I WANT YOU TO KNOW HOW SORRY I AM.
FOR WHAT?
FOR NOT TRUSTING YOU ENOUGH. I CALLED OUT TO THE 'DARKNESS' BECAUSE I WAS SCARED. SCARED I WAS GOING TO LOSE YOU.
YOU DON'T HAVE TO SAY...
I KNOW, BUT I WANT TO. I NEED YOU TO HEAR THIS. I KNOW YOU WANTED TO SAVE EVERYONE FROM WHAT HAPPENED BUT YOU'RE JUST ONE MAN.
BUT YOU SAVED ME, AND I'VE BEEN THANKFUL FOR THAT EVER SINCE. SO, WHATEVER
AND

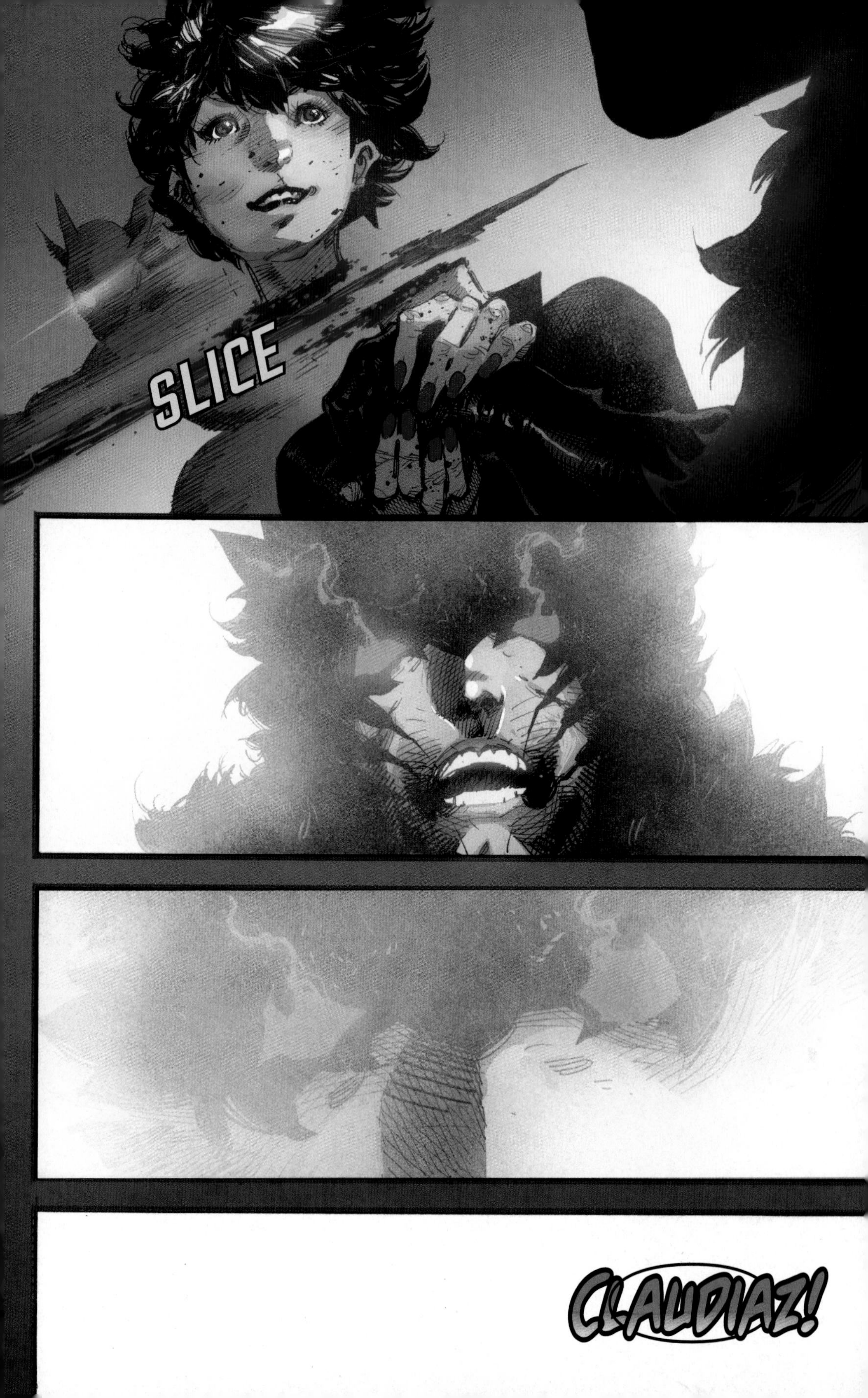
SLICE
CLAUDIAZ!

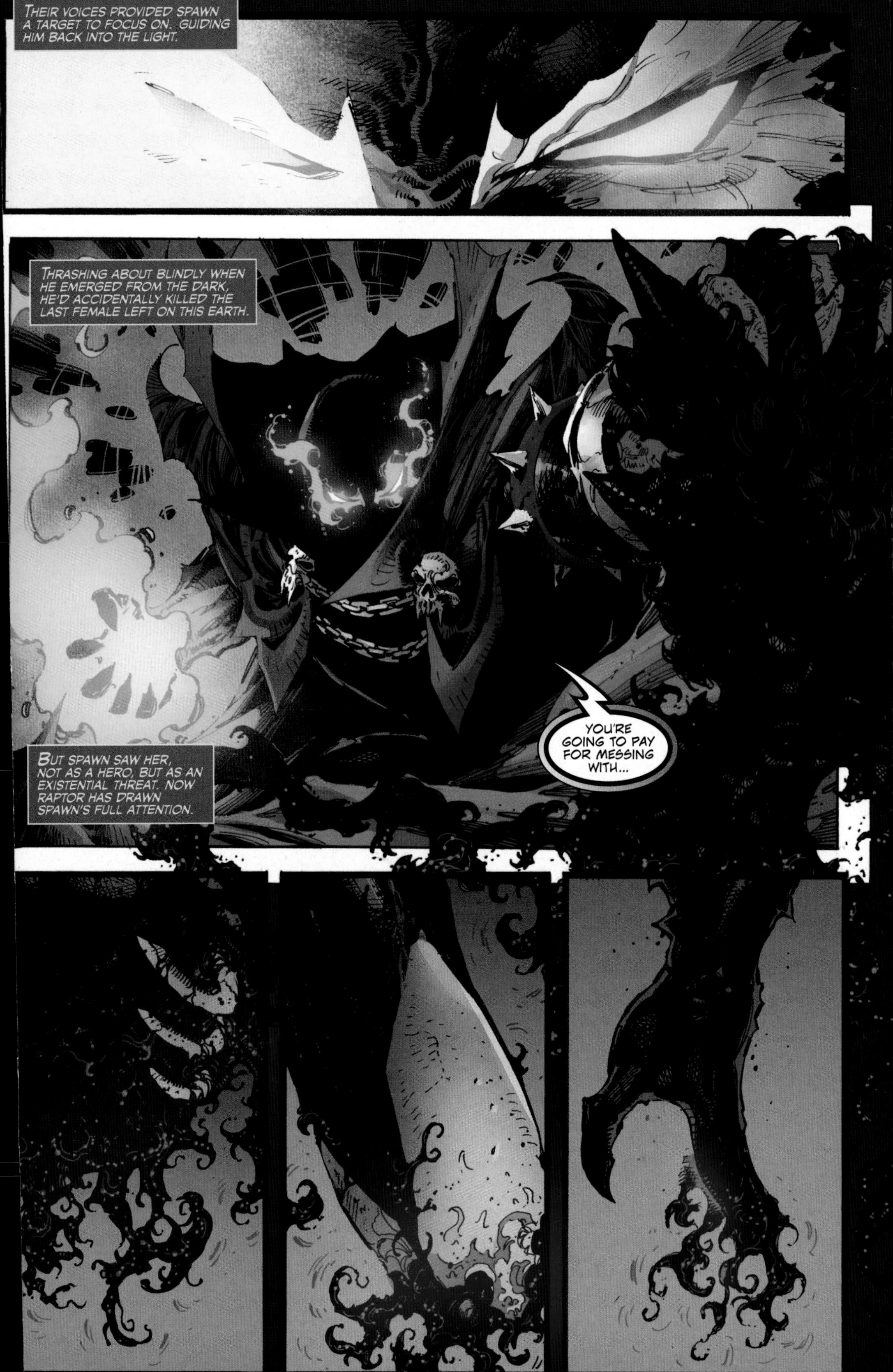
THEIR VOICES PROVIDED SPAWN A TARGET TO FOCUS ON. GUIDING HIM BACK INTO THE LIGHT.
THRASHING ABOUT BLINDLY WHEN HE EMERGED FROM THE DARK, HE'D ACCIDENTALLY KILLED THE LAST FEMALE LEFT ON THIS EARTH.
YOU'RE GOING TO PAY FOR MESSING WITH...
BUT SPAWN SAW HER, NOT AS A HERO, BUT AS AN EXISTENTIAL THREAT. NOW RAPTOR HAS DRAWN SPAWN'S FULL ATTENTION.

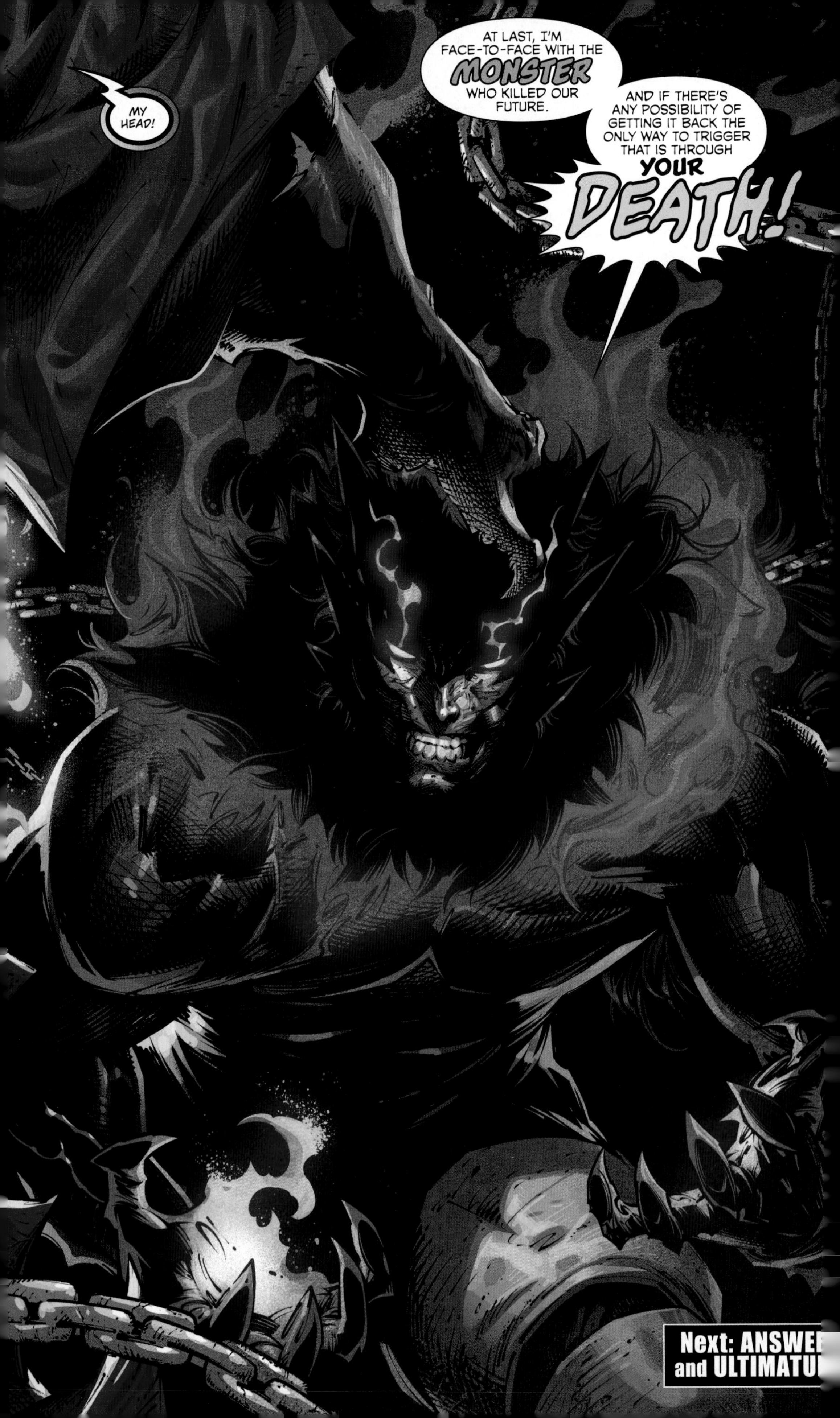
MY HEAD!
AT LAST, I'M FACE-TO-FACE WITH THE MONSTER WHO KILLED OUR FUTURE.
AND IF THERE'S ANY POSSIBILITY OF GETTING IT BACK THE ONLY WAY TO TRIGGER THAT IS THROUGH YOUR DEATH!
Next: ANSWE and ULTIMATU

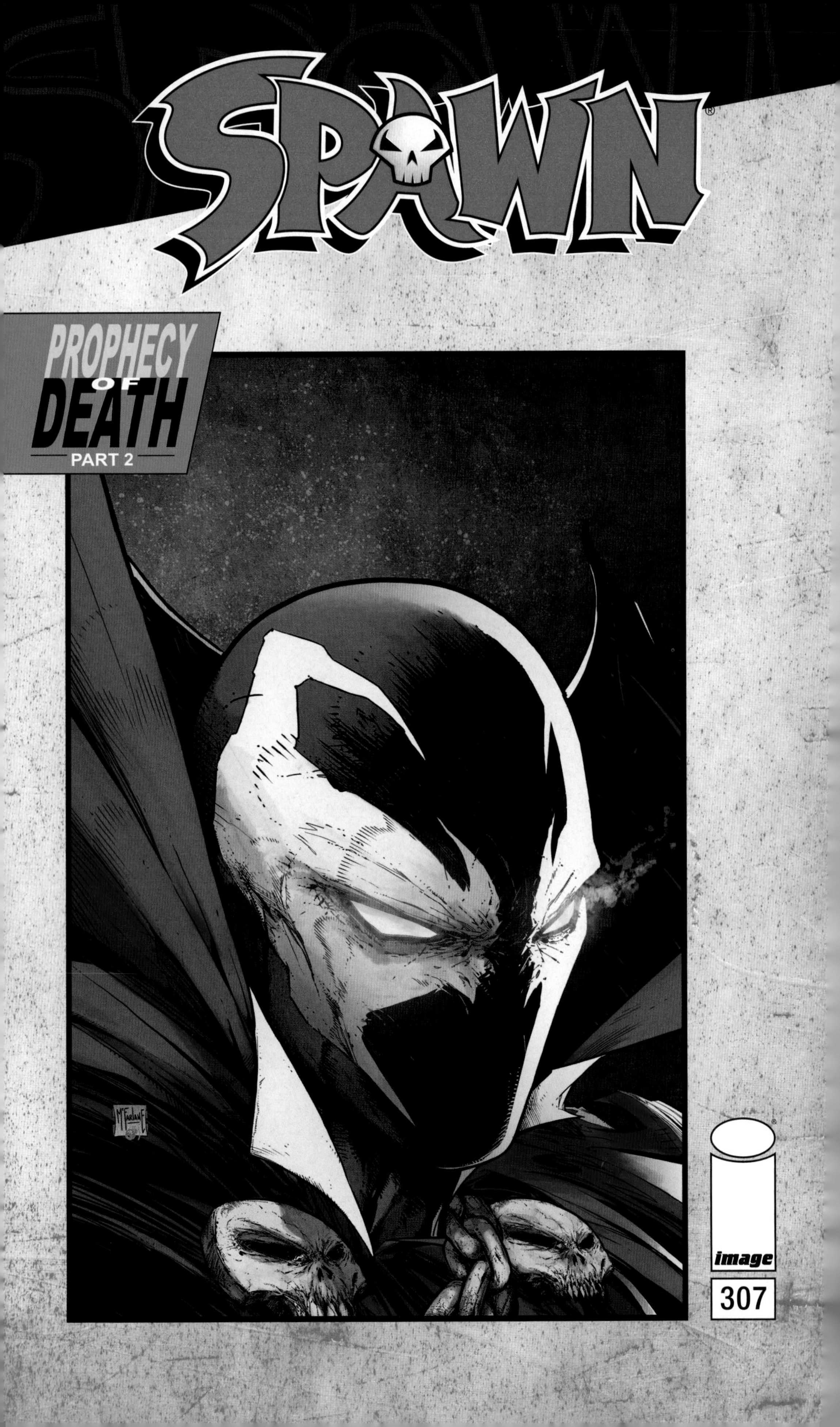
SPAWN
PROPHECY OF DEATH
PART 2
image
307

THEY ALWAYS HAVE
A RATIONALE --
A REASON FOR THEIR
ACTIONS. EVEN WHEN
MILLIONS OF HUMANS
SUFFER IN THE WAKE
OF THOSE ACTIONS,
BECOMING NOTHING
BUT COLLATERAL
DAMAGE IN THEIR
WAR.

SO, IF CENTURIES OF THEIR
CALLOUS SLAUGHTER COULD
SO EASILY BE DISMISSED, THEN
SPAWN IS EQUALLY UNMOVED
BY THE FACT HE'S JUST KILLED
THE ONLY WOMAN LEFT ALIVE
IN THIS NEW REALITY. *

EARTH IS MERELY A
NUISANCE. GETTING
IN THEIR WAY AS
HEAVEN AND HELL
WAGE THEIR ENDLESS
WAR AGAINST ONE
ANOTHER.

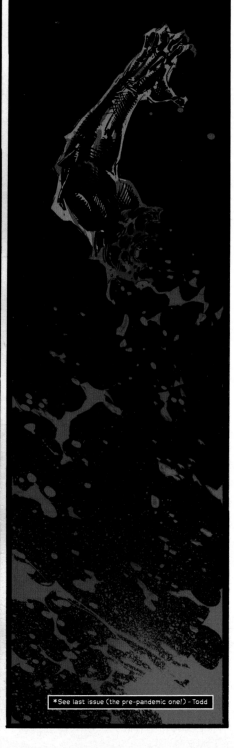

*See last issue (the pre-pandemic one!) - Todd

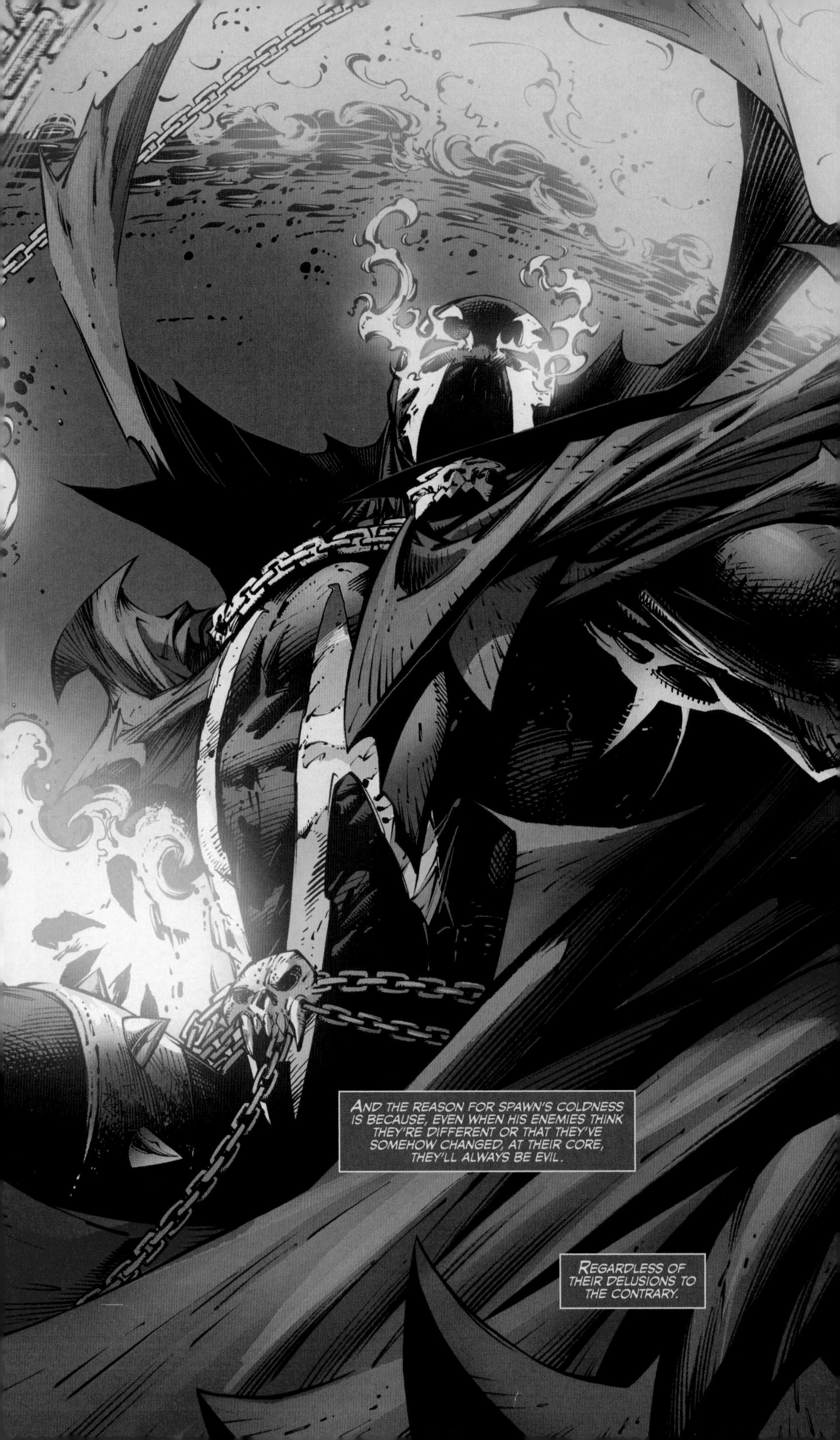
AND THE REASON FOR SPAWN'S COLDNESS IS BECAUSE, EVEN WHEN HIS ENEMIES THINK THEY'RE DIFFERENT OR THAT THEY'VE SOMEHOW CHANGED, AT THEIR CORE, THEY'LL ALWAYS BE EVIL.
REGARDLESS OF THEIR DELUSIONS TO THE CONTRARY.

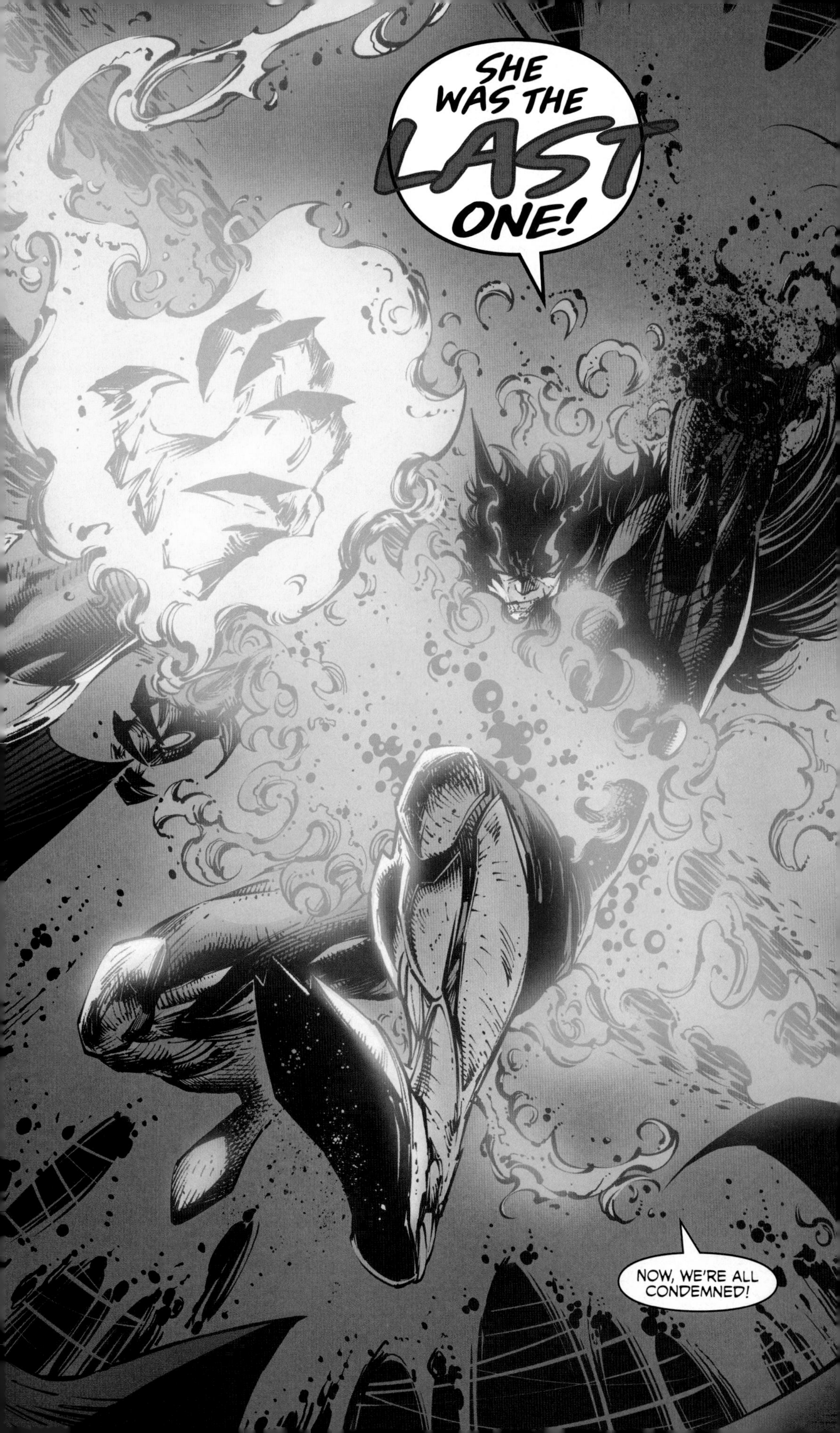
SHE WAS THE LAST ONE!
NOW, WE'RE ALL CONDEMNED!

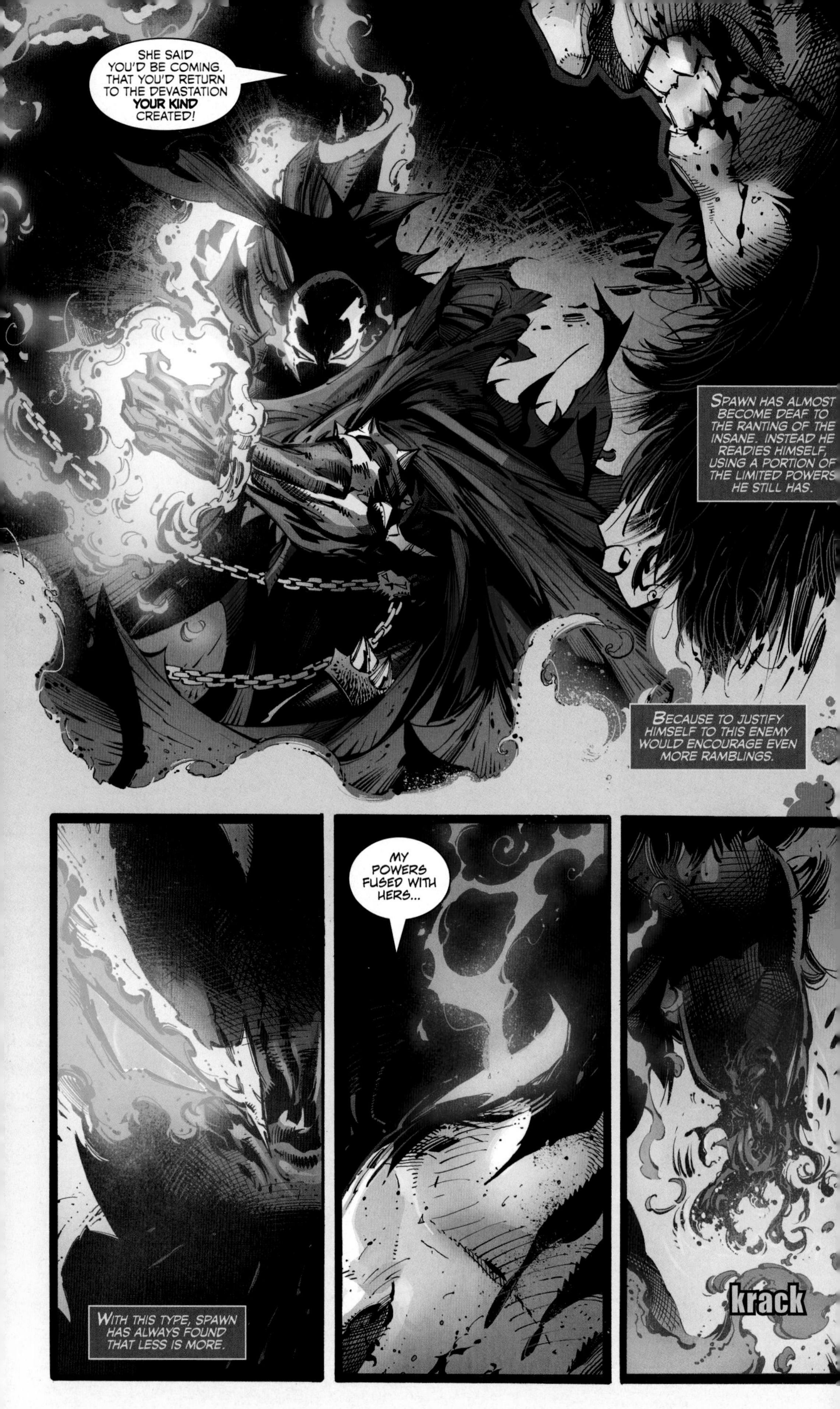
SHE SAID YOU'D BE COMING. THAT YOU'D RETURN TO THE DEVASTATION **YOUR KIND** CREATED!
SPAWN HAS ALMOST BECOME DEAF TO THE RANTING OF THE INSANE. INSTEAD HE READIES HIMSELF, USING A PORTION OF THE LIMITED POWERS HE STILL HAS.
BECAUSE TO JUSTIFY HIMSELF TO THIS ENEMY WOULD ENCOURAGE EVEN MORE RAMBLINGS.
WITH THIS TYPE, SPAWN HAS ALWAYS FOUND THAT LESS IS MORE.
MY POWERS FUSED WITH HERS...
krack

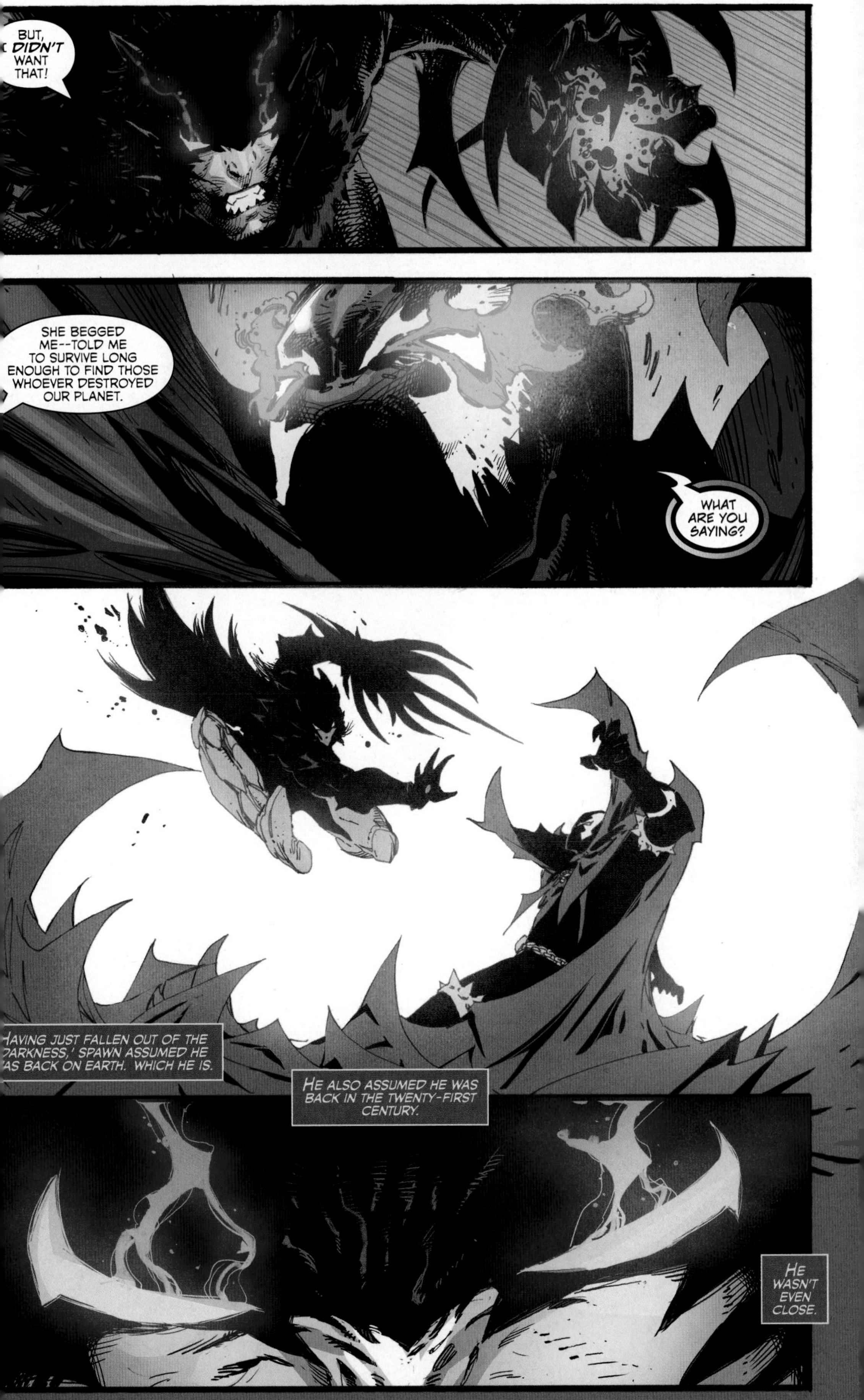

BUT, I DIDN'T WANT THAT!
SHE BEGGED ME--TOLD ME TO SURVIVE LONG ENOUGH TO FIND THOSE WHOEVER DESTROYED OUR PLANET.
WHAT ARE YOU SAYING?
HAVING JUST FALLEN OUT OF THE 'DARKNESS,' SPAWN ASSUMED HE WAS BACK ON EARTH. WHICH HE IS.
HE ALSO ASSUMED HE WAS BACK IN THE TWENTY-FIRST CENTURY.
HE WASN'T EVEN CLOSE.

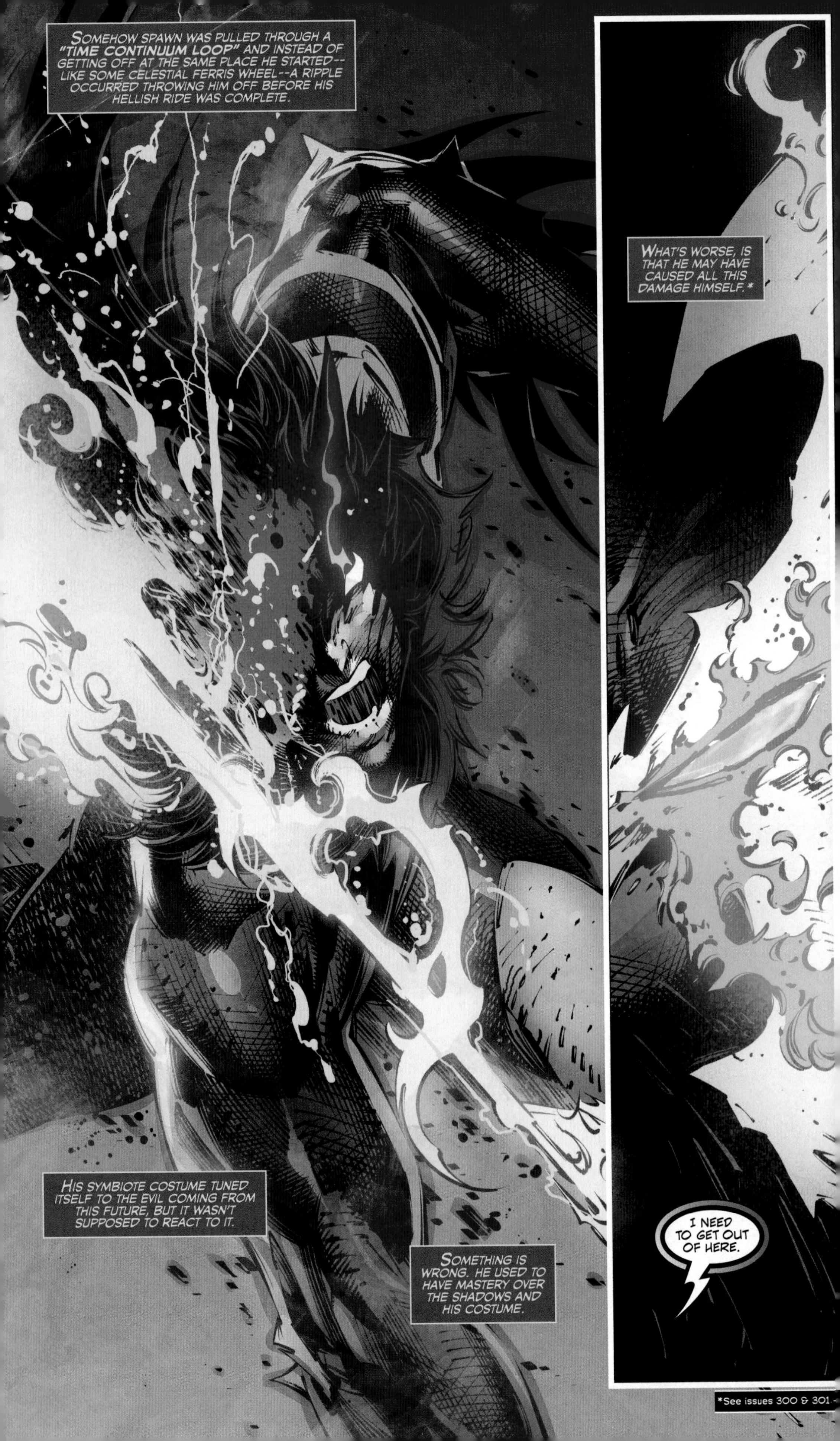
SOMEHOW SPAWN WAS PULLED THROUGH A "TIME CONTINUUM LOOP" AND INSTEAD OF GETTING OFF AT THE SAME PLACE HE STARTED--LIKE SOME CELESTIAL FERRIS WHEEL--A RIPPLE OCCURRED THROWING HIM OFF BEFORE HIS HELLISH RIDE WAS COMPLETE.
HIS SYMBIOTE COSTUME TUNED ITSELF TO THE EVIL COMING FROM THIS FUTURE, BUT IT WASN'T SUPPOSED TO REACT TO IT.
SOMETHING IS WRONG. HE USED TO HAVE MASTERY OVER THE SHADOWS AND HIS COSTUME.
WHAT'S WORSE, IS THAT HE MAY HAVE CAUSED ALL THIS DAMAGE HIMSELF.*
I NEED TO GET OUT OF HERE.
*See issues 300 & 301

THE PROBLEM IS, SPAWN DOESN'T KNOW WHERE TO GO. IF HE TELEPORTS BACK INTO THE SHADOWED DARKNESS, WILL HE JUST GET LOST AGAIN?

BUT IF HE DOESN'T GO NOW, HE MIGHT NOT HAVE THE POWER TO TRY AGAIN.

DEVIL! WHY HAVE YOU MADE ME SO WEAK?

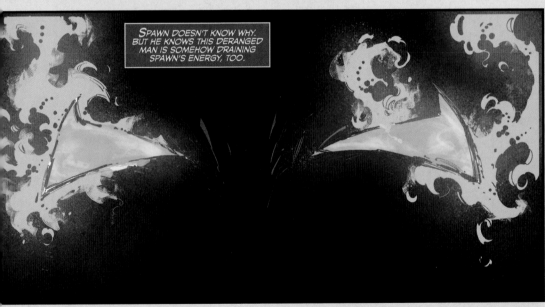

SPAWN DOESN'T KNOW WHY. BUT HE KNOWS THIS DERANGED MAN IS SOMEHOW DRAINING SPAWN'S ENERGY, TOO.

THESE TWO ARE SOMEHOW FEEDING OFF EACH OTHER'S LIFE FORCE.

IF I'M GOING TO DIE, THEN YOU'RE COMING WITH ME!

SPAWN'S BEGINS TO FEEL WHAT LITTLE POWER HE STILL HAS--START TO DRAIN FROM HIS BODY. THIS PLANET IS SLOWLY EATING THEM BOTH ALIVE LIKE EVERYTHING ELSE THAT'S CONNECTED TO IT. THE HEARTBEAT OF THIS WORLD IS EBBING ITS WAY TO EXTINCTION.

AND SOMEHOW, HE AND THIS MADMAN ARE A PART OF THIS INSANE PUZZLE. THOUGH SOMETHING ELSE IS AT PLAY HERE. SOMETHING THAT ISN'T HEAVEN OR HELL.

THE CHILL GOING DOWN SPAWN'S SPINE IS THAT DEEP IN THE RECESSES OF HIS MIND IS THE KNOWLEDGE THAT MANKIND MAY NOT SURVIVE IN THE LONG RUN.

IT'S BIGGER THAN THOSE TWO. **MUCH BIGGER!**

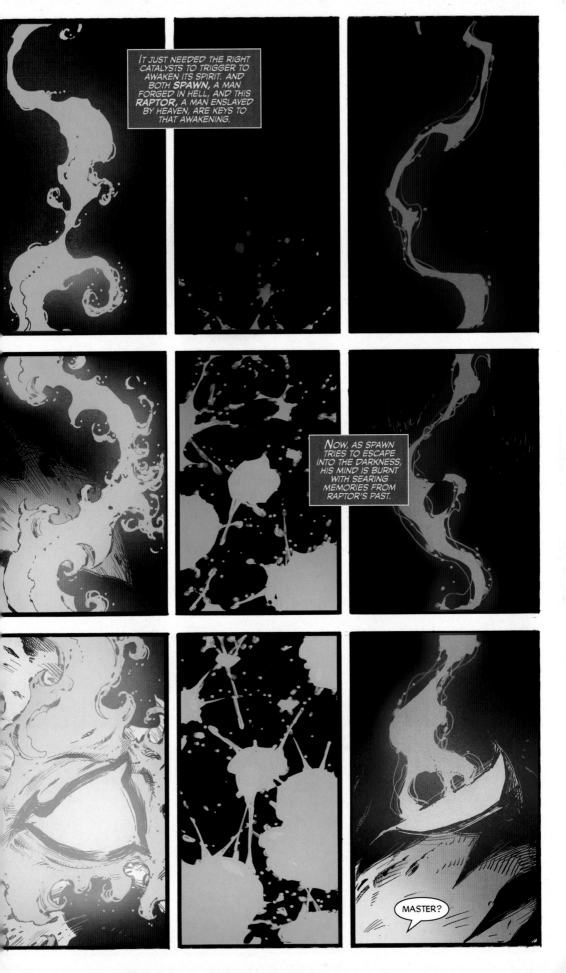

IT JUST NEEDED THE RIGHT CATALYSTS TO TRIGGER TO AWAKEN ITS SPIRIT. AND BOTH **SPAWN**, A MAN FORGED IN HELL, AND THIS **RAPTOR,** A MAN ENSLAVED BY HEAVEN, ARE KEYS TO THAT AWAKENING.

NOW, AS SPAWN TRIES TO ESCAPE INTO THE DARKNESS, HIS MIND IS BURNT WITH SEARING MEMORIES FROM RAPTOR'S PAST.

MASTER?

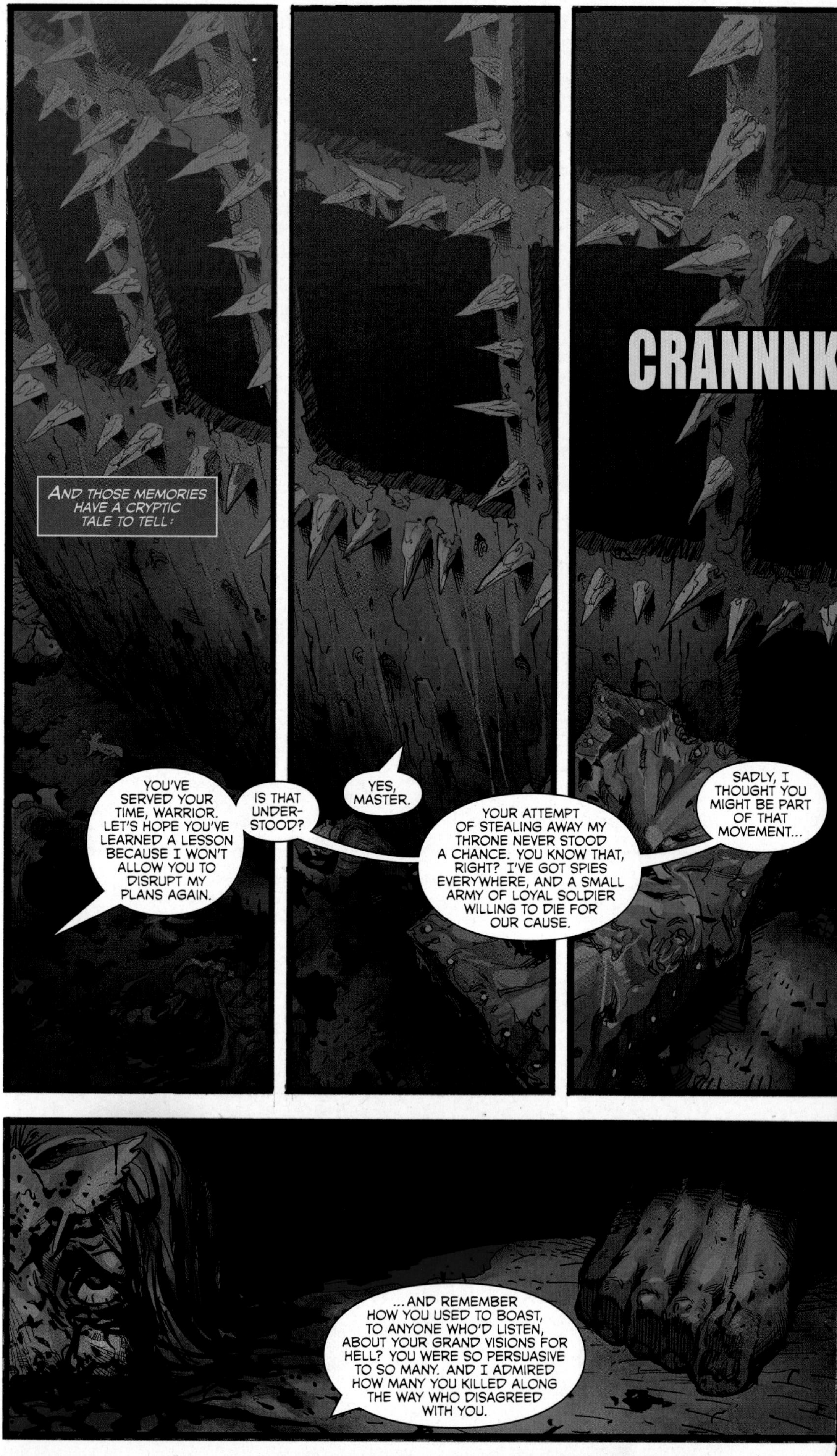
AND THOSE MEMORIES HAVE A CRYPTIC TALE TO TELL:
CRANNNK
YOU'VE SERVED YOUR TIME, WARRIOR. LET'S HOPE YOU'VE LEARNED A LESSON BECAUSE I WON'T ALLOW YOU TO DISRUPT MY PLANS AGAIN.
IS THAT UNDER-STOOD?
YES, MASTER.
YOUR ATTEMPT OF STEALING AWAY MY THRONE NEVER STOOD A CHANCE. YOU KNOW THAT, RIGHT? I'VE GOT SPIES EVERYWHERE, AND A SMALL ARMY OF LOYAL SOLDIER WILLING TO DIE FOR OUR CAUSE.
SADLY, I THOUGHT YOU MIGHT BE PART OF THAT MOVEMENT...
...AND REMEMBER HOW YOU USED TO BOAST, TO ANYONE WHO'D LISTEN, ABOUT YOUR GRAND VISIONS FOR HELL? YOU WERE SO PERSUASIVE TO SO MANY. AND I ADMIRED HOW MANY YOU KILLED ALONG THE WAY WHO DISAGREED WITH YOU.

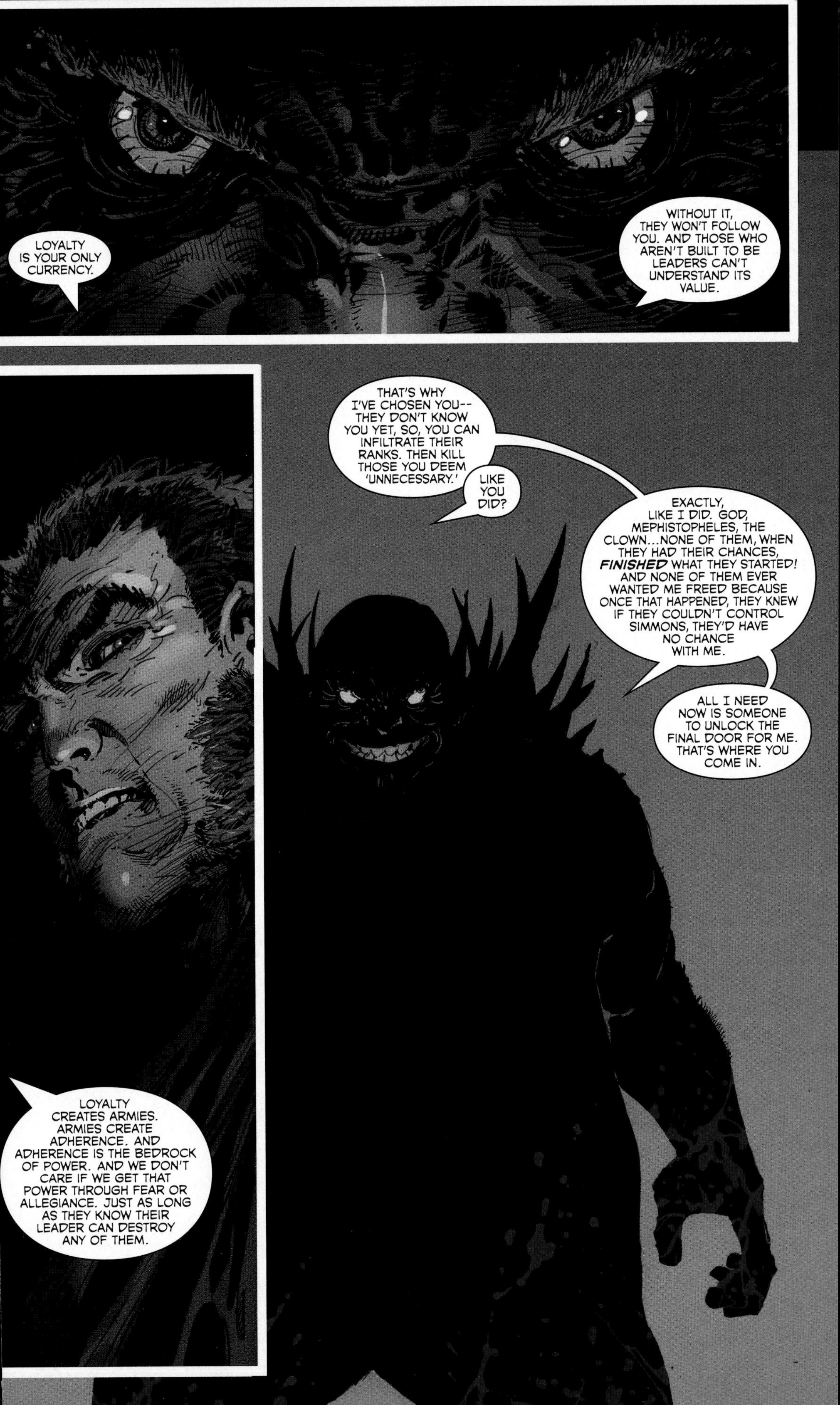

LOYALTY IS YOUR ONLY CURRENCY.
WITHOUT IT, THEY WON'T FOLLOW YOU. AND THOSE WHO AREN'T BUILT TO BE LEADERS CAN'T UNDERSTAND ITS VALUE.
THAT'S WHY I'VE CHOSEN YOU-- THEY DON'T KNOW YOU YET, SO, YOU CAN INFILTRATE THEIR RANKS. THEN KILL THOSE YOU DEEM 'UNNECESSARY.'
LIKE YOU DID?
EXACTLY, LIKE I DID. GOD, MEPHISTOPHELES, THE CLOWN...NONE OF THEM, WHEN THEY HAD THEIR CHANCES, ***FINISHED*** WHAT THEY STARTED! AND NONE OF THEM EVER WANTED ME FREED BECAUSE ONCE THAT HAPPENED, THEY KNEW IF THEY COULDN'T CONTROL SIMMONS, THEY'D HAVE NO CHANCE WITH ME.
ALL I NEED NOW IS SOMEONE TO UNLOCK THE FINAL DOOR FOR ME. THAT'S WHERE YOU COME IN.
LOYALTY CREATES ARMIES. ARMIES CREATE ADHERENCE. AND ADHERENCE IS THE BEDROCK OF POWER. AND WE DON'T CARE IF WE GET THAT POWER THROUGH FEAR OR ALLEGIANCE. JUST AS LONG AS THEY KNOW THEIR LEADER CAN DESTROY ANY OF THEM.

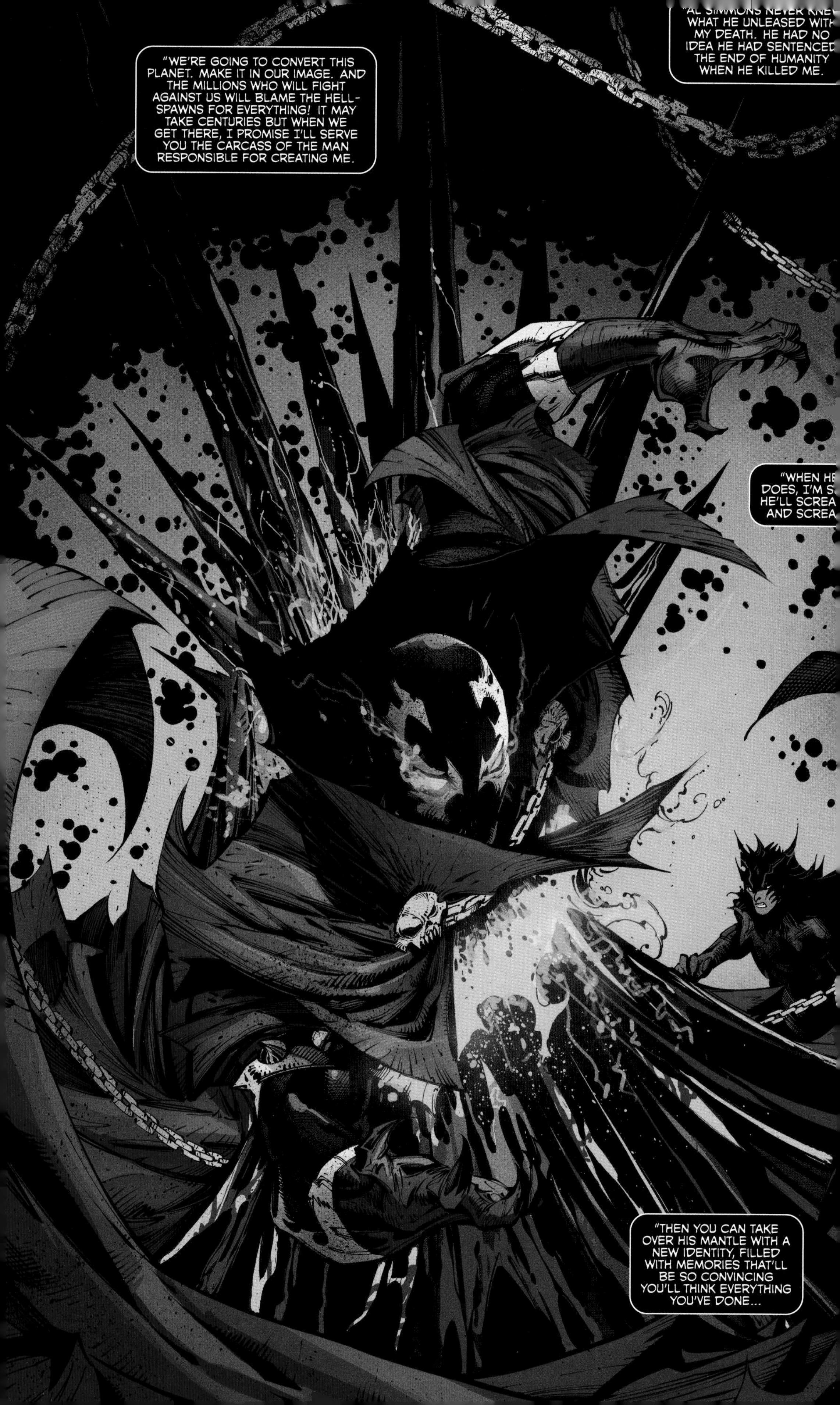
"WE'RE GOING TO CONVERT THIS PLANET. MAKE IT IN OUR IMAGE. AND THE MILLIONS WHO WILL FIGHT AGAINST US WILL BLAME THE HELL-SPAWNS FOR EVERYTHING! IT MAY TAKE CENTURIES BUT WHEN WE GET THERE, I PROMISE I'LL SERVE YOU THE CARCASS OF THE MAN RESPONSIBLE FOR CREATING ME.
"AL SIMMONS NEVER
WHAT HE UNLEASED
MY DEATH. HE HAD NO
IDEA HE HAD
THE END OF HUMANITY
WHEN HE KILLED ME.
"WHEN
DOES, I'M
HE'LL
AND
"THEN YOU CAN TAKE OVER HIS MANTLE WITH A NEW IDENTITY, FILLED WITH MEMORIES THAT'LL BE SO CONVINCING YOU'LL THINK EVERYTHING YOU'VE DONE...

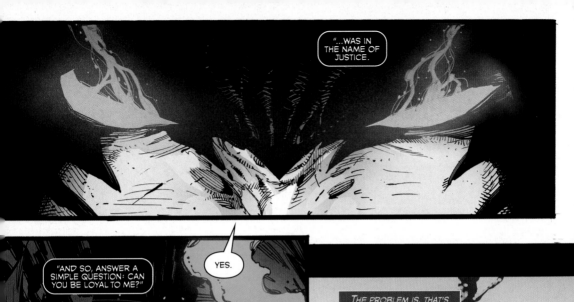

"...WAS IN THE NAME OF JUSTICE.

"AND SO, ANSWER A SIMPLE QUESTION: CAN YOU BE LOYAL TO ME?"

YES.

WITH THAT SINGLE WORD, THE ATTEMPTS AT INTERSECTING THE FUTURE AND THE PAST BEGAN.

THE PROBLEM IS, THAT'S NOT HOW NATURE WORKS. IT WON'T TOLERATE BEING FORCED INTO SOMETHING THAT ISN'T 'NATURAL.'

SO, WHEN HELL'S AMBITIOUS GOAL WERE THRUST UPON THE WORLD, TRYING TO DESTROY MAN AND CONQUERING HEAVEN, IT ALSO WOKE A *SLEEPING GIANT.* THAT RESULT WILL SOON MAKE ITS PRESENCE KNOWN.

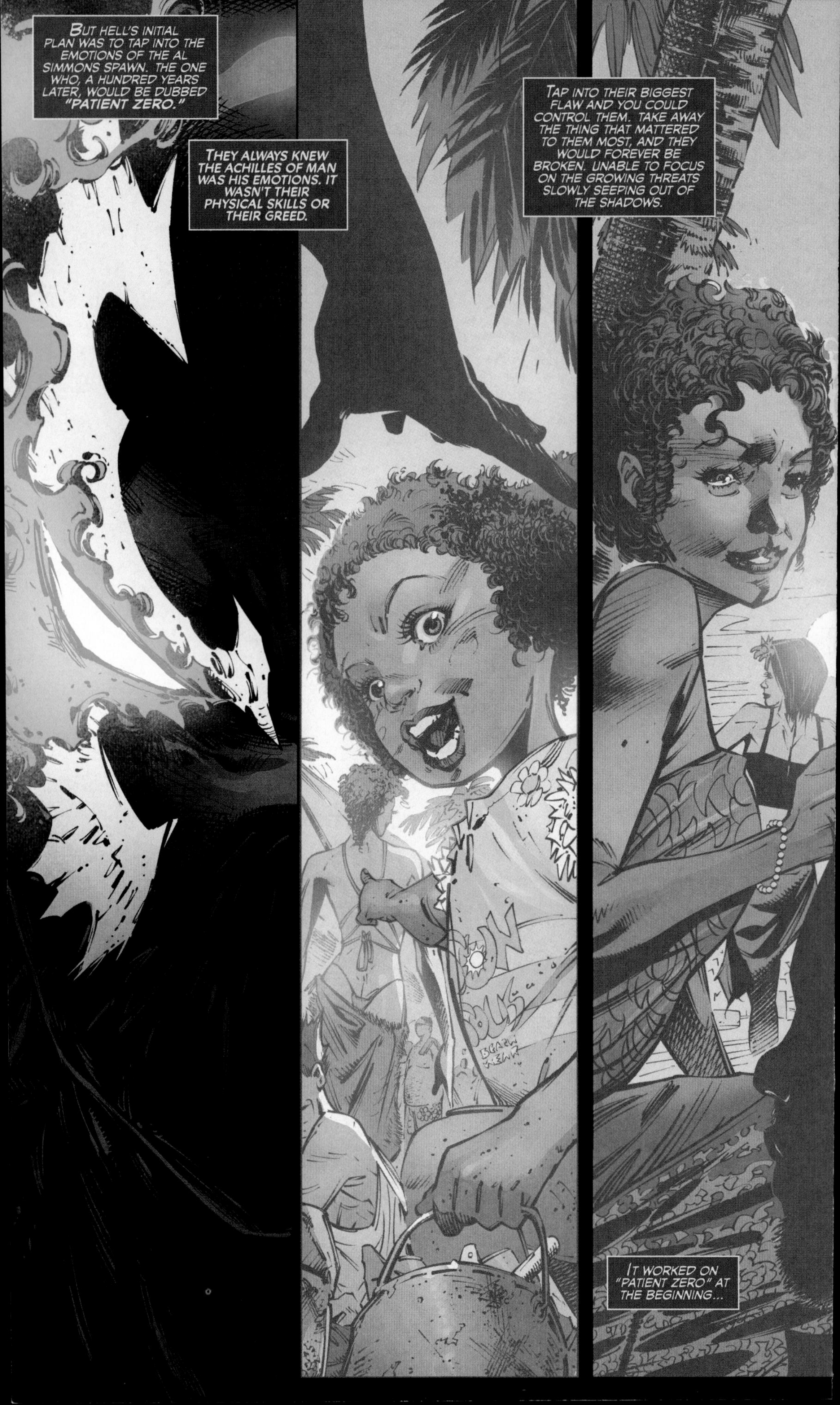

But hell's initial plan was to tap into the emotions of the Al Simmons Spawn. The one who, a hundred years later, would be dubbed "Patient Zero."
They always knew the Achilles of man was his emotions. It wasn't their physical skills or their greed.
Tap into their biggest flaw and you could control them. Take away the thing that mattered to them most, and they would forever be broken. Unable to focus on the growing threats slowly seeping out of the shadows.
It worked on "Patient Zero" at the beginning...

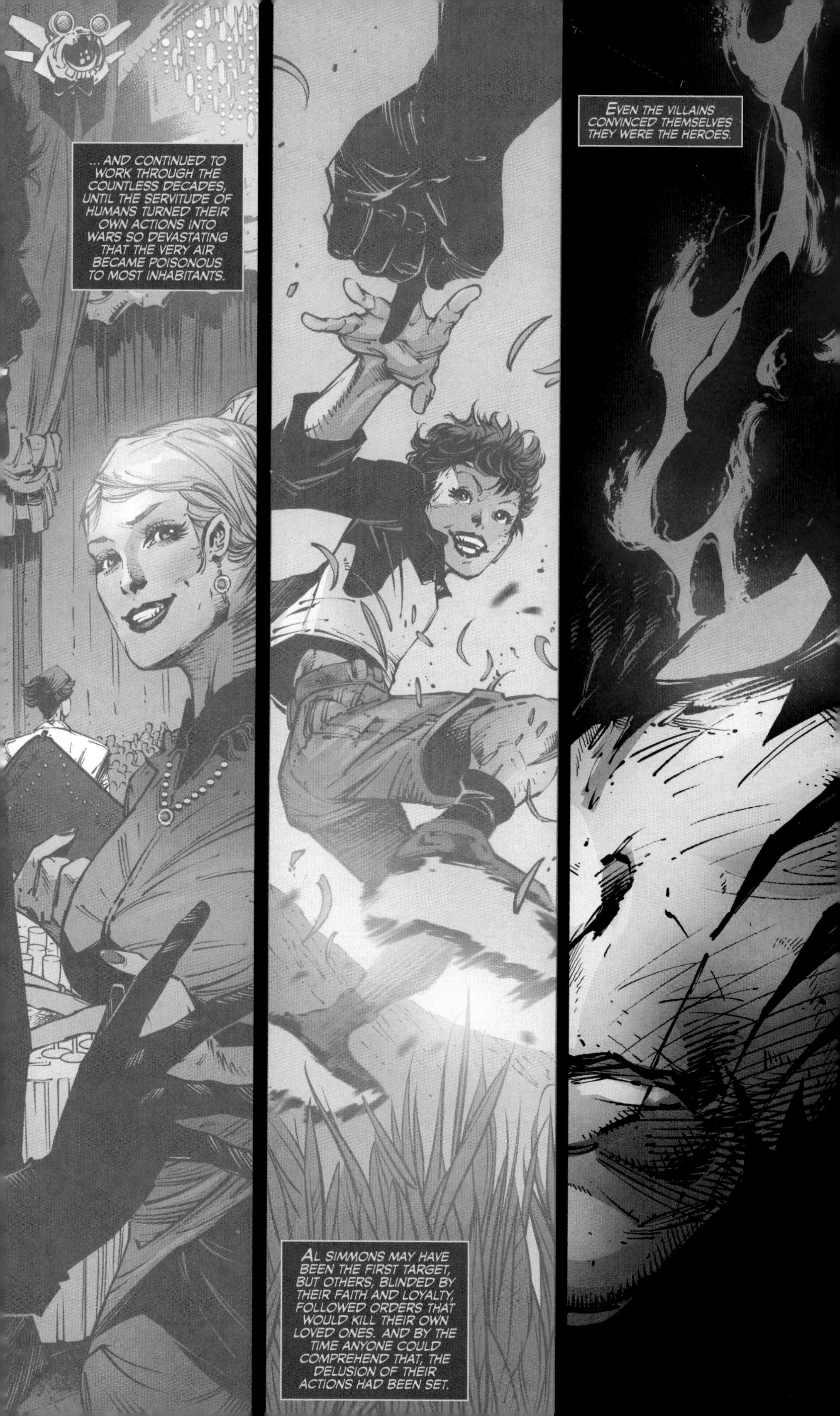
...AND CONTINUED TO WORK THROUGH THE COUNTLESS DECADES, UNTIL THE SERVITUDE OF HUMANS TURNED THEIR OWN ACTIONS INTO WARS SO DEVASTATING THAT THE VERY AIR BECAME POISONOUS TO MOST INHABITANTS.
AL SIMMONS MAY HAVE BEEN THE FIRST TARGET, BUT OTHERS, BLINDED BY THEIR FAITH AND LOYALTY, FOLLOWED ORDERS THAT WOULD KILL THEIR OWN LOVED ONES. AND BY THE TIME ANYONE COULD COMPREHEND THAT, THE DELUSION OF THEIR ACTIONS HAD BEEN SET.
EVEN THE VILLAINS CONVINCED THEMSELVES THEY WERE THE HEROES.

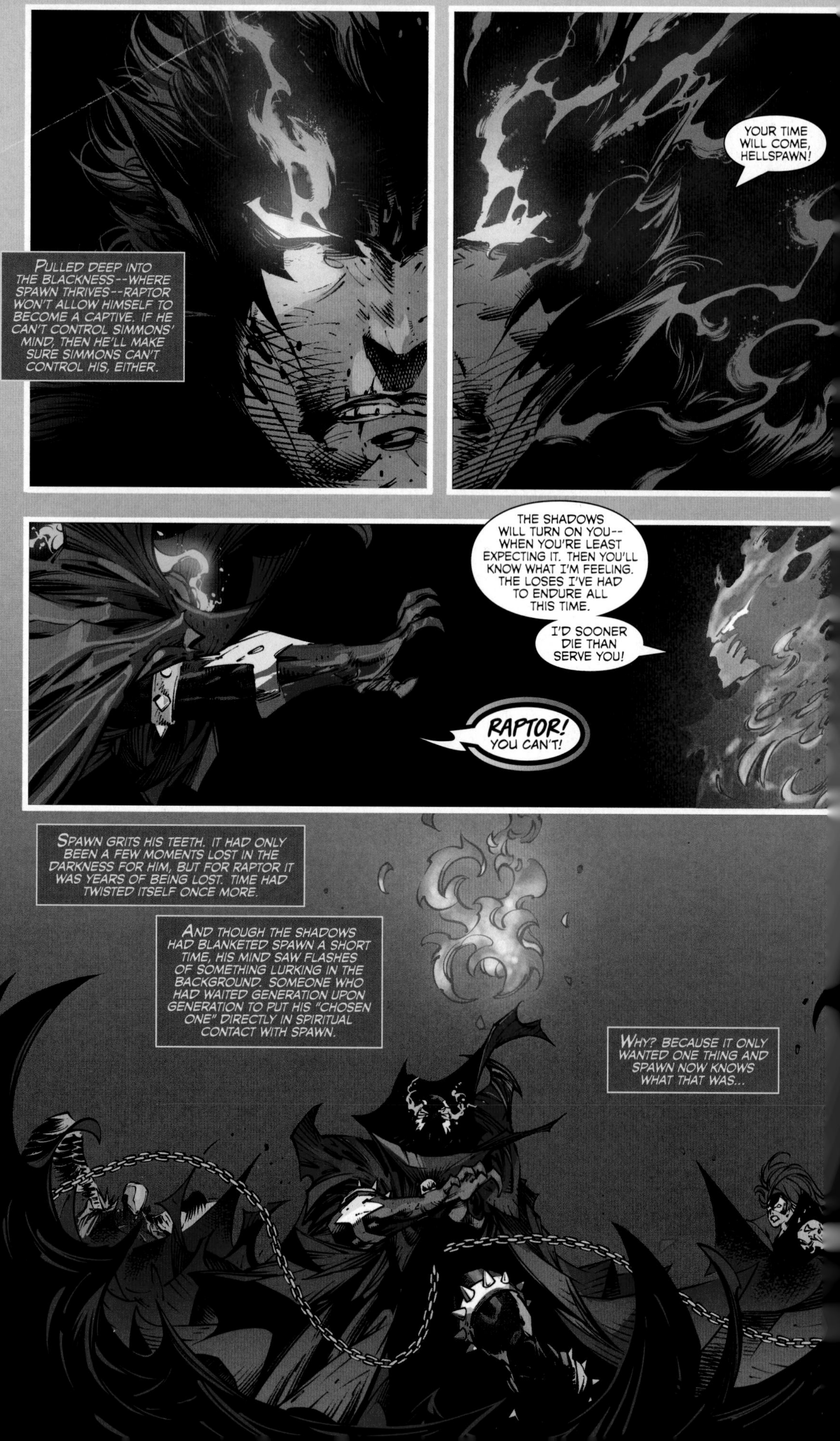
PULLED DEEP INTO THE BLACKNESS--WHERE SPAWN THRIVES--RAPTOR WON'T ALLOW HIMSELF TO BECOME A CAPTIVE. IF HE CAN'T CONTROL SIMMONS' MIND, THEN HE'LL MAKE SURE SIMMONS CAN'T CONTROL HIS, EITHER.
YOUR TIME WILL COME, HELLSPAWN!
THE SHADOWS WILL TURN ON YOU-- WHEN YOU'RE LEAST EXPECTING IT. THEN YOU'LL KNOW WHAT I'M FEELING. THE LOSES I'VE HAD TO ENDURE ALL THIS TIME.
I'D SOONER DIE THAN SERVE YOU!
RAPTOR! YOU CAN'T!
SPAWN GRITS HIS TEETH. IT HAD ONLY BEEN A FEW MOMENTS LOST IN THE DARKNESS FOR HIM, BUT FOR RAPTOR IT WAS YEARS OF BEING LOST. TIME HAD TWISTED ITSELF ONCE MORE.
AND THOUGH THE SHADOWS HAD BLANKETED SPAWN A SHORT TIME, HIS MIND SAW FLASHES OF SOMETHING LURKING IN THE BACKGROUND. SOMEONE WHO HAD WAITED GENERATION UPON GENERATION TO PUT HIS "CHOSEN ONE" DIRECTLY IN SPIRITUAL CONTACT WITH SPAWN.
WHY? BECAUSE IT ONLY WANTED ONE THING AND SPAWN NOW KNOWS WHAT THAT WAS...

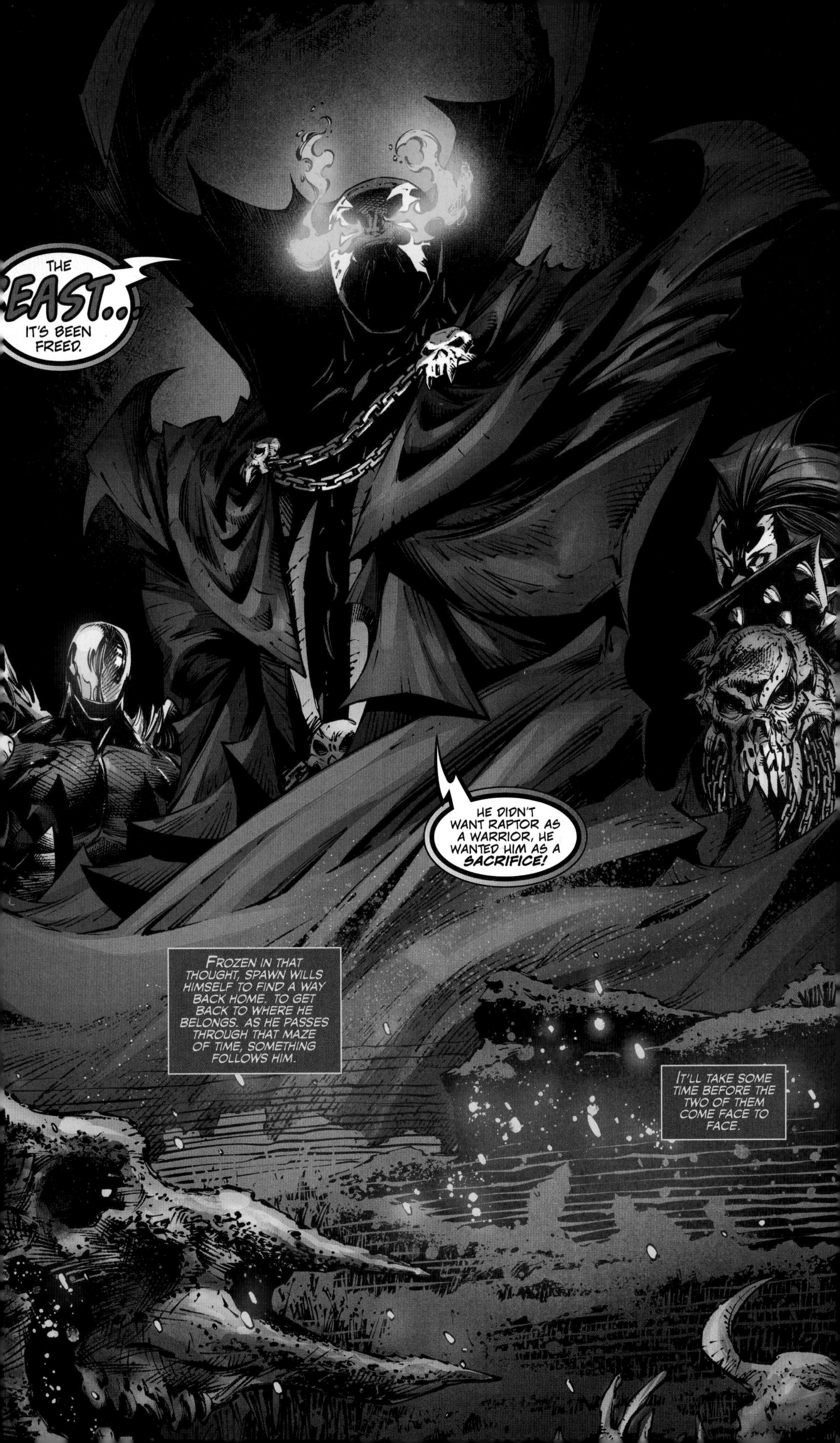

THE BEAST... IT'S BEEN FREED.
HE DIDN'T WANT RAPTOR AS A WARRIOR, HE WANTED HIM AS A SACRIFICE!
FROZEN IN THAT THOUGHT, SPAWN WILLS HIMSELF TO FIND A WAY BACK HOME, TO GET BACK TO WHERE HE BELONGS. AS HE PASSES THROUGH THAT MAZE OF TIME, SOMETHING FOLLOWS HIM.
IT'LL TAKE SOME TIME BEFORE THE TWO OF THEM COME FACE TO FACE.

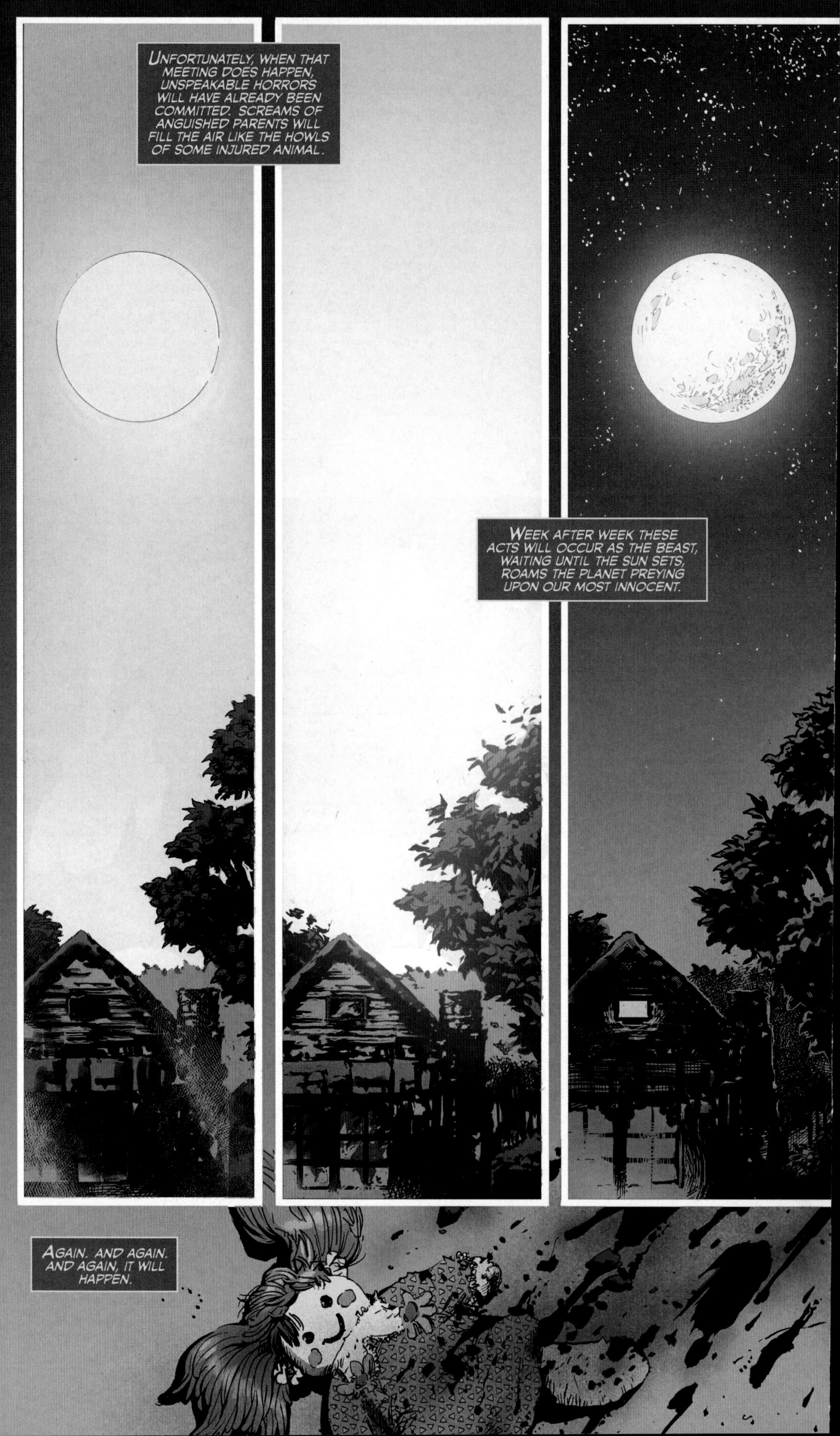
Unfortunately, when that meeting does happen, unspeakable horrors will have already been committed. Screams of anguished parents will fill the air like the howls of some injured animal.
Week after week these acts will occur as the beast, waiting until the sun sets, roams the planet preying upon our most innocent.
Again. And again. And again, it will happen.

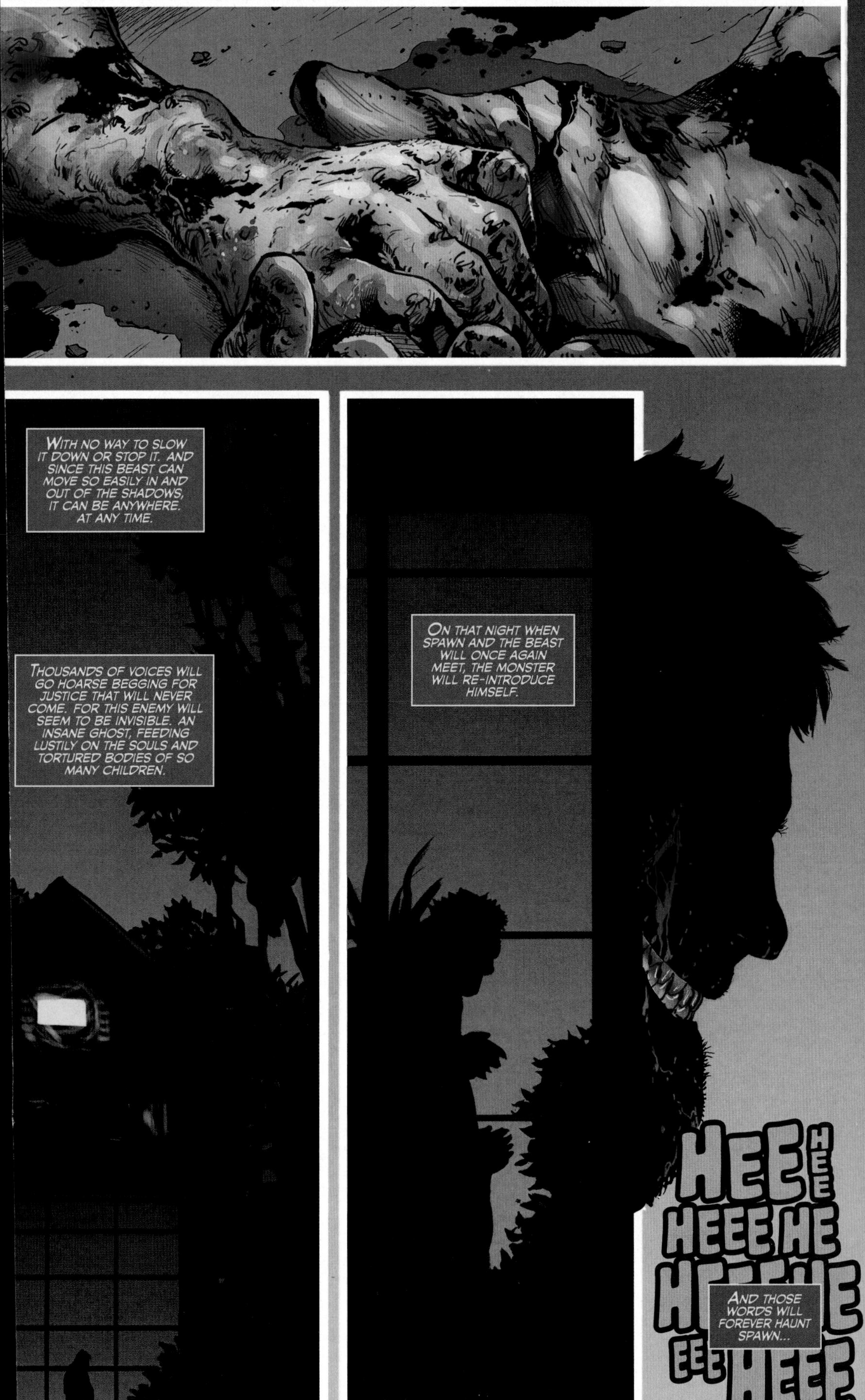

WITH NO WAY TO SLOW IT DOWN OR STOP IT. AND SINCE THIS BEAST CAN MOVE SO EASILY IN AND OUT OF THE SHADOWS, IT CAN BE ANYWHERE. AT ANY TIME.
THOUSANDS OF VOICES WILL GO HOARSE BEGGING FOR JUSTICE THAT WILL NEVER COME. FOR THIS ENEMY WILL SEEM TO BE INVISIBLE. AN INSANE GHOST, FEEDING LUSTILY ON THE SOULS AND TORTURED BODIES OF SO MANY CHILDREN.
ON THAT NIGHT WHEN SPAWN AND THE BEAST WILL ONCE AGAIN MEET, THE MONSTER WILL RE-INTRODUCE HIMSELF.
HEE HEE
HEEE HE
AND THOSE WORDS WILL FOREVER HAUNT SPAWN...
EEE HEEE

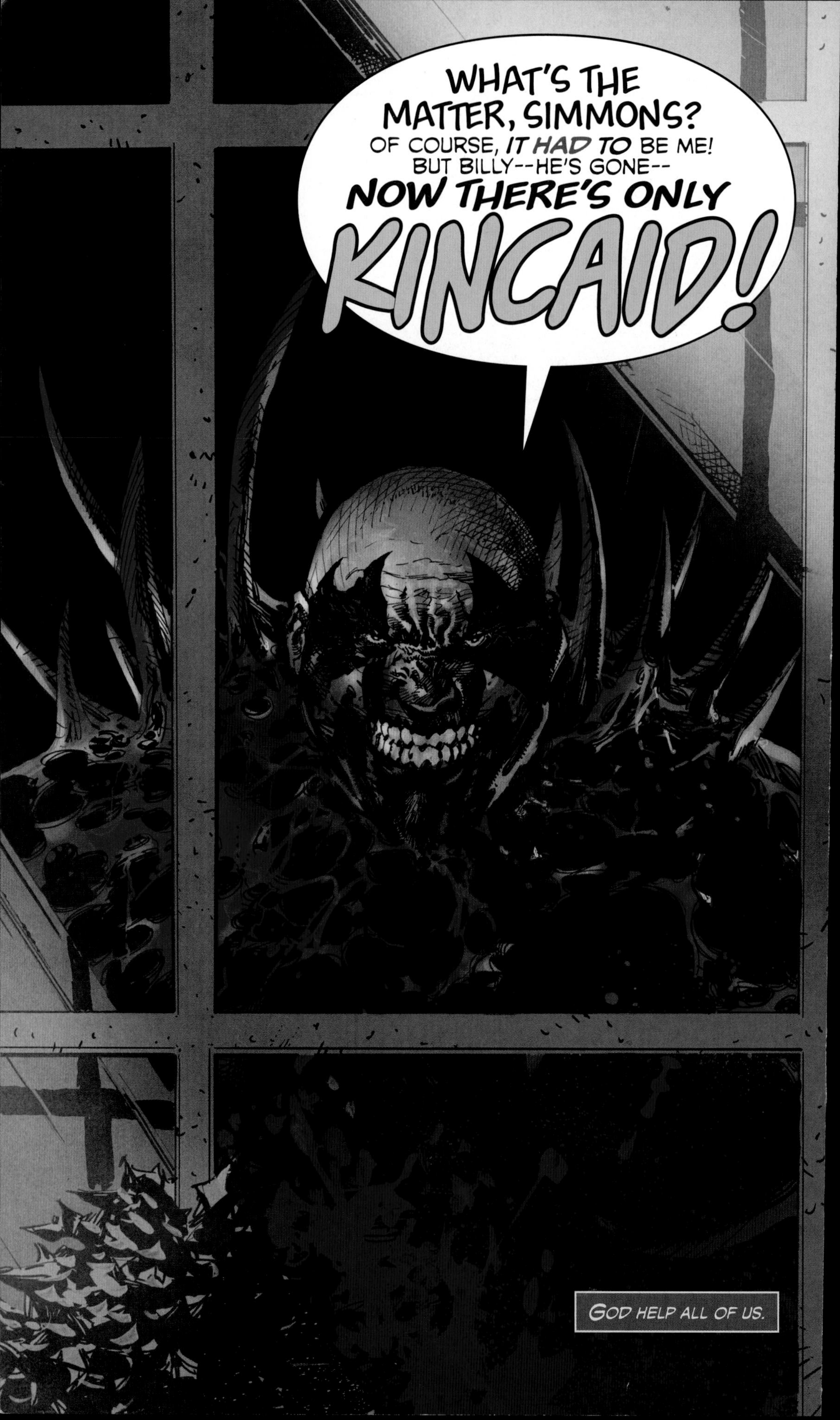
WHAT'S THE MATTER, SIMMONS? OF COURSE, IT HAD TO BE ME! BUT BILLY--HE'S GONE-- NOW THERE'S ONLY KINCAID!
GOD HELP ALL OF US.

SPAWN

302-307 COVER GALLERY

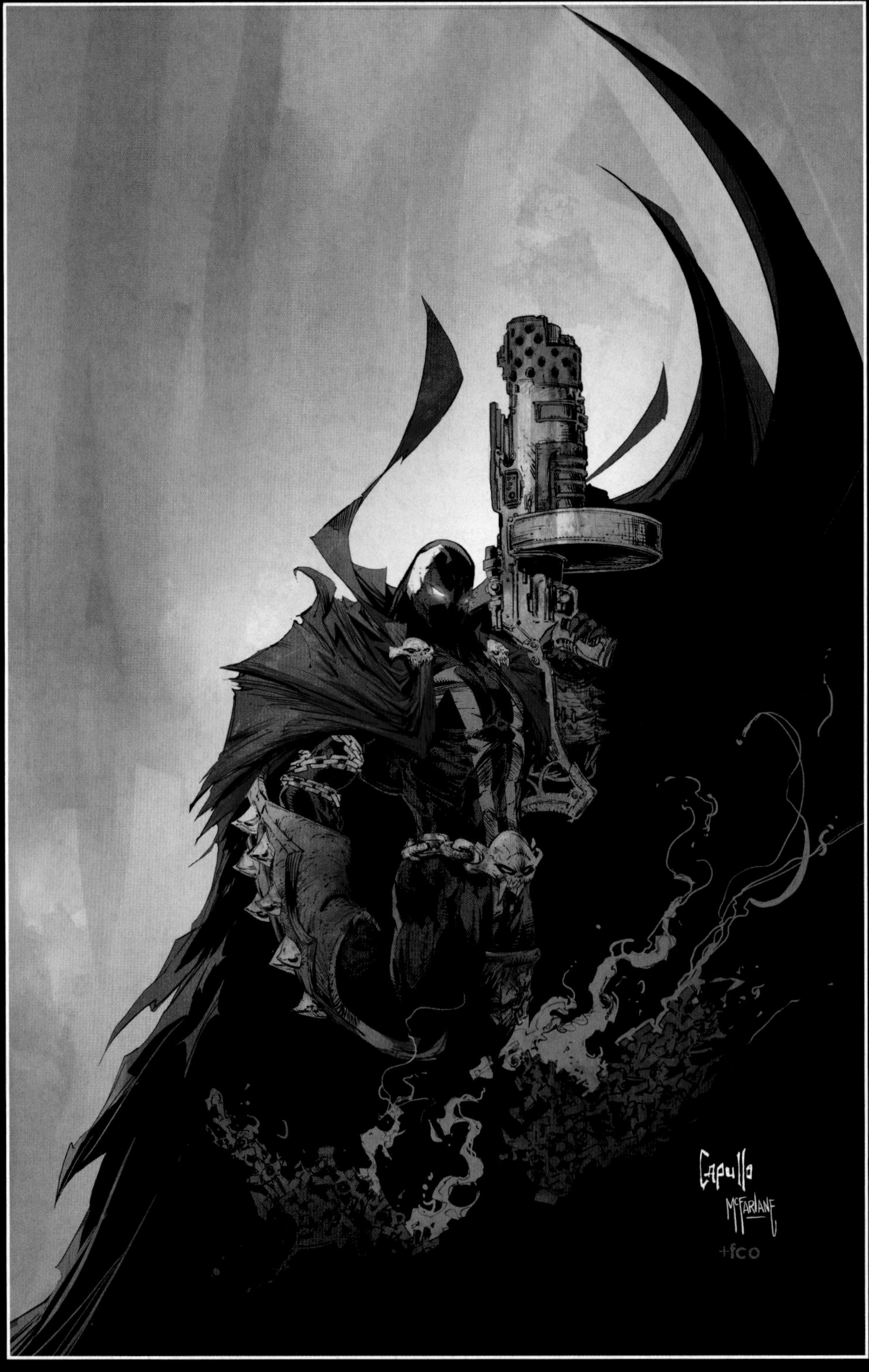

Capullo
McFarlane
+fco

SPAWN 302 by Greg Capullo & Todd McFarlane

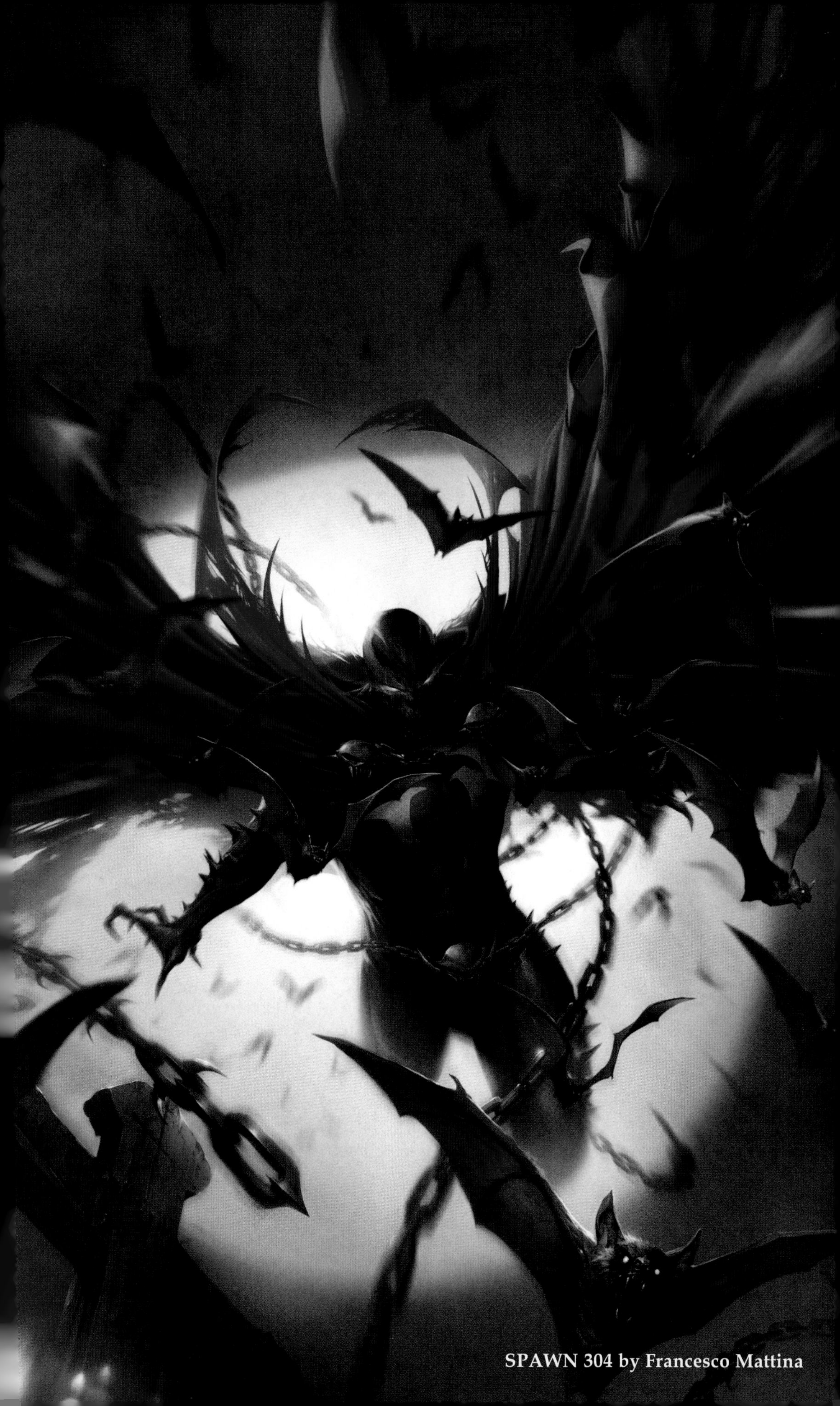

SPAWN 304 by Francesco Mattina

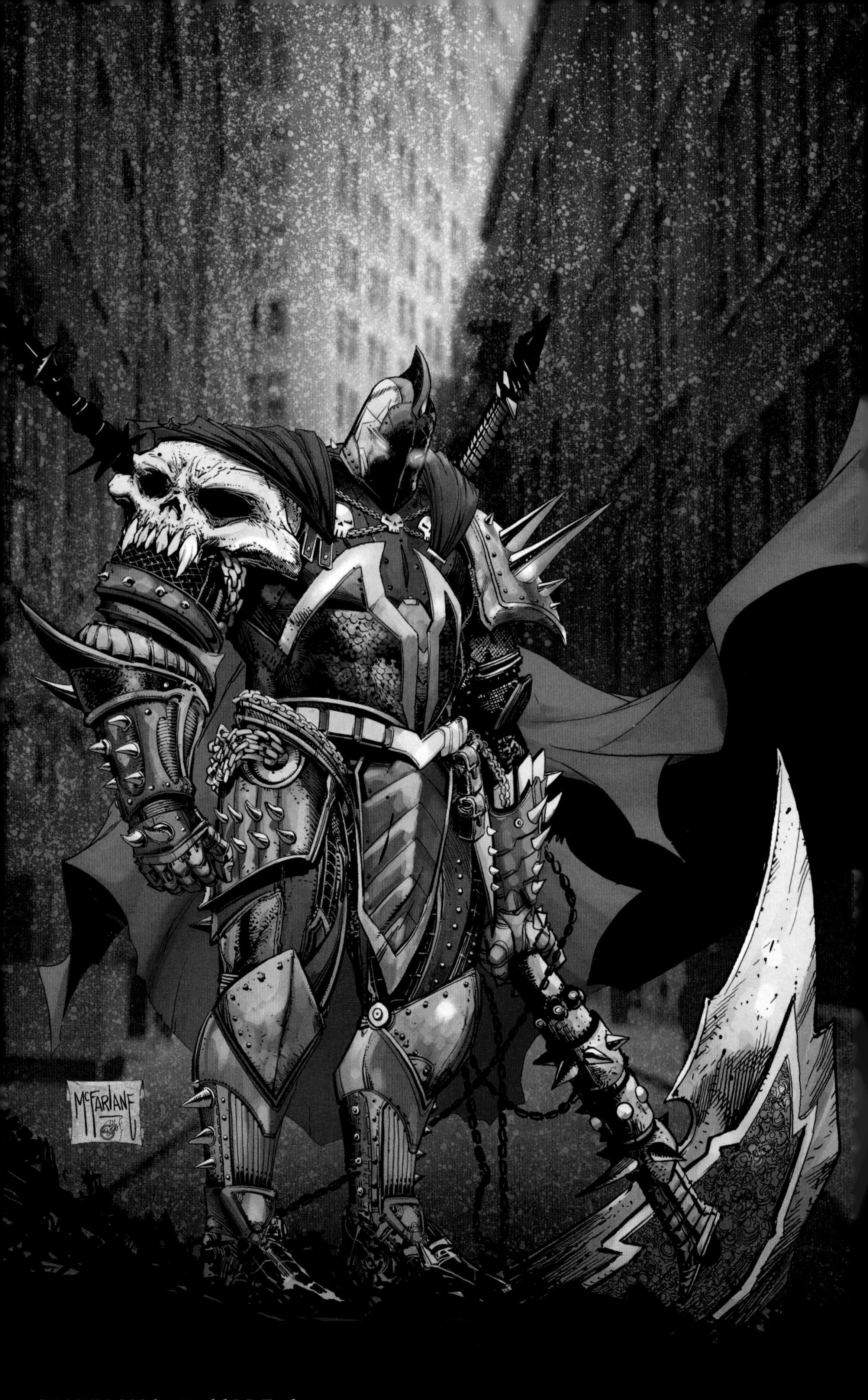
McFARLANE

SPAWN 303 by Todd McFarlane

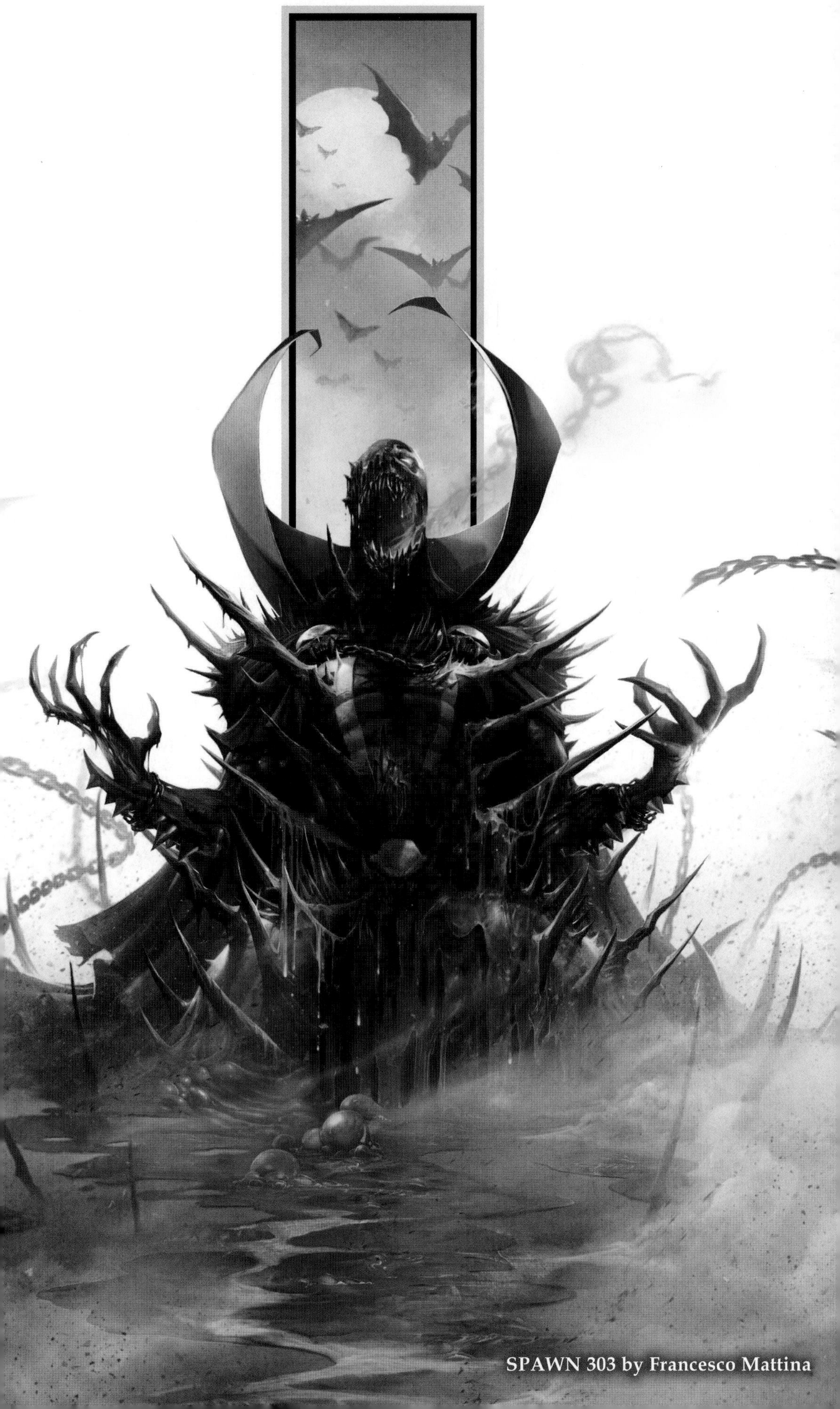

SPAWN 303 by Francesco Mattina

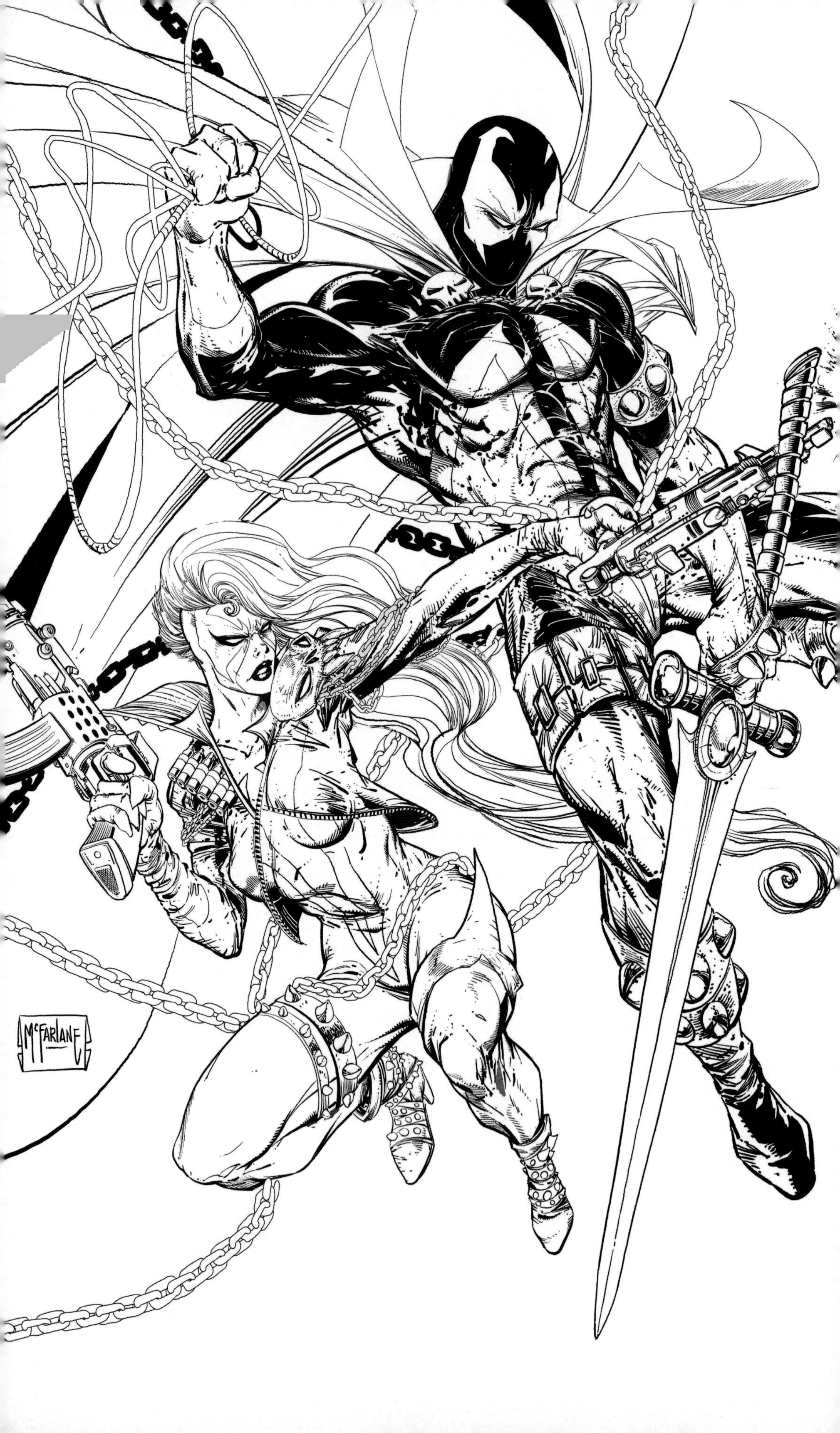
McFARLANE

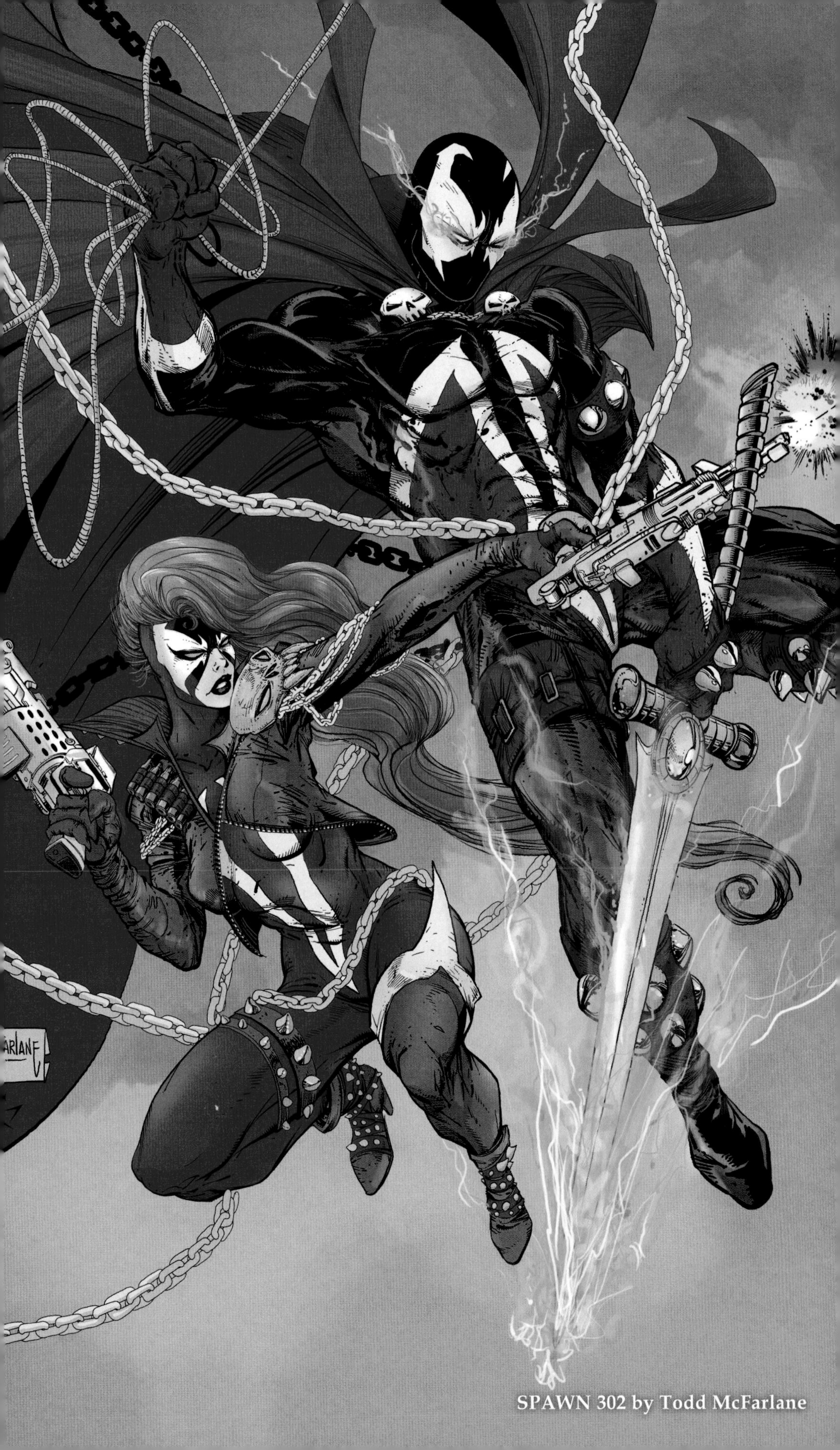

SPAWN 302 by Todd McFarlane

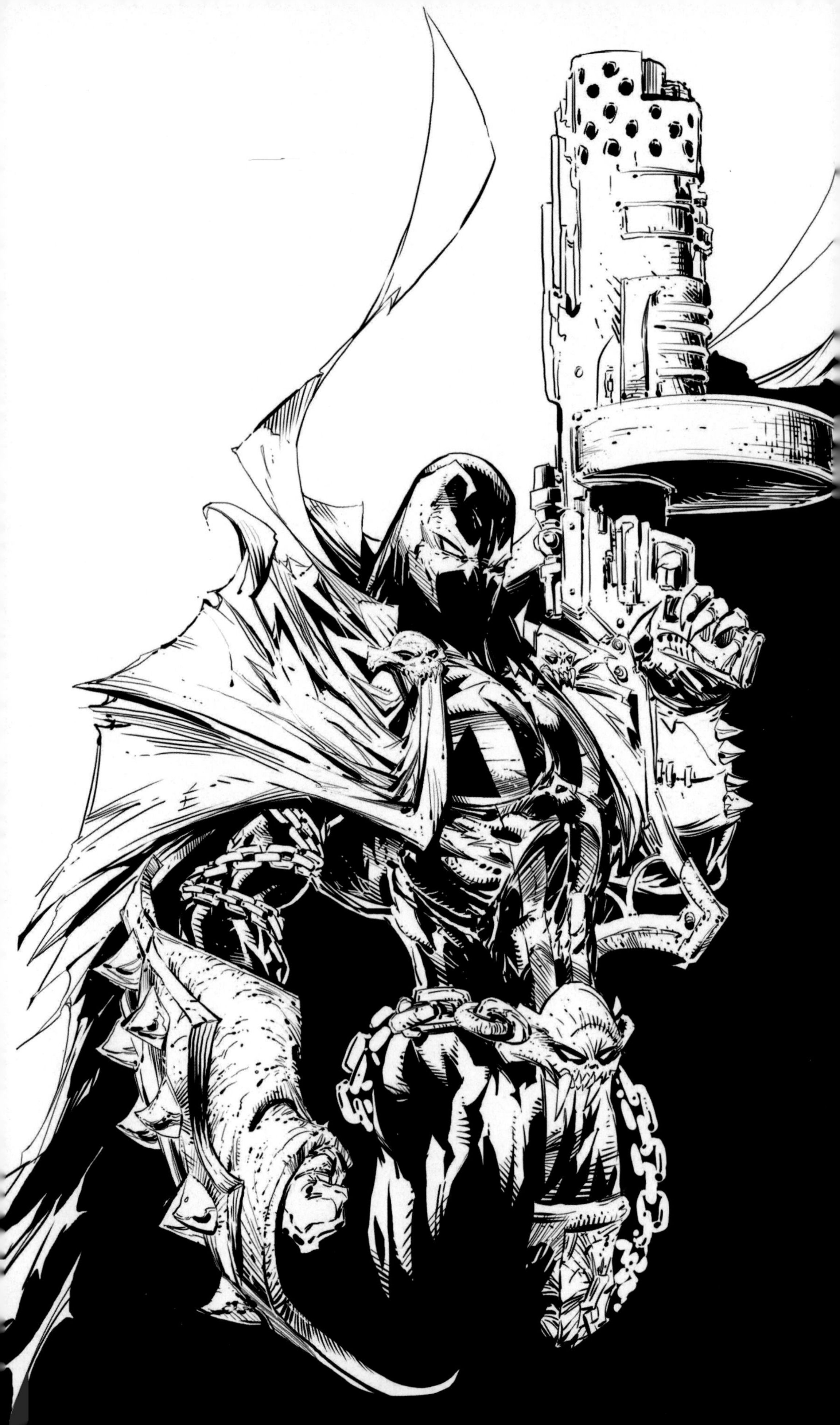

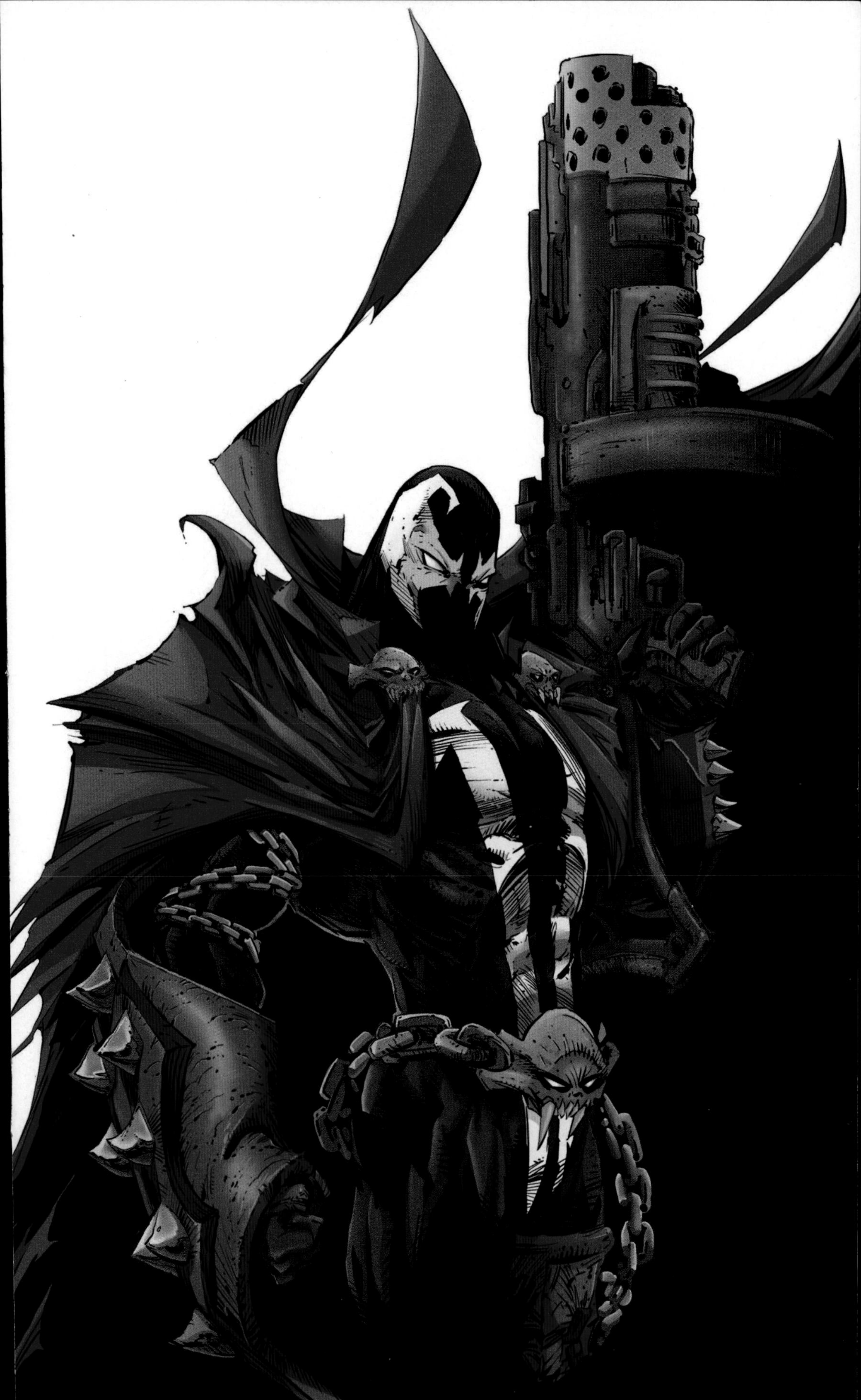

SPAWN 302 by Greg Capullo & Todd McFarlane

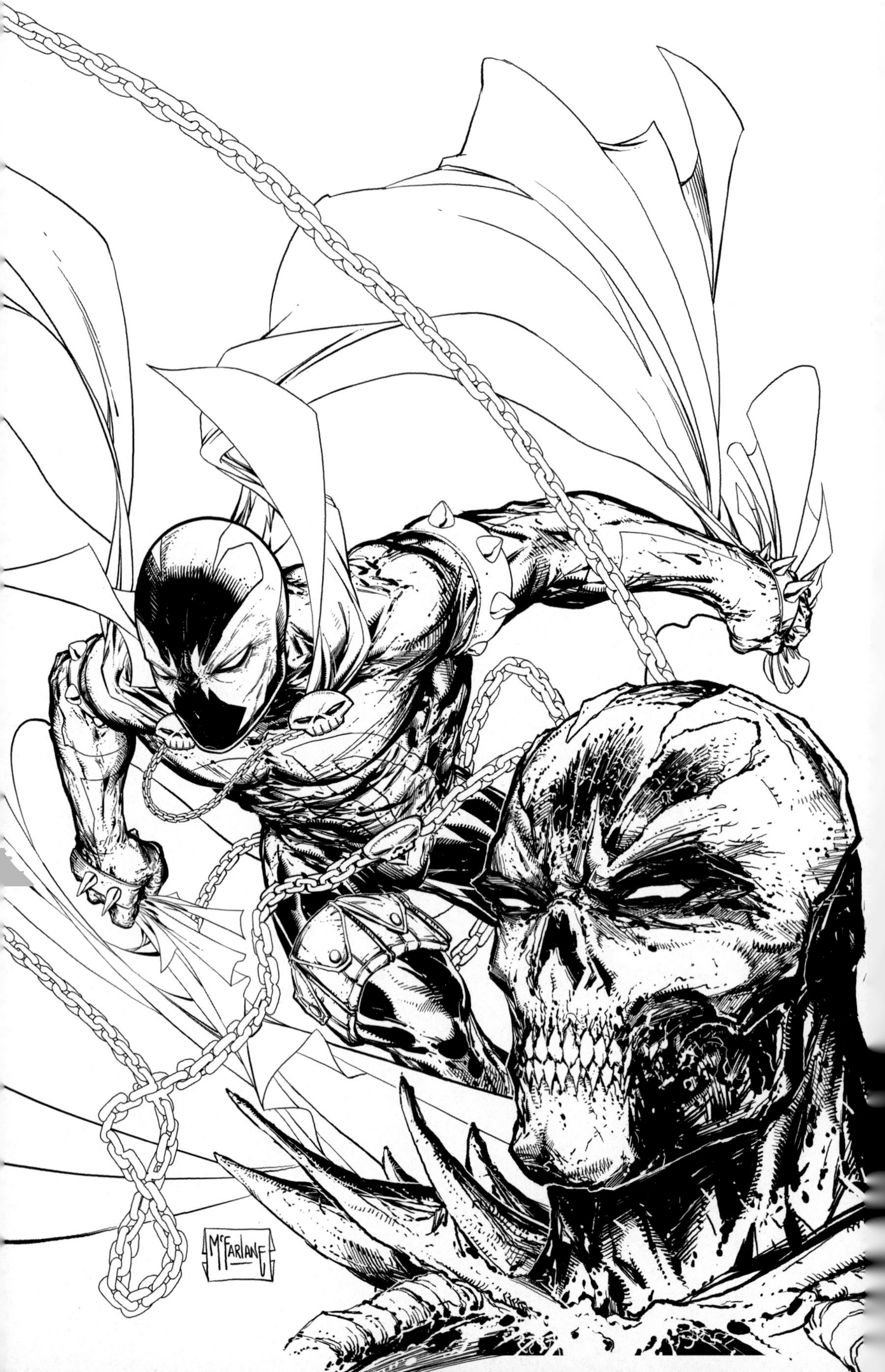
McFARLANE

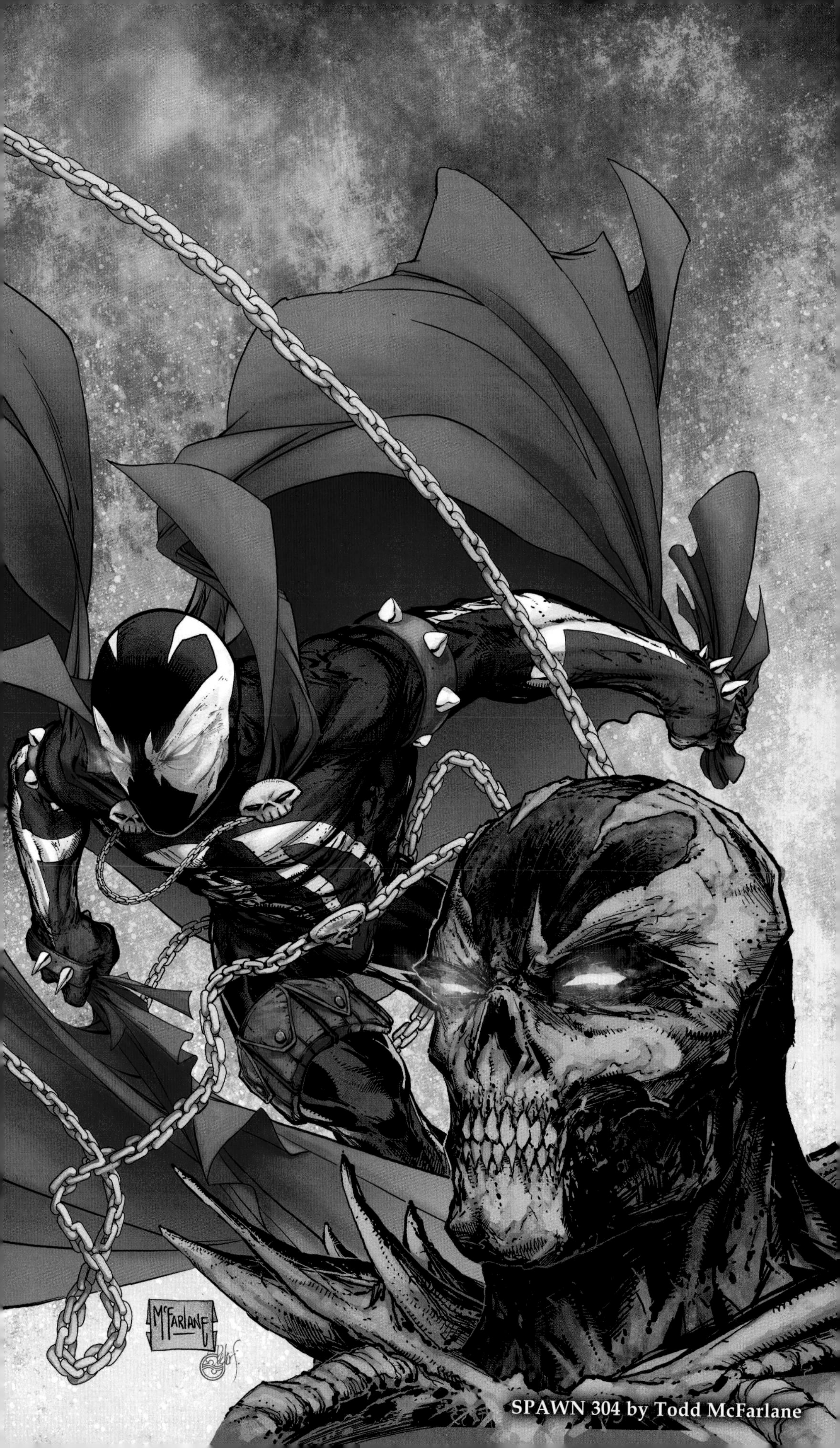

SPAWN 304 by Todd McFarlane

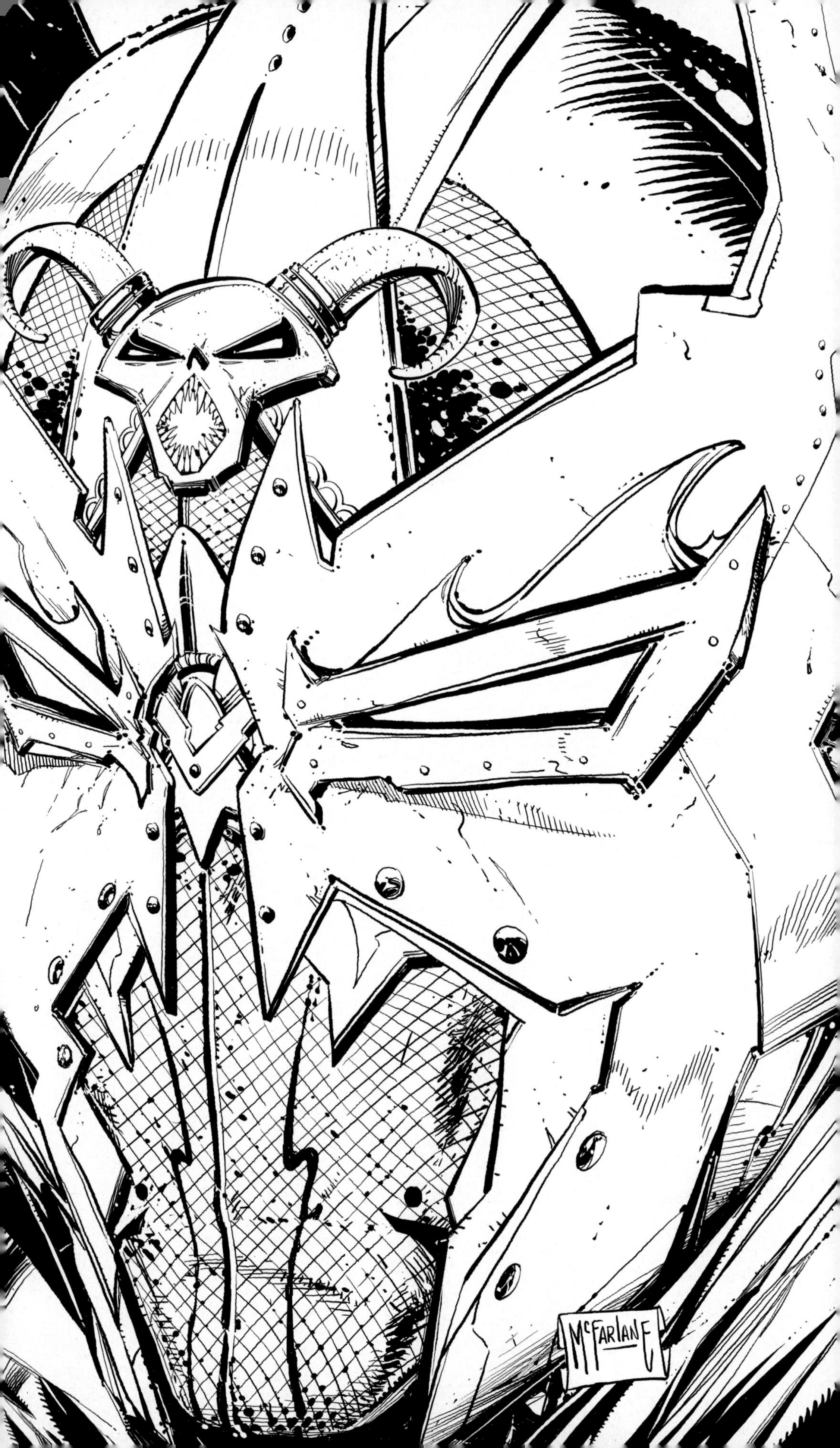
McFARLANE

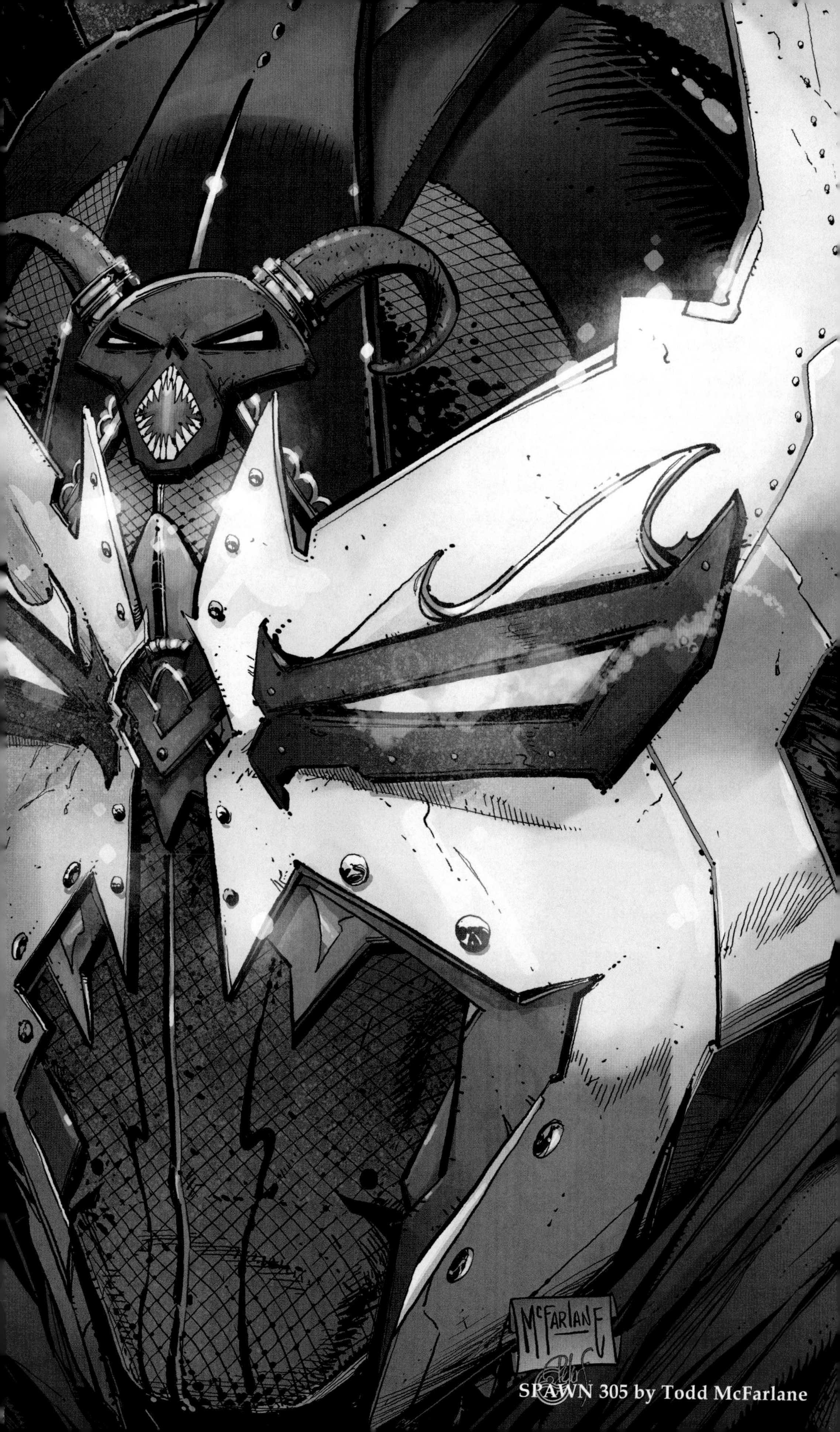
McFARLANE

SPAWN 305 by Todd McFarlane

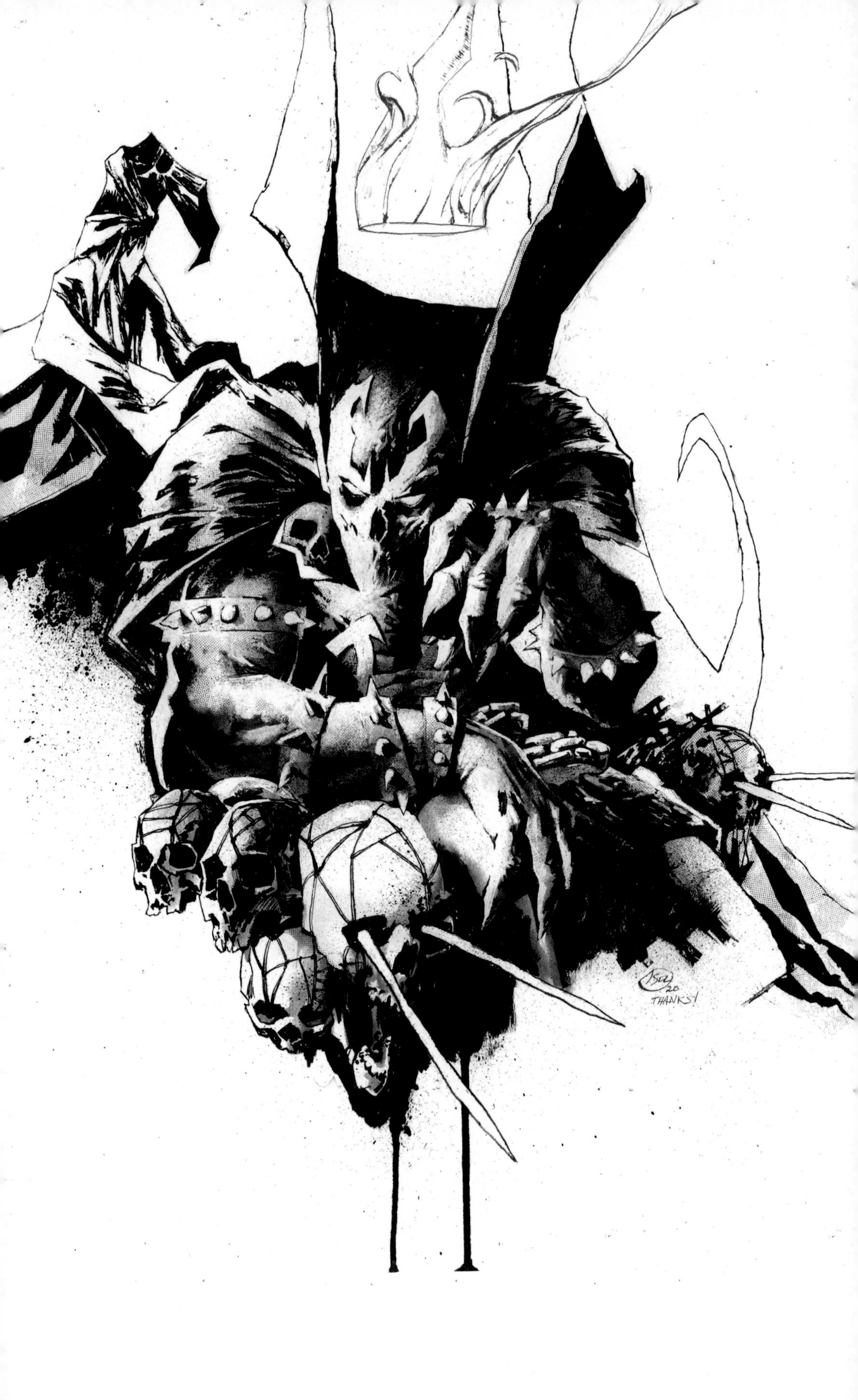
THANKS!

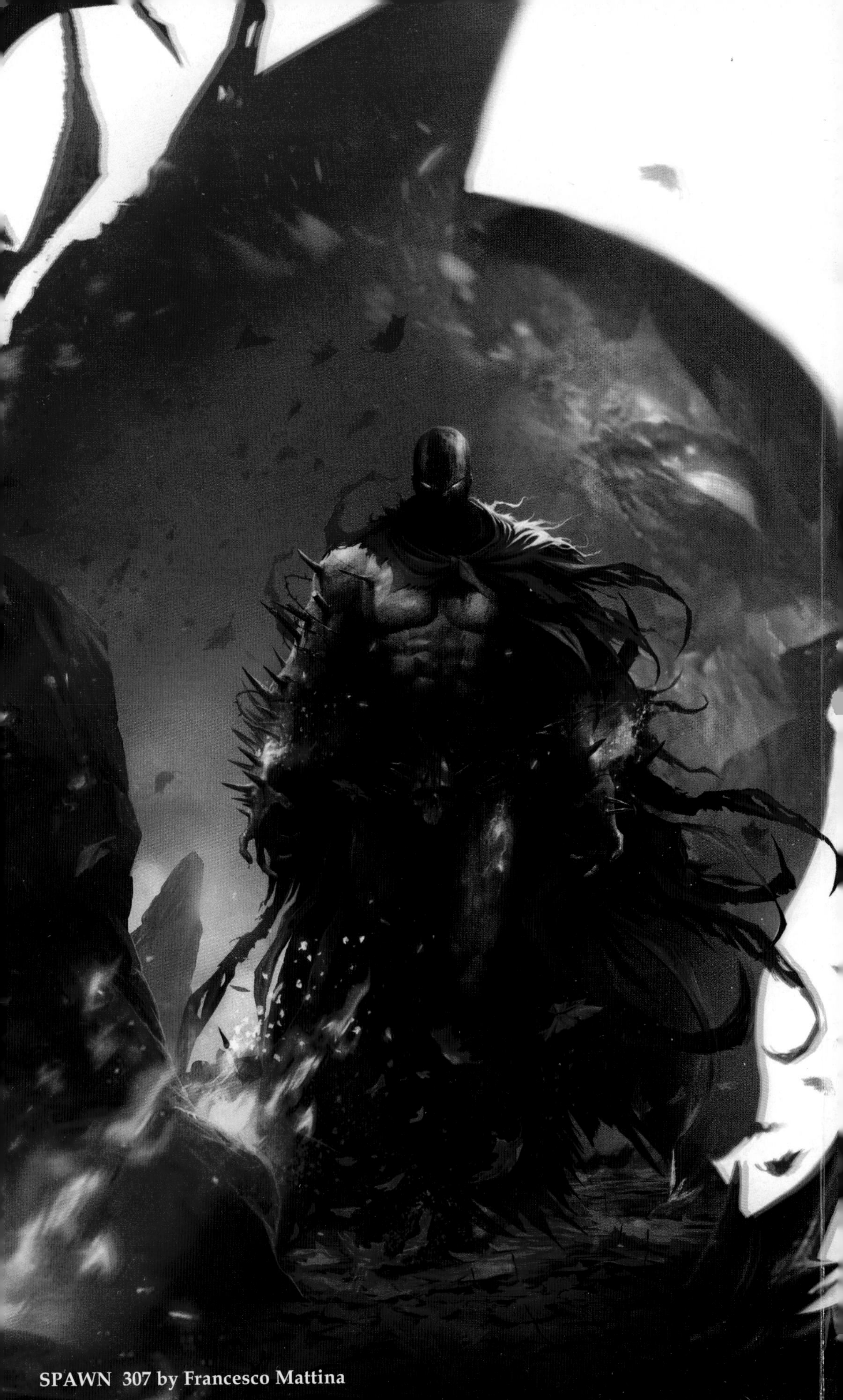

SPAWN 307 by Francesco Mattina

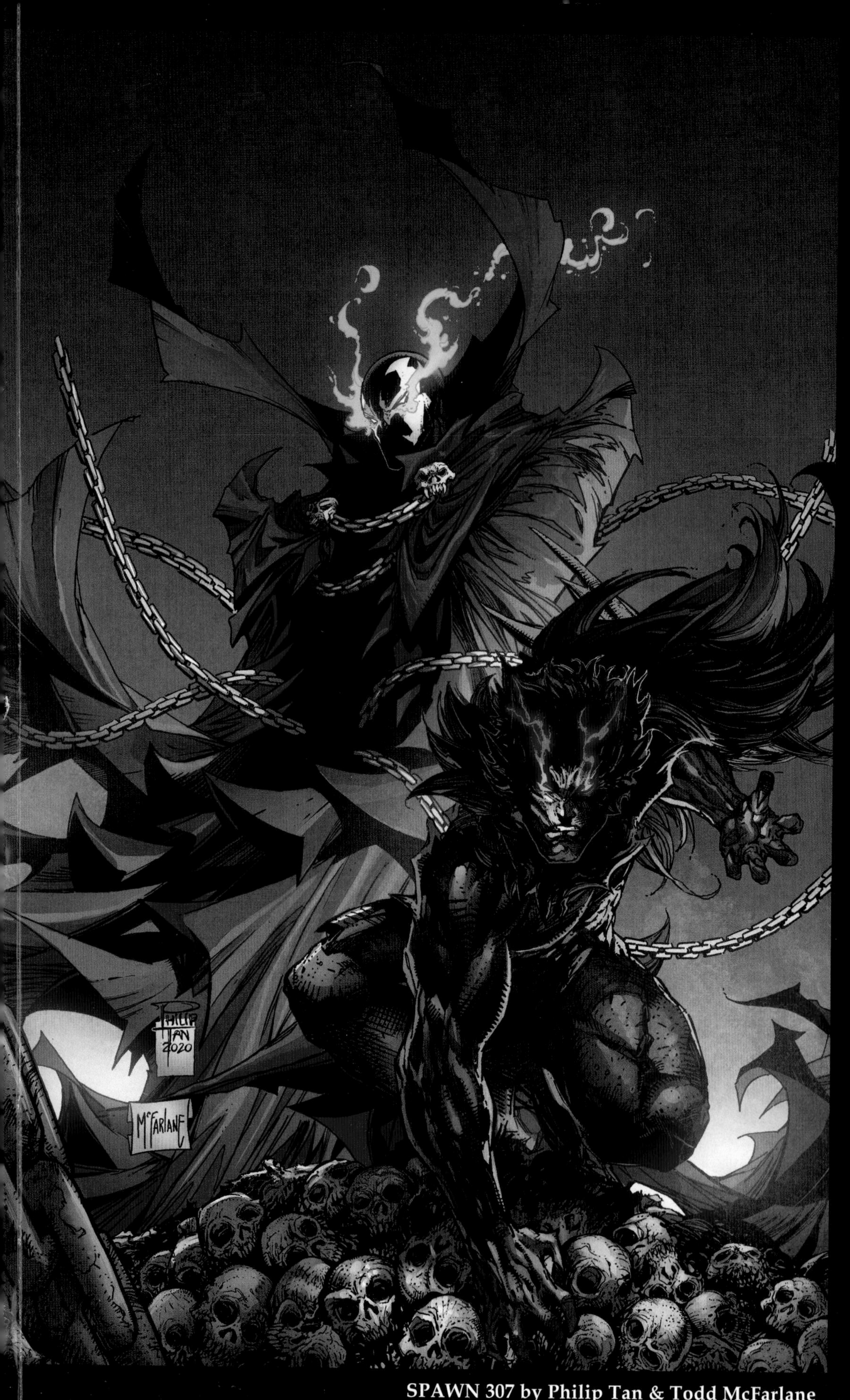
PHILIP
TAN
2020
McFARLANE

SPAWN 307 by Philip Tan & Todd McFarlane

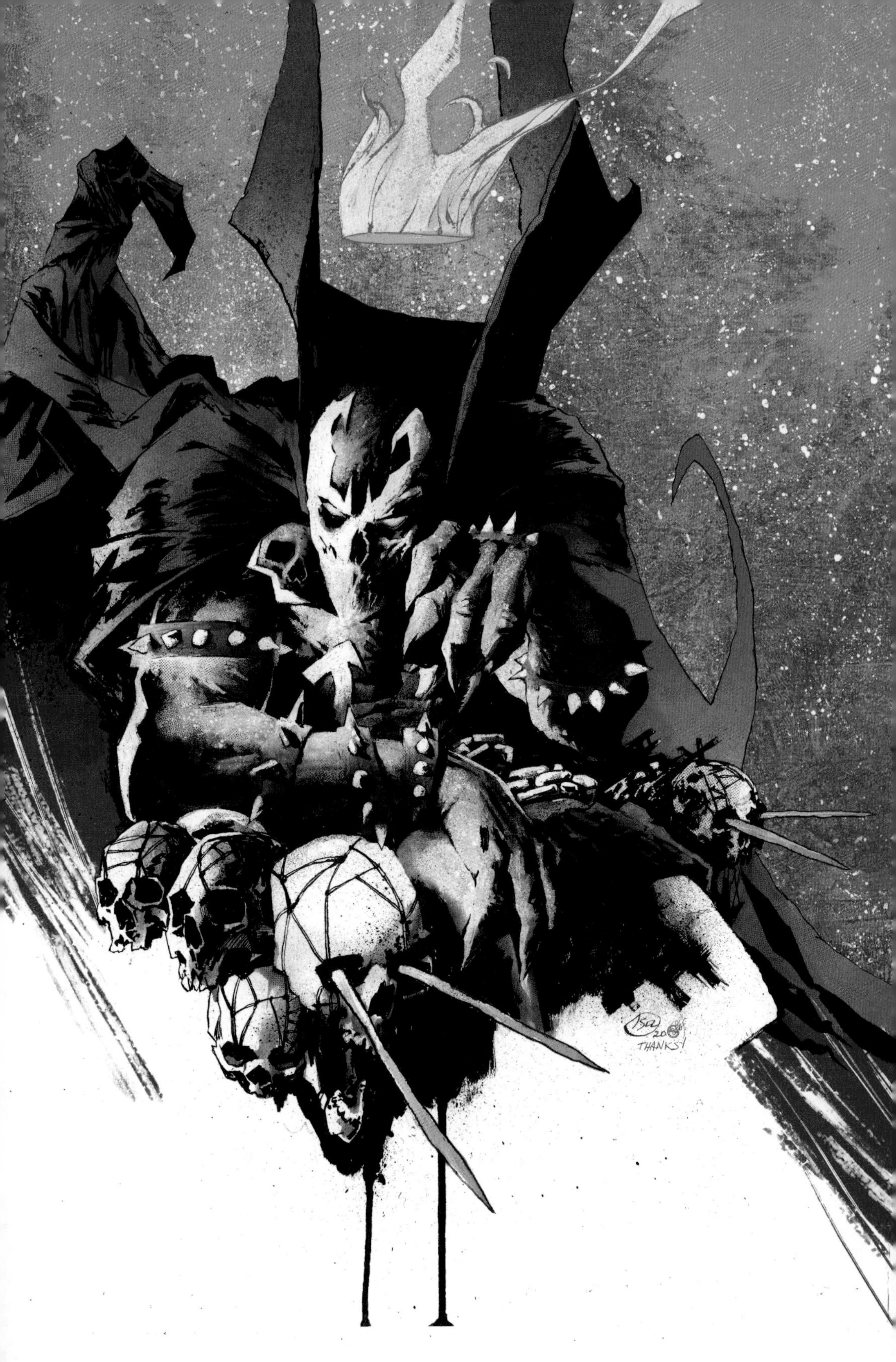
THANKS!

SPAWN 305 by Jason Shawn Alexander

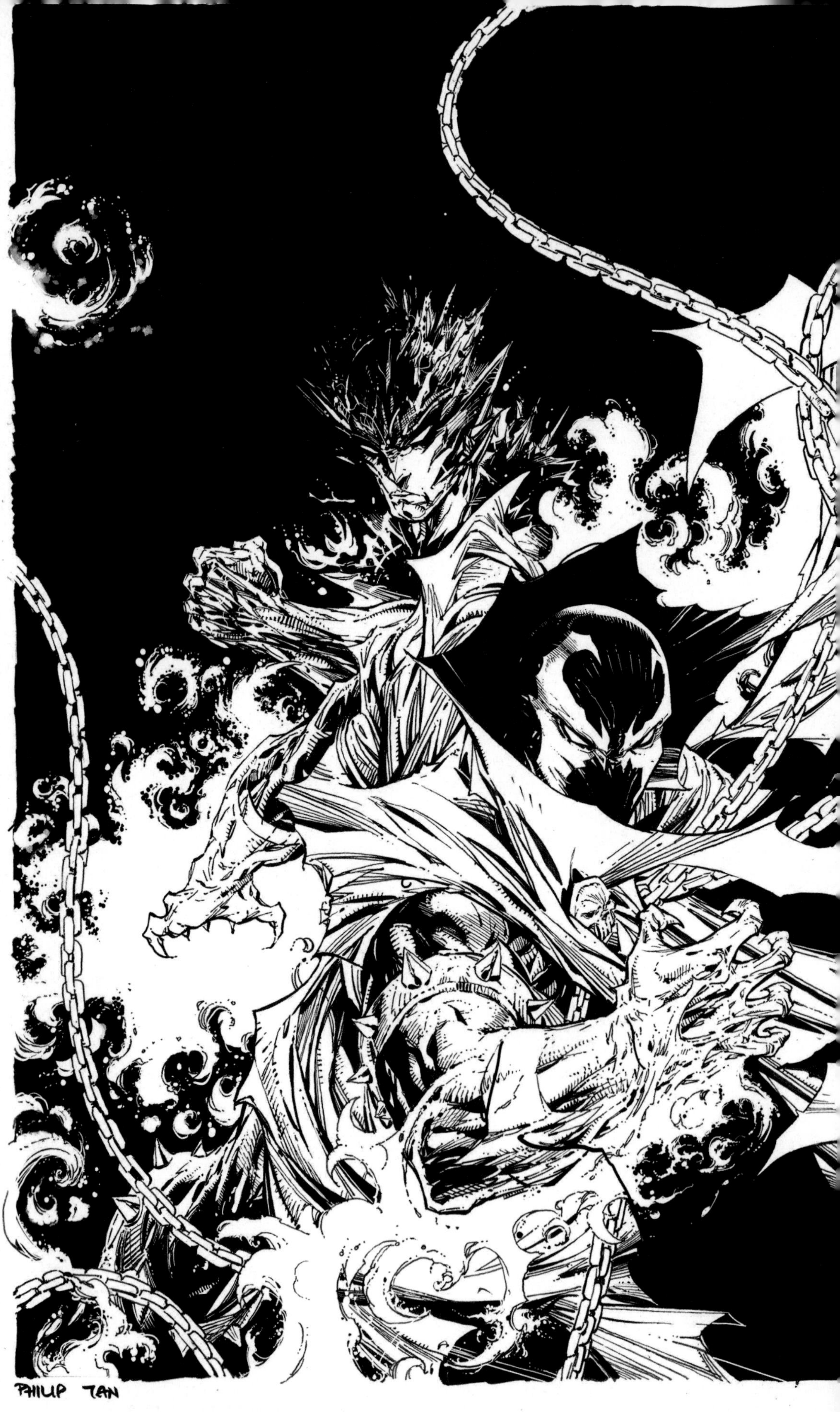
PHILIP TAN

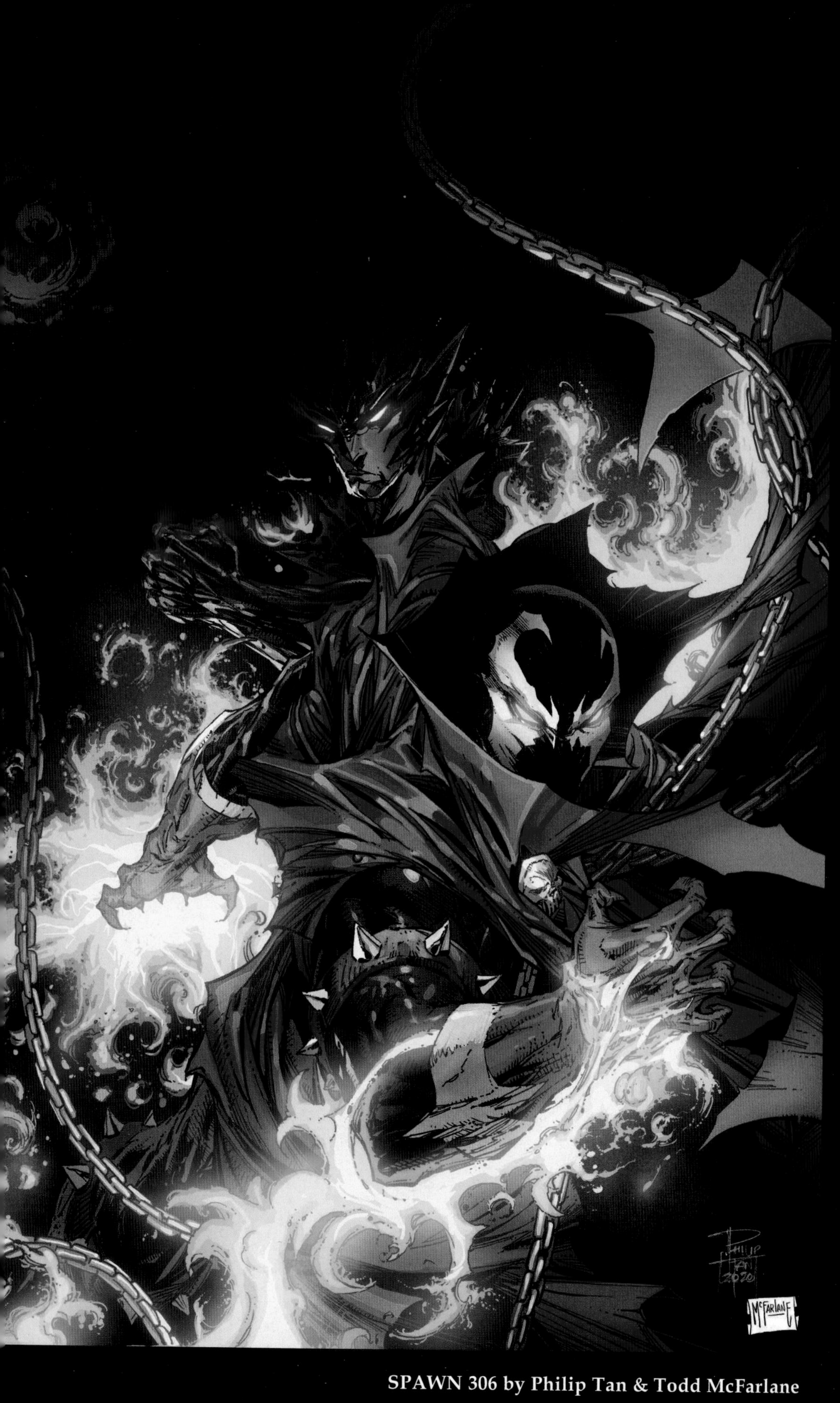
PHILIP TAN 2020
McFARLANE

SPAWN 306 by Philip Tan & Todd McFarlane

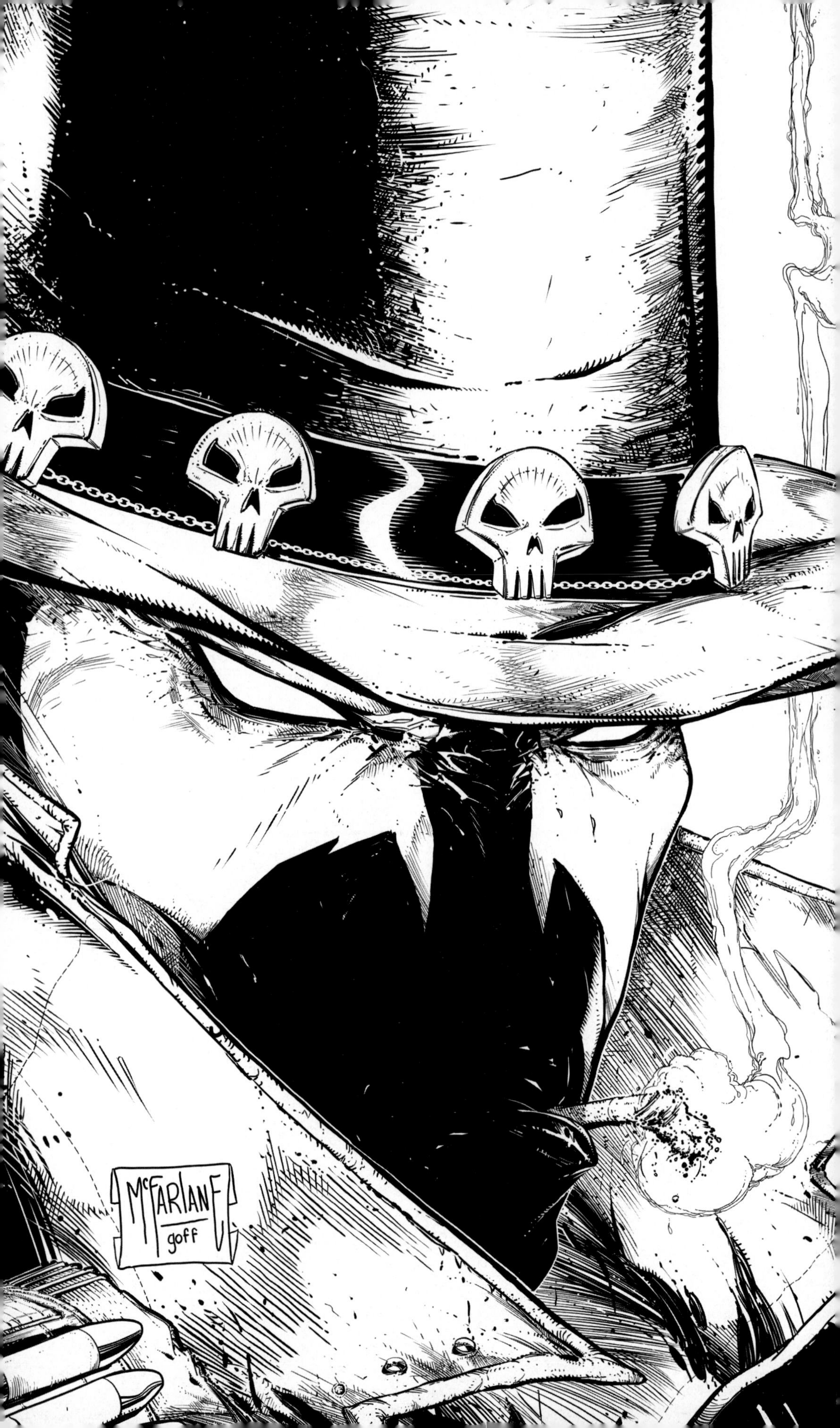

McFARLANE
goff

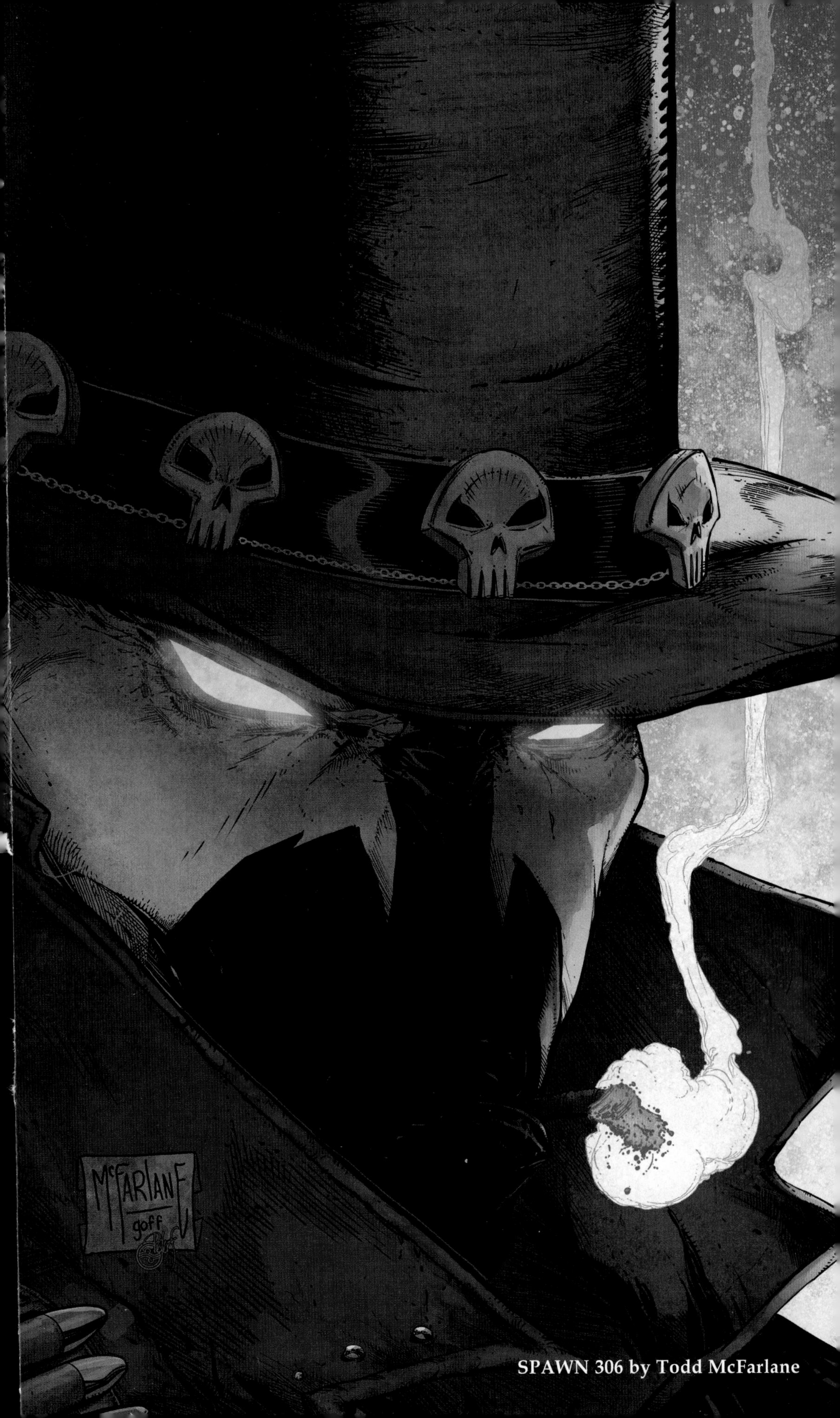
McFARLANE
goff

SPAWN 306 by Todd McFarlane

SPAWN COVER B

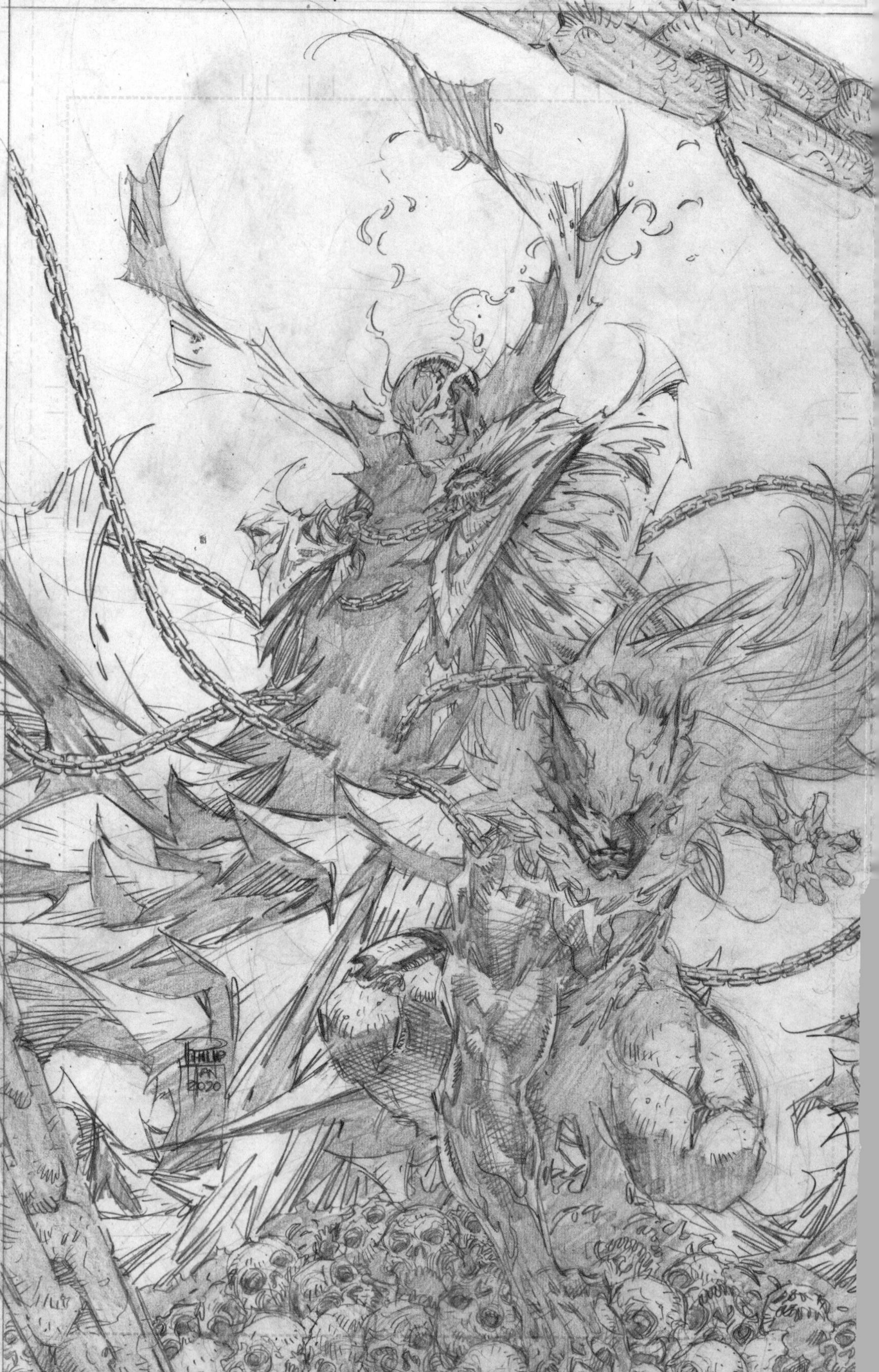
PHILIP TAN 2020

PHILIP TAN